Student-Centered Learning

Nine Classrooms in Action

EDITED BY BILL NAVE

Harvard Education Press
Cambridge, Massachusetts

Library of Congress Control Number 2015936477

Paperback ISBN 978-1-61250-821-4
Library Edition ISBN 978-1-61250-822-1

Published by Harvard Education Press,
an imprint of the Harvard Education Publishing Group
Harvard Education Press
8 Story Street
Cambridge, MA 02138

Cover Design: Saizon Design
Cover Photos: Steve Debenport/E+/Getty Images (top and bottom);
©zerocreatives/Westend61/Corbis (middle)
The typefaces used in this book are Garamond Premier Pro and Futura

Student-Centered Learning

Kevin Grover

1972–2012

> Just as ripples spread out when a single pebble is dropped into water, the actions of individuals can have far-reaching effects.
>
> —Dalai Lama

Kevin's ripple effects on the education community in Maine have been far-reaching and long lasting. Known for his disco parties and rocket launches, he made learning magical and engaging. An advocate of lifelong service, he established relationships between his second-graders and "senior teachers" at Oceanview Retirement Center in Falmouth. As Maine Teacher of the Year in 2010, Kevin traveled the state, sharing his message of parents as partners. During that year, he also created Bring Your Rep to School Week, a program encouraging teachers to invite their local representatives into their classrooms. His goal of connecting lawmakers to classrooms is still rippling across the state of Maine in the form of the law passed in his honor, Invite Your Legislator to School Month.

Known to many as "Super Grover," he often carried a small figure of the beloved character from Sesame Street. He loved to take photographs of his mini Grover with people he met on his Teacher of the Year journey, including President Obama.

Kevin lived each moment to the fullest and made connections with every person who was fortunate to cross his path. It is with honor that we dedicate this book to a superhero in student-centered education, Kevin Grover.

—Shelly Moody

CONTENTS

INTRODUCTION   1

Bill Nave

CHAPTER 1

Kindergarten   13

Preparing for a Lifetime of Learning

Suzen Polk-Hoffses

CHAPTER 2

Grade Four   33

Building Relationships with Whole-Heart Teaching

Mary Graziano-Glynn

CHAPTER 3

Grade Four/Five Multiage   57

A Journey of Transformation: Redesigning the Classroom for Students

Shelly Moody

CHAPTER 4

Grade Five   81

Modeling a Passion for Learning

Susan Carpenter O'Brien

CHAPTER 5

Grades Six and Seven Looping   107

Real-World Tasks for an Authentic Audience

Karen MacDonald

CHAPTER 6

Grade Seven 133

Transparency, Efficiency, and Acceleration
Cynthia Raymond

CHAPTER 7

Grade Eight Special Education 151

Charting the Course to Proficiency-Based Learning
Shannon Shanning

CHAPTER 8

High School English and Speech 179

People First, Things Second
Alana M. Margeson

CHAPTER 9

Sophomore English 203

Creating Meaning
Christiane Cullens

CONCLUSION

"Yet" 235

Bill Nave

Notes 245

About The Editor 249

About The Contributors 251

Index 255

Introduction

BILL NAVE

> Burn 'em all down and start from scratch with just one question: What do we need to do to make sure that each and every student reaches his or her full potential?

This was the opening line of my presentations as I traveled around the state as 1990 Maine Teacher of the Year and finalist for National Teacher of the Year. I used this line as an attention grabber because I wanted my audiences to take that one question very seriously. What *would* a school look like if it were to be designed to make sure every single student reached her or his maximum potential? It is the quintessential student-centered question. This was not a theoretical question for me, because just a couple of years earlier, I had helped to create from scratch a school that was built on this very question.

This book is a next step in my forty-six-year journey (so far—I'm not done yet) to create and document ways of teaching that work best for students by putting the students in control of their own learning. This idea was well outside mainstream thinking when I began teaching, but the science of learning and the science of how the brain works have come to confirm what has always seemed to me to be common sense—people learn when they are in charge of their learning, when they are learning what they want to learn. Our goal with this book is to show how student-centered learning can and is being done. Nine teachers have composed word pictures of their classrooms, learning environments within which their students are learning and thriving because the students are in the driver's seat of their own learning.

MY JOURNEY IN STUDENT-CENTERED LEARNING, AND MAINE'S JOURNEY

When I entered the teaching profession in New York City in 1968, I quickly became a champion of accelerating learning for students stuck in the lowest tracks of public schools. As a science teacher, I soon discovered that my students were eager to learn and that their placement in the lower tracks did not reflect their ability or their motivation to learn. I made sure they felt welcomed and respected in my classroom, because they were all hypersensitive to feeling disrespected (or "dissed," in their terms). If they felt dissed, a literal or figurative fight ensued.

Then, in the late 1980s, after I had moved to Auburn, Maine, and was teaching all four major subjects in a special class for the lowest twenty students in the ninth grade, the school district next door decided to create an alternative program for high school dropouts. It was clear from my first interview with the district planners that their plans at that early stage were not much beyond agreeing that "this is the right thing to do for our dropouts." But it was a challenge I couldn't resist. Mark (the other teacher in the program) and I created what would become the River Valley School, taking our cue from our potential customers—the students.

We divvied up the list of all the students who had dropped out of the district high school during the previous three years, and we spent the first part of the summer driving around the woods and farmlands of the three-town rural district to visit each former student. We found all of them, telling each that we were designing a school just for them so that they could earn their high school diploma. They were invited to help design the school by describing what characteristics a school should have if they were to think about giving it another try.

Most of the students mentioned three categories of ideas. First, they would need a flexible schedule. Some had jobs, some had child-care needs, and many just did not do mornings. Second, they wanted to study what they were interested in and thus wanted a flexible curriculum. Similarly, they had no interest in sitting through a class that they had already mastered, but for which they had not earned credit because of excessive absenteeism, for example. Third, they did not want to be invisible. When we looked into what they meant, we discovered that every student had stopped attending school partly because he or she had felt invisible. As long as they did not make trouble, teachers left them alone, and when the students were absent, no one seemed to care or call to find out if they were okay. If they were to come to our new school, they wanted to be seen, acknowledged, respected, and cared about.

Our initial design for River Valley School included two major characteristics, which we called credit by appointment and credit by objective. *Credit by appointment* meant that we created the school schedule for each student individually according to her or his personal schedule of job responsibilities or family responsibilities such as child care. *Credit by objective* meant that our students earned credit for a course as soon as they demonstrated that they had mastered the course objectives. We obtained copies of the course learning objectives for every course at the high school and developed several options for students to demonstrate their mastery of the course objectives. For example, students could sit for a written assessment that covered the entire course, they could participate in an oral exam if appropriate, or they could enroll in and pass a similar course at a local college. In math courses, for example, most students opted for the exam because they knew the material but had been absent too frequently. If they scored 80 percent or better, the course went on their transcript immediately. We also encouraged students to pursue their interests through classes at the local technical college, the local extension school of the University of Southern Maine, or Bates College. These courses counted as electives on their transcripts.

We also emphasized relevance before a student was accepted to the school. As part of the screening process, I would interview each student. I would begin by asking the student to imagine that for the next five or ten years, life worked out exactly as it should and nothing bad happened. "Where will you be then, and what will you be doing?" I would ask. This question is, of course, one way to frame the "What do you want to be when you grow up?" question. Most of the students were a little taken aback, and most said that no one had ever asked them that question in a serious way. Nevertheless, each had an answer within seconds. Whatever it was that students described as their dream job, I honored the response as a serious one and began a process of helping the student plan backward from that future state to map out the path from here to there, beginning with high school courses to work on beginning now.

We were fully aware of the backgrounds and reputations that our students carried with them, and we made it one of our goals to begin to change those reputations and to provide opportunities for the students to see themselves in a different light as well. Therefore, we scheduled community service activities for our students to participate in, and we always invited local media (newspaper reporters and the local television station) to document the students' work. The media did not always show up, but when some newspaper pieces about a student's good deed began to appear, we observed subtle changes in the students' attitudes and demeanors as they could grasp how the community began to see them a little differently.

Many of our students lived in challenging home situations, and often, the parents did not have a positive experience in school—indeed many students were on track to become the first in their families to earn a high school diploma. Therefore we instituted another tradition—monthly family dinners. Mark possessed considerable culinary skills, so he worked with the students to create a menu, shop, and prepare a meal for students and their families. The students learned about nutrition, comparison shopping, modifying recipes for larger groups, cooking from scratch, creating semiformal table settings, and participating in an unhurried family meal with easy discussions around the table.

During the first three years of quietly running our little alternative school and working with the students, 75 percent of our graduates went on to pursue postsecondary training, ranging from college to trade school to the military. Then I was selected as Maine's 1990 Teacher of the Year (and subsequently selected as one of four finalists for National Teacher of the Year). Suddenly we had lots of visitors who wanted to see what we were doing and how we were doing it. It could have been disruptive to have so many visitors, but our students saw this as a chance to learn from these visitors as well as to evangelize, if you will, about how and why River Valley School worked for them.

In retrospect, the success of River Valley and the naming of an alternative education teacher as Teacher of the Year was probably instrumental in the creation of more than fifty alternative programs across the state in 1990 and 1991. Apparently, we had made it safe for districts to let the existence of their at-risk students and dropouts become visible and then to take the next step of meeting the needs of these students in a public way. The Maine Department of Education even created a position that employed a professional educator to advise and support districts as they developed their own homegrown alternative programs.

In addition, when a new school district was formed in a nearby town and its new high school was established (Poland Regional High School), it was designed from the ground up, both physically and organizationally, to make sure that every student reached his or her learning potential. Derek Pierce, the founding principal, hired his new staff according to their commitment to that goal, namely, proficiency-based learning for every student. In fact, this principal acknowledges that he based the school's design on the philosophy of the River Valley School, and he has since created Casco Bay High School, an award-winning alternative high school in Portland, Maine, based on the same principles, most importantly, that of proficiency-based teaching and learning.

River Valley School also influenced the transformation of King Middle School in Portland in a roundabout sort of way. During the summer of 1990, I hosted an educators' camping retreat at the Mountain Outward Bound Center in Newry, Maine. During our several days together, I led the participants through some thought experiments and planning sessions focused on my question of how to build a school where all students succeed. The principal of King Middle School, along with eight of his teachers, attended the session. A year or two later, the school became the first school in Maine to join the new Outward Bound Expeditionary Learning school reform movement. You will read about this movement in chapter 5—Karen MacDonald was one of those teachers, and the principal is still there guiding the school.

At present, student-centered, proficiency-based learning is the law in Maine. The legislature passed, and the governor signed, LD 1422 in 2012, a law that requires all schools to implement proficiency-based teaching and learning for all students.[1] The graduating class of 2018 will be the first class of Maine students to earn proficiency-based diplomas. All graduates will be required to demonstrate proficiency in eight areas of study to receive their diplomas. These areas of study are those described in the Maine Learning Results: career and education development, English language arts, health education and physical education, mathematics, science and technology, social studies, visual and performing arts, and world languages.[2]

In addition, in order to graduate, students also must demonstrate proficiency in the guiding principles that undergird the Maine Learning Results. Each student must demonstrate proficiency as a clear and effective communicator, a self-directed and lifelong learner, a creative and practical problem solver, a responsible and involved citizen, and an integrative and informed thinker.[3]

The teachers in the nine classrooms we feature here are leading in their schools and districts in this transition, and they represent all corners of the state, from the northern tip of Maine (Aroostook County) to the far Downeast coast (Washington County) to the high-poverty region of Central Maine to the city of Portland with its substantial immigrant population in the south of the state. The majority of the nine schools have a high percentage of students living in poverty. Yet, because of the teachers' skills in creating student-centered classrooms, the educators succeed in raising their students' achievement levels and in closing achievement gaps, as you will see.

THE BIRTH OF THIS BOOK

Fast-forward to Wednesday, August 28, 2013, when I received an invitation from Rebecca Wolfe, a colleague and former student, to attend a panel discussion of *Anytime, Anywhere*, a newly published book she had co-edited.[4] The timing could not have been better. I was already scheduled to be in Cambridge, Massachusetts, the day of the panel discussion (September 12) to consult on a program evaluation project, and I stayed on to join the discussion at the Harvard Graduate School of Education that evening before returning to Maine late that night.

Anytime, Anywhere provides a comprehensive summary of the research that supports the efficacy of student-centered teaching and describes six high schools where student-centered teaching is the norm.[5] Eight major characteristics are common across these six schools (see the sidebar "Characteristics of Student-Centered Schools"). The book also lists student-centered teaching practices that are supported by how the brain learns (see the sidebar "Student-Centered Learning Practices").

CHARACTERISTICS OF STUDENT-CENTERED SCHOOLS

Teachers in the six schools highlighted in *Anytime, Anywhere* weave the following eight characteristics into the in-school and out-of-school experiences of their students. These characteristics could thus reasonably be described as facets of the school culture:

- Strong relationships with students
- Personalization and choice in curricular and instructional tasks
- Appropriate challenge levels for each learner
- Support for students' social and emotional growth and identity development
- Anytime, anywhere, and real-world learning
- Technology that is integral to teaching and learning
- Clear, timely assessment and support
- Practices that foster autonomy and lifelong learning

Source: Rebecca E. Wolfe, Adria Steinberg, and Nancy Hoffman, eds., *Anytime, Anywhere: Student-Centered Learning for Schools and Teachers* (Cambridge, MA: Harvard Education Press, 2013).

STUDENT-CENTERED LEARNING PRACTICES

These eight teaching practices derive directly from recent research findings about how the brain learns:

- Individualized instruction
- Formative assessment
- Planning out-of-school experiences
- Active learning
- Progressing at student's own pace
- Serving youth who may learn differently
- Attending to emotion
- Teaching executive functioning

Source: Rebecca E. Wolfe, Adria Steinberg, and Nancy Hoffman, eds., *Anytime, Anywhere: Student-Centered Learning for Schools and Teachers* (Cambridge, MA: Harvard Education Press, 2013).

Finally, *Anytime, Anywhere* demonstrates that these teaching practices fit perfectly with what we know about how to increase students' sense of agency, their motivation to achieve, their engagement with the school, and their voice in what happens at school. All of this makes perfect sense, but can ordinary teachers in ordinary schools do student-centered teaching? Is it possible only in special schools?

As the panelists described the book and the evidence supporting student-centered learning, I kept thinking about a group of colleagues in Maine and how their instructional practices exemplified exactly the sort of strategies that the book was advocating.[6] It seemed to me that a book describing a set of student-centered classrooms flourishing in ordinary public schools would be the perfect follow-up, especially if it were to be written by teachers so it embodied their perspective.

I approached Rebecca and told her that I personally knew all sorts of K–12 teachers who were putting student-centered teaching into active, effective practice. These teachers could provide other teachers across the nation with excellent examples of what student-centered teaching looks like in real, live classrooms— in elementary schools, middle schools, special education classrooms, and high schools. I had come to know these teachers through my program evaluation work that included classroom observations across the state and through my mentoring of nominees in the Maine Teacher of the Year process.

I suggested that I introduce these teachers to her so that she could create the perfect follow-up book. Rebecca looked me in the eye and said, "Bill, I don't have time to do that. Why don't you do it?" After a brief pause, I thought, yes, why don't I do that? I'll select some of the teachers whose classrooms I knew to be thoroughly student-centered, and I'll ask them if they would be interested in joining me in such a project. They were interested, enthusiastically so. These teachers had developed student-centered classroom strategies that worked for their students, were committed to continuing to improve those strategies, and were excited about the opportunity to share their work with others beyond their schools and districts.

Rebecca introduced me to her editor from Harvard Education Press, and my colleagues and I began crafting a book proposal. Thus began this book's gestation. We envisioned a set of classroom portraits, with each teacher describing in some detail how she organizes her classroom instruction and why she does it that way, and we planned to include detailed descriptions of some of the strategies that each teacher uses to support student-centered teaching. Our goal was to inspire other teachers to begin to shift to more student-centered teaching and to help them get started by sharing some of the classroom strategies that we knew worked for our students. The first question raised by one of the teachers was a good one—in fact, it was probably the best question raised during our entire process. "What is student-centered teaching?" she asked. "I need to know because I'm not sure I'm doing it and I don't want to work on this book if I'm not doing student-centered teaching."

I knew they were all doing student-centered teaching, because I had read the essays they wrote for their Teacher of the Year nomination packet. I had conversed with them at length as I mentored them through the Teacher of the Year process, and I had visited some of their classrooms. I responded to that question with other questions. "Do you work to make sure every one of your students learns what you intend? Do you work to get to know each student well enough to know where their growing edges are so that you can start them from where they are?" All the answers were yes.

So we began. I asked the teachers to keep a daily journal if they were not already doing so, so that they would have examples to use in their chapters. We agreed to meet in person or virtually about every five or six weeks to monitor our progress. I suggested that the chapters be so vivid that readers could feel as if they were sitting in the classroom observing a lesson. One of my early ideas was that the chapters might be sort of like a screenplay, capturing what students were doing and saying.

At our first meeting, all my colleagues told me that the screenplay idea wasn't working and they couldn't see how they could make it work. I withdrew the suggestion, and then we brainstormed what to include in each chapter. A consensus emerged; we should describe the strategies that we consider the foundational pieces of our practice. We should include stories about how students respond to these strategies. The teachers should describe their individual journeys that led them to their student-centered practice. We agreed that these journey descriptions would be extremely important because they would provide readers with nine maps showing them "how to get there from here," that is, how to get to student-centered teaching from where they were at present.

The teachers began writing with a new focus, and they shared with me and with each other what they were writing. We provided ongoing feedback to each other. We continued to meet every six weeks or so to share our progress, sort of like a book group—only we were writing a book, not reading one. During this time, I also spent a full day in eight of the nine classrooms and, occasionally, more than one day.[7] These observations allowed me to see firsthand the strategies the teachers were using and how the students were responding, to *feel* the culture of the classroom and the school, and to chat with students about the work they were doing when I was there. The visits also provided me with several ideas for specific activities or strategies that I asked the teacher to include in her chapter. As I edited each chapter, my classroom observations helped, because I had witnessed the strategies the teacher was describing. All student names have been changed to protect their privacy.

WHOM THIS BOOK IS FOR

It is often assumed that student-centered teaching can happen only in very special schools that were designed from the beginning to be fully student-centered, have strong outside institutional support, and can hire special teachers who sign on to the student-centered approach when they are hired. In short, student-centered teaching can supposedly happen only in schools that are not ordinary public schools.[8]

The nine teachers whose classroom portraits are included here work in ordinary public schools. These teachers began their careers as ordinary teachers, but as you will see, somewhere along the way, they made a commitment to become more student-centered, and in doing so, they became extraordinary. The point about ordinariness is important to understand. For the most part, our nine teachers have developed their student-centered teaching practices over time, building on their commitment both to students and to their own learning and professional growth. Three of the teachers work in schools undergoing schoolwide transformations to become fully student-centered and proficiency-based in their instruction. These include Karen MacDonald's King Middle School (chapter 5), which embarked on its relationship with the Outward Bound Expeditionary Learning school reform model more than twenty years ago, and Shelly Moody's and Cindy Raymond's schools (chapters 3 and 6), which are part of Maine's original cohort of schools working to implement mass customized learning.

It might feel intimidating at first for a teacher to think about trying to do student-centered teaching. Thoughts like these come to mind: "I teach eighty students a day—how can I possibly individualize for all of them?" Or, "What about my slow learners? I have a curriculum to cover, and there's only so much time." Or, "I have to teach all subjects to my twenty-five students. I can't imagine the time it would take to individualize instruction for all of them in all the subjects. I couldn't physically work that hard, even if I wanted to." The nine chapters in this book address those questions and more as the teachers describe how they work with their students and, just as important, what has influenced the evolution of their practice over time. To repeat: the nine teachers whose classroom portraits are included in the book began their careers as ordinary teachers, but somewhere along the way, they made a commitment to become more student-centered, and in doing so, they became extraordinary. *Any teacher* can work to become a student-centered teacher and, as a result, can evolve to become an extraordinary teacher. You can too.

These chapters show that student-centered teaching can be done in ordinary schools with ordinary students and ordinary teachers. You will read about powerful student-centered strategies, how students respond, and evidence that the strategies do lead to improved student achievement.

In the conclusion, I note the commonalities across the nine classrooms in terms of the strategies teachers use and the cultures they cocreate with their students. I also point out how readers can respond by working to support student-centered teaching wherever they may be and from whatever role they currently play in relationship with their local schools.

CLOSING COMMENTS

Some very thoughtful comments and questions from the blind reviewers of our proposal included some misgivings about the value of a book about teachers in Maine. For example, the descriptions of Maine teachers' classrooms may be of interest to other Maine teachers, but would the book benefit teachers in other places that are more diverse and more urban? The short answer is yes.

We responded to these queries by describing the diversity that would be evident in our teachers' classroom portraits. For example, our kindergarten teacher is second-generation Mexican American who grew up living in poverty in the projects of San Francisco. She now teaches kindergartners in a small town in Downeast Maine, where many of her students are English language learners, children of migrant farm workers who settled in the community rather than returning to Central America, and where 75 percent of her students live below the poverty line. One of our middle school teachers works in a school where twenty-nine languages are spoken and where many of the students live in the nearby projects (yes, Portland, Maine has projects). Seven of the nine teachers are in schools with a high percentage of students living below the poverty line. One of the schools is in a town where many of the students face myriad problems: a parent lost to a drug overdose, fathers or older brothers in prison, alcoholism within the family, or parents who have not graduated from high school.

In short, we believe that the teaching strategies described here can benefit any teacher in any classroom, be it urban, rural, suburban, or exurban. Indeed, we invite, we implore you, the teachers who read these chapters, to try out these strategies in your own classrooms with your own students. No special tools are required. Adapt the strategies to your own situation, and watch what happens.

CHAPTER ONE

Kindergarten

Preparing for a Lifetime of Learning

SUZEN POLK-HOFFSES

The family was standing in front of a vegetable garden. As the mother spoke to her children about the importance of eating vegetables and the various types of vegetables that were being grown in the garden, one of her children turned to his mother and said, "I already know all that. I learned all about gardening and vegetables in kindergarten."

A PERSONAL HISTORY

The Three R's

When I was in grade school in the early 1970s, I had a teacher who would always remind my class of the three R's. She would say, "Remember, class, we are here to learn the three R's: reading, writing, and arithmetic. We are here to learn. We are not here to fool around." I too had my own three R's as a student. My three R's were rats, roaches, and rent.

From the age of three until the age of twenty-one, I grew up in an inner-city housing project in San Francisco. Rats, roaches, and rent were just a part of my daily life. It would not be uncommon for me to see rats around the garbage cans in front of my housing project on my way to school or as I came home from school. When it came to roaches and school, I was always afraid that one day, I would open up my book bag and have roaches from my home crawl out of my book bag for all my classmates to see. Yet, even with the rats, roaches, and violence that surrounded me in the projects, I was always very aware that if my divorced mother, who was raising two children on her own, did not pay the rent, then we would all be forced to live in a homeless shelter. The thought of having to live in a homeless shelter was terrifying.

My teacher who believed in the three R's was right. School was a place of learning. It wasn't a place for me to fool around, become unfocused, or be a behavior problem. My job was to learn. My job was to focus. My job was to pull it together socially and emotionally when I was at school. Yet, my chaotic home life prevented me from doing any of those things. As a student, I was unable to turn off that part of my brain that stored the memories of what I was experiencing outside of school daily. Every day I would bring my home life into school. And every day, my teachers were not happy to see how my home life was interfering with their teaching. When it came to academics, I wasn't setting the world on fire. To be honest, I was always near the bottom of my class academically.

A Slide Show That Changed My Life

When I was in the tenth grade, I saw a slide show that changed the course of my life. A guest speaker came to one of my classes and put on a slide show of her experience as a Peace Corps volunteer. She talked about the work she did setting up an elementary school in an African country. I had always wanted to travel and see places other than the housing projects that I lived in. I knew there was a better world outside of my depressing and dead-end world. But there was a problem. I didn't know how to leave the only world I knew. Sure, I knew I could take a bus outside of my neighborhood. But what would I do once I got off the bus? I needed answers. I needed a plan.

After the slide show, I asked the guest speaker what I needed to do to become a Peace Corps volunteer. She told me that I needed to go to college and that, once I finished college, I could then apply to become a Peace Corps volunteer. Okay, I needed to go to college. Yet, how could I go to college if I was barely passing my classes in high school? Getting into the Peace Corps and out of the housing projects by attaining a college degree became my goal. Through years of hard work, moral support from friends, and connections with very supportive teachers, both in high school and throughout my college years, I was able to graduate from both high school and college. I also realized my dream of becoming a Peace Corps volunteer. As I was growing up in the projects, I always felt looked down upon because of my Mexican heritage and my poverty. Yet, when I boarded that plane to begin life as a Peace Corps volunteer, I knew that the hardships I had endured as a child had showed me that I had the grit and self-control that I needed to be successful in life.

HOW POVERTY SHAPES HOW I TEACH

I shared my personal story of how I grew up and my experiences as a student to give you a better understanding of how my living in poverty and being a struggling student of color has affected the way I teach. My role as a kindergarten teacher is to create in my young students a foundation of knowledge and skills that will prepare them for a lifetime of learning. I also realize that sometimes life gets in the way of my young students' learning. Thus, early on in my career as a teacher, I needed to make a choice. Was I to become the type of teacher who would focus only on the three R's, that is, only on academics? Or would I focus on academics, with an understanding that my students' home life does affect their learning?

The learning environment in my kindergarten classroom does focus on academics, but I also maintain a deep understanding that my young students are coming to me with very different skills and abilities because of the circumstances of their home life. A few students have had a Head Start or nursery school experience, but most students have little or no exposure to a structured early childhood program. Nineteen of my twenty-five students this year (76 percent) qualify for free or reduced-price lunch. With this understanding in mind, I have created a classroom that is academically based, yet also has a strong focus on embedding learning opportunities into my curriculum—opportunities that may not have been present, *yet*, in the lives of my young students. My personal understanding of the poverty that some of my students are living in gives me a framework to decide what kinds of learning opportunities I need to provide. These opportunities will help my students build that all-important solid foundation they will need to be successful in school and, later, in life.

As a teacher, I have thought long and hard about how to close the achievement gap between wealthy and poor students. As I reflected on my own experiences as a student living in poverty, I began to see that I lacked the exposure or learning opportunities or experiences that my more affluent classmates had. My mother would have loved to take my brother and me to a museum or symphony to learn about art or classical music, yet the cost of admission to these types of cultural outings was not something that our household budget could afford. This personal understanding has allowed me to look at my students not through the lens of a *deficit model*, but rather through the lens of an *opportunity to learn* model. My students could benefit from opportunities and experiences that they have not yet had.

This is why I plan rich and varied experiences and opportunities throughout the year for my students. I want them to be exposed to experiences that can open them to new concepts. I decided that our classroom would be a place of experiences and opportunities that support learning.

VOCABULARY AND REAL-WORLD LEARNING

Besides growing up in poverty, many of my students have a speech or language delay or don't speak English as their primary language at home. These challenges have a major impact on my students, especially when it comes to their understanding of the meaning of words and the concepts embedded in those words. If my students aren't growing up in an environment that is rich in oral language, whether it's English or their native home language (usually Spanish for my students), they come to school with gaps in their understanding of various concepts and in their ability to communicate. A limited vocabulary is a huge barrier to their understanding of basic concepts.

I have discovered that one way to hook and engage my students when I'm teaching a new topic, concept, or vocabulary word is by reading a great picture book. Picture books are a wonderful way to encourage my young students to visually tune in when they are listening to a story. Yet, what happens when the story I am reading has vocabulary that is unfamiliar to my students? To help them understand unfamiliar words, I front-load these words and their meanings. On a large piece of chart paper that I have divided into four equal boxes, I write one vocabulary word at the bottom of each box. For example, in Aleksei Tolstoi's story *The Great Big Enormous Turnip*, which focuses on perseverance, the vocabulary words I would write on the large chart paper would be *seed, turnip, enormous*, and *pulling*.[1]

Before I read the story to my students, I first explain the meaning of each vocabulary word. Next, I ask my students to give me a thumbs-up when they hear the vocabulary words in the story. By having the children do this, I can see if they are connecting the vocabulary word to what was happening in the story.

At the end of the story, I give my students their own mini version of the vocabulary chart. Like my large chart, the students' paper is divided into four equal boxes with a vocabulary word at the bottom of each box. In the blank space in each box, I ask my students to draw a picture icon for each of the vocabulary words after I have modeled this on the big chart paper. By having my students draw a picture icon for each vocabulary word, I give them the opportunity to learn the meaning of the word in a visual and creative manner. In addition to hearing me explain the definition of the vocabulary words, hearing the words in the context of a story, and drawing an icon of the words, the students also act out the words using movement, like pretending to pull up a turnip. I also make sure to embed the newly learned vocabulary words into my own oral vocabulary as I am interacting with my students. My oral use of the various vocabulary words that my students are learning in class gives the children the opportunity to begin using and incorporating the new words into their own vocabulary.

Teaching new vocabulary words doesn't stop with oral language. My students will refer to vocabulary words that they learned in a story and will include the words in their writing.

I encourage my students to use their newly learned vocabulary words in the student lunchroom, on the playground, in their homes, and beyond. Students need to be adventurous when it comes to incorporating new words into their oral communication. New vocabulary words cannot be relegated only to the four walls of the classroom. These new words need to be shared with others.

INDIVIDUALIZING WITH IPADS

Sometimes I plan a lesson with specific objectives in mind—things that I really want my students to learn. I might also have a clear picture of how to present the lesson. But I have found that sometimes my students are much better at thinking outside the box than I am, especially when using technology in their learning.

A few days after the first day of spring, I announced to the class, "All right, everyone, we are going to be detectives today. Using our iPads, we are going outside to take pictures of signs of spring. Before we go outside, what signs do you think we are going to see that would tell us that spring is here?"

Various students said, "Green grass," "Birds," "Buds on trees."

As the students interacted with their peers and me, I noticed that Cesar, one of my English language learners, sat quietly. Cesar would rarely talk in class, although he could speak and understand English. After my students had taken pictures of signs of spring using iPads, I had them break up into small groups to look at the pictures they had taken and talk about what they had seen when they were outside. As I walked around the classroom, Cesar looked at the pictures on the iPad in his group, but didn't interact with his peers.

When I was about to wrap up our lesson, a student asked if he could draw a picture of what he had seen outside. "Great idea," I said. As my students began drawing what they had seen outside, I started looking at the pictures my students had taken using their iPads. I saw blades of green grass, a picture of a seagull, the sun, and melting snow. But what really caused me to stop and think was a video that a student had recorded on the iPad. The student had recorded and narrated his quest for signs of spring. I thought, "Wait a minute, my students know how to video-record information using an iPad?"

After my students had finished their drawings of what they had seen outside, I decided to extend the activity. I paired up students and gave them one iPad per pair. I told them that not only were they going to tell their partner what they saw outside, using their drawings as a visual prompt, but they were also going to record each other as they talked. As I walked around the room, I saw my young students fully engaged, either recording or sharing with their partner what they had drawn.

When I walked over to Cesar and his partner, I was shocked. Cesar was facing his partner and talking. No, Cesar was doing more than talking. He was smiling and animatedly speaking in Spanish about what he had seen outside. As Cesar pointed to his drawing, he did it with such joy and a sense of happiness that it took my breath away. We had been in school for over hundred school days then, yet this was the first time that I had seen Cesar really happy and engaged as he participated in a classroom activity. Cesar laughed and had a huge smile on his face as he watched his image playback on the iPad explaining what he had seen outside.

After seeing this, I thought that it would be a good idea to have my students record each other on the iPads as they read their weekly decodable books from our reading series. They loved the idea of being recorded as they read. So my students began to regularly record each other as they read. Over time, I noticed some interesting things beginning to happen.

One day, I saw Jorge and Julian sitting at a table with three pencil boxes stacked on top of each other in front of them. On top of the pencil box was an iPad. I said, "Jorge, what are you and Julian doing with the iPad?" Jorge replied, "We can read together at the same time and film ourselves reading when the iPad is up high." These two students had devised a way to record themselves reading at the same time by figuring out how many pencil boxes they needed to stack on top of each other.

Josette also took her reading and using her iPad to another level. Instead of just reading to the iPad, Josette had her partner record her as she read to her doll. Josette would sit on the rug with a doll and read to the doll with great expression. After Josette was finished reading, she would watch her recorded image playback on the iPad as she held her doll. I could hear Josette tell her doll from time to time as she viewed herself reading, "Look at me reading to you. You did a good job listening to my story." This is strong support for her developing reading skills.

However, the most powerful thing I saw happen with one of my students and an iPad was with Connie. Connie was so shy that she would rarely speak while at school. One day during our reading and iPad time, the classroom was quite loud. Because of the high noise level, I decided to have my teacher's aide stay in the classroom while I took Connie out of the room and read to her in the quiet hallway. Since she was struggling in the area of sight-word identification and phonemic awareness, I would read the decodable stories to her. Whenever I or someone else would read to Connie, she would always sit silently and listen to the story. That day in the quiet hallway, Connie sat next to me on a bench as I began recording myself reading to her on the iPad. As I began to read, Connie began to repeat what I had read. Out of Connie's mouth came this very tiny, mousy type of voice. Connie would look at the story and then look at the iPad as she repeated what I had just read. I very slowly turned the iPad away from me and focused it on Connie. After we had read the story, I showed Connie what I had recorded. When she heard and saw herself reading, she turned to me, pointed to her frozen image on the iPad and said, "That's me reading. Can we read another story?" Somehow, being outside of the noisy classroom and in the quiet of the hallway, Connie felt comfortable enough to repeat the words she was hearing me read. She loved seeing and hearing herself read. From that day forward, I made sure that Connie was allowed to go out in the hallway when it was our iPad reading time.

GARDENING AND ACTIVE LEARNING

Fifty years ago, it was very common to see vegetable gardens in the backyards of homes in the town where I teach. Lettuce, cucumbers, beans, peas, carrots, potatoes, beets, and tomatoes were just some of the crops traditionally planted. Yet, because of the hectic lifestyles of today's families and the convenience of stopping by the local grocery store to buy vegetables, the art of vegetable gardening has become a distant memory for some of my students' families. Knowing that vegetable gardening used to be a part of some of my students' family culture, I decided that my young students should have the opportunity to experience what their grandparents and great-grandparents did when they grew vegetables in their own home gardens.

My goal in building two raised beds for a vegetable garden was twofold. First, I wanted my students to experience the whole picture of growing food. Second, I wanted to use the vegetable garden as a tool for teaching math, science, language arts, and social skills.

It was late April 2013 by the time the garden beds were built and ready to be used. In order for my students to harvest the crops before the end of the school year, we needed to plant quick-growing crops. As a math activity, I presented my students with a math problem. Which vegetables would be suitable to grow and harvest in the short amount of time we had left at school? Using lengths of string to represent the number of days we had left at school and different lengths of string representing the various number of days it would take certain vegetables to grow, my students were able to figure out that lettuce and radishes would be the best quick-growing crops to plant in our vegetable garden. Before the students planted the lettuce and radish seeds, they compared and contrasted the seeds by color, shape, and size. Once the students were to plant the seeds, we studied the concept of length. Using their index finger, students learned that the seeds they were planting could be planted only up to the first joint of their index finger. If the seed was planted too deep, it wouldn't be able to grow; if planted too shallow, it would be washed away or eaten by birds.

We also did vocabulary activities during our gardening lessons. Students learned the names of the parts of the plants and labeled the parts on their drawings. When the first sprouts began popping out of the soil, students would shout, "Look, Mrs. Hoffses, I see a sprout!" as they looked at rows of sprouts popping out.

Learning teamwork was also a big part of caring for the vegetable garden. Students understood that to grow vegetables, they needed to water, weed, and thin out the seedlings. Students worked together to haul out the heavy garden hose to the garden beds. They learned that if they put too much water on the plants, the plants would rot and not grow. *Rot* was another vocabulary word that became a part of their oral language. I would hear students say, "Not too much water or the lettuce will rot." During the thinning of the seedlings, the students worked together in small groups. The students understood that if the plants were too crowded, they wouldn't have room to properly grow. As the plants began to grow, I would have my students go out and measure them. Using plastic connecting cubes, they measured how tall the plants were growing. At the end of that school year, my students were able to eat the lettuce that had matured. They couldn't believe that they had grown lettuce. Even though the radishes didn't mature as quickly as we had thought they would, I was able to send home small Baggies filled with ten small radish plants.

That summer, I planted green beans and peas in the vegetable garden beds. When my students came to school in September, I gave them the task of caring for the maturing plants. Bean pods had begun to form on the plants. As I did with previous year's crop of kindergarten students, I did the same types of vocabulary, math, and teamwork activities with these students. The only difference was that with this group, my students got the opportunity to measure the length of mature green bean and pea pods. They counted the number of beans and peas that were in the pods they had picked. And most importantly, they were able to eat fresh-picked beans and peas that they had helped grow.

What evidence do I have that having my students growing vegetables in raised garden beds seeped into my students' academic learning? In our science unit about plants, my students already had firsthand knowledge and experience identifying and labeling the parts of a plant. In the past, before I had incorporated gardening as a tool for learning, my students used only worksheets to learn the names of the parts of a plant. Using the garden, my students had hands-on experience in touching and naming the parts. The students were able to keep this information in their memory bank because of this hands-on experience. When it came to math vocabulary terms such as *longer, shorter, top, bottom, more, less, big, little,* and so forth, the students could recall this information as well. Having the real-world experience of using these terms as they worked in the garden allowed the students to make personal connections with the meaning of the words, which is especially helpful for my English language learners.

INCORPORATING NUTRITION INTO THE LEARNING ENVIRONMENT

It is no secret that nutrition plays a significant part in a student's ability to learn, focus, and engage in a classroom setting. It is not uncommon for one of my kindergarten students to tell me that he or she is hungry or that his or her belly hurts. Some of my students can't always connect that when their belly hurts, it could mean that they are hungry. In April 2013, I decided to incorporate into my classroom some lessons that would somehow feed my students both physically and academically. I needed to find a way not only to bring food into my classroom, but also to somehow turn the act of eating into an academic activity. Fruits and vegetables are expensive. Where I live in Maine, oranges can cost $0.50 apiece, and three kiwis can run $1.99. When I discovered that the federal government gave qualifying schools funding to purchase fresh fruits and vegetables through the US Department of Agriculture's Fresh Fruits and Vegetables Program, I knew I had found a way to bring healthy fresh fruits and vegetables as a daily snack not only for my kindergarten students, but also for all the students at my school. Through this program, all the students have the opportunity to eat a fresh fruit or a fresh vegetable as a snack every day. The fruits and vegetables that the students eat are more than just carrots, celery, bananas, or apples. Our students are eating star fruit, cherimoyas, prickly pears, blood oranges, kumquats, Bella mushrooms, leeks, European cucumbers, turnips, mixed lettuce, baby greens, arugula, mini sweet tomatoes, rainbow carrots, and parsnips, just to name a few of the fruits and vegetables that the students eat for their daily snacks.

Where does the learning come in when my students are eating these fruits and vegetables? I do brief "infomercials" on that day's fruit or vegetable. As my students are eating, I talk about where that day's fruit or vegetable was grown. I use the classroom globe to show where the food was grown and show how far that fruit or vegetable had to travel to get to our school (social studies and math). I tell my students how the food is grown, such as above the ground or underground or on a vine, bush, or tree (science). I will also ask my students to think about and share what they think the food might look like inside if the food has a peel. What color is the flesh under the peel? Are there seeds? If so, how many seeds, and what is the size of the seed or seeds (making predictions)? I will write the name of the fruit or vegetable on the board and have the students identify the letters, vowels, and how many letters are in the word (letter identification and math).

I also explain how the growing seasons are different in the southern part of our world from where we live in Maine. This year, my students learned that the grapes that they were eating in February didn't come from the United States, but came from Chile, South America, where it is hot and sunny in February and not cold and snowy like it is during February here in Maine. I used my classroom globe and a flashlight to demonstrate how the sun shines on different parts of our world during different times of the year. One of my students said, "Do you mean that it isn't cold and snowy everywhere in the world right now?" while another student asked, "If it is hot where the grapes came from, when does it get cold there?" Again, my students were surprised to learn that while they will be on summer vacation from school in June, July, and August, enjoying playing outside in the warm sunshine, eating ice cream, and wearing shorts, Chilean children will still be going to school and wearing winter clothing because of the cold and snow in June, July, and August in Chile.

This school year, I secured a grant that allowed me to do a weekly nutrition lesson with my students as well. I wanted my students to have a deeper understanding of the importance of eating healthy foods. Again, I was very aware that some students might not always have healthy food choices at home because healthy foods often cost more than processed foods. For those students, I wanted to make sure that they had the opportunity to learn about and eat a variety of healthy foods that would help their young, developing brains and bodies grow. Thus, each week, I read a story or did a nutrition activity that illustrated eating healthy food and also involved math, science, and language arts components.

How did doing a year-long nutrition program in my kindergarten classroom have value academically? I saw evidence when my students were using toy food items during their social play. The grant allowed me to buy a wide variety of toy food items such as breads, meats, vegetables, fruits, pita pocket sandwiches, burrito-making kits, and eggs. My students incorporated language, math, and nutritional understandings into their language as they played with the various toy food items. One student came up to me with a plate of hard-boiled eggs and said, "Here, Mrs. Hoffses, you need to eat your protein so you can stay strong and have your brain work." Another student sat me down and made me a salad. As he gathered up the ingredients, the student would identify each item as he placed it on my plate. "Here is a lettuce. A red bell pepper. You need some onions. Onions grow under the ground." Another student would gather up the fruits and vegetables and count how many items he had placed on his plate.

These toy food items also allowed my students who had speech/language delays or who were English language learners to use during their social play language that they were learning during our nutrition lessons. My students weren't just playing with the food items. Through their social play, they were demonstrating to their peers and me that they had understood and retained the concepts learned through our weekly nutrition lessons.

LEARNING OUTSIDE OF SCHOOL

When I was in the fifth grade, I remember taking a school field trip to the Muir Woods, a national park located in Marin County, just north of the Golden Gate Bridge. I lived south of the bridge, in the projects. Even though that field trip happened so very long ago, two things stand out quite clearly. I remember pressing my face against the window of the school bus as it crossed the Golden Gate Bridge. I remember looking out the window and thinking how beautiful the bridge looked as it spanned high over the waters of the Pacific Ocean and San Francisco Bay. Even though I had lived in San Francisco all my life and the bridge was only seven miles from where I lived, I had never seen the Golden Gate Bridge in person. I had only seen this world-famous bridge in pictures.

I also remember eating pine nuts in the Muir Woods. This might not seem like such a big deal, but being surrounded by a forest of towering redwood trees was a new and exciting experience. As the adult in the group began passing around pine nuts to my classmates and me to eat, he began talking about how the Native Americans in these same woods over a century ago had gathered up pine nuts and cooked them to make food. I can still remember the wonderful taste of pine nuts in my mouth as I ate them while I stood with my friends in the middle of a forest of stately redwood trees thinking of the Native Americans that had lived there long ago.

The school where I teach is located in a rural fishing village on the Downeast coast of Maine. Lobstering and digging clams, mussels, and bloodworms are just some of the types of fishing-related jobs that people do in the area. Depending on which school bus students take to and from my school, they may see lobster boats traveling on the water going out to haul, lobster buoys floating on top of the water, or lobster boats tied up on their mooring. Even though my students might live in a fishing village, some of them have never experienced up close and personal what a lobster, clam, mussel, or seaweed looks or feels like. Like me and the Golden Gate Bridge, some of my students have only seen lobsters, clams, mussels, or seaweed in pictures.

This year, I experimented with raising both clams and lobsters in the classroom, with only a modicum of success. Our classroom was too hot in the winter to grow the algae needed to feed the clams, and later in the year, unbeknownst to my kindergartners, I had managed to accidently kill our classroom juvenile lobster, the beloved Louie. When the opportunity arose to have students from my school visit the Downeast Institute of Marine Research, I jumped at the chance to expose my students to what real-world hands-on marine research looks like. After getting my principal's permission to set up the field trip, I decided that it made sense for the seventh-graders to accompany my kindergarten students to the marine institute. By partnering with my students, the seventh-graders would become teacher-leaders and would help my kindergarten students learn firsthand how algae is grown and how marine scientists measure water and clams. All the students would have the chance to check out a marine life touch tank and would learn how juvenile lobsters are grown outside of an ocean environment.

Before we went on our field trip, I first spoke to my students about the type of work that goes on at a marine institute and the types of jobs people do there.

I also asked the children to do me a favor. I asked them to look out the window as we traveled the thirty-five miles to the institute and to really look at what they could see along the road. I wanted my students to notice that there was another world beyond where they lived and went to school.

Once at the institute, each kindergarten student found his or her seventh-grade teacher-leader and began doing the activities at the various learning stations. One station had the students measure a specific amount of ocean salt-water using different types of graduated cylinders. At another station, students measured various sizes of clam shells using calipers. This station had the students model how marine researchers measure clam shells. And in the very active part of the institute, students saw how algae are grown in huge glass tanks that lined the walls. One of my students was so mesmerized by the large amount of algae and the bubbles he was seeing in the huge glass tank that he began to pound on the tank and said in a very excited voice, "Look at all the bubbles! Look at all the algae!"

The station that got the most action was the sea life touch tank. Both kindergarteners and seventh-graders would scream with delight as they would touch and hold various sea creatures. Sea stars, sea cucumbers, clams, lobsters, mussels, and a flounder were some of the creatures that the students had the opportunity to touch, handle, and learn about. The biggest hit was the sea cucumber. A sea cucumber looks like a pale green pickle that is very soft and slimy. It is also very smelly when opened. Sea cucumbers are harvested and processed by some of my students' parents in a sea cucumber processing plant located in the same town as our school. Once processed, the sea cucumbers are exported overseas to various Asian countries as food. Because I knew that some of my students' family members either harvested or processed sea cucumbers, I wanted my students to view a sea cucumber up close.

As I picked up a sea cucumber out of the touch tank, I began talking to my students about how sea cucumbers crawl into lobster traps, where they become trapped. As I was holding the sea cucumber in my hand, a huge stream of liquid shot out of one end of its body onto my jacket. As the stream of liquid was shooting out, the students began to scream and point at me. Thinking that the stream of liquid was just seawater, I put down the sea cucumber and began to wipe away the liquid off my jacket with my bare hands. As I was wiping off my jacket, one of the seventh-graders asked the marine researcher at the touch tank why the sea cucumber shot out liquid as I held it in my hand. The researcher replied in a very matter-of-fact voice, "Oh, they do that when they are scared. Sea cucumbers shoot out their urine as a defense mechanism." When the students heard the word *urine*, they all looked at me in silence for a second. They then began to say, "Yuck!" and told me that I had "sea cucumber pee" all over my hands and jacket.

The day after our field trip to the marine institute, I asked my students to write about, and draw a picture of, their favorite part of the field trip. Some students wrote about being on the school bus and what they had seen on the way to the institute. But the sentences and pictures I remember most vividly are the ones that involve my getting urinated on by a sea cucumber.

Coast Guard Visit

In the late 1970s, one of the requirements for graduating from high school in San Francisco was knowing how to swim. As an eleventh-grade teenage girl, the last thing I wanted to do for a semester was to put on a bathing suit and learn how to swim in front of eleventh-grade teenage boys. Yet, learning how to swim in high school taught me how to be safe and confident when around lakes, ponds, and the ocean.

Only a few students at my present school know how to swim. The barriers that students and their families at my school face when it comes to taking swimming lessons are the price of the lessons and the fact that the lessons are held far out of town. Nevertheless, people living and working in a fishing village need to understand how to be safe on and around the water. A few local families have experienced firsthand how, in an instant, the ocean has taken the life of a family member who was working on the water. That is why I arranged for a local Coast Guard station to visit my school. The goal of the Coast Guard's visit was to teach water safety tips and how lighthouses are maintained in the twenty-first century and to allow the students to tour a twenty-eight-foot Coast Guard boat.

It was a warm and sunny May spring morning when the Coast Guardsmen pulled into the school's parking lot towing their boat. Like a well-oiled machine, the Coast Guard personnel quickly and efficiently set up the learning stations. Instead of having one class at a time tour the stations, I created multiage groupings of our school's students to experience the stations. The older students would take on the role of the teacher and explain what was happening at each station. The job of the classroom teachers was to make sure that the groups moved from one station to the next. The teachers were like sheep herders that day. They would move their group along in an orderly manner, yet would stand in the back of the group and let the older students do the teaching or answering of any questions the younger students had about what they were seeing.

As I followed my group along from station to station that day, I could see the excitement in the students' faces as they interacted with the Coast Guard personnel. The students had great questions when they were at the various stations. I remember one of my students asking at the water safety station, "What happens if a shark bites the life raft? Will the raft sink?" At the lighthouse navigation station, where we learned that lighthouses are now powered by solar energy, another of my students asked, "Will the lighthouse still make a light if it is a foggy day?" The best comment I heard from one of my students was when we were on the twenty-eight-foot Coast Guard boat. As my young student was standing at the wheel of the boat steering the wheel vigorously from left to right, he looked up at the Coast Guard person who was giving the tour and said, "Hey, this is really cool. I want to be just like you. I want to drive this kinda boat when I get older."

As I heard these words, I thought, "I have this Coast Guard visit all wrong." I was pushing the water-safety aspect of the visit. I wanted the students at my school to be aware of how to be safe on and around the water. I hadn't considered that some students would find being in the Coast Guard an interesting career choice. Suddenly, I remembered as if it were yesterday what had happened to me the day a guest speaker came to one of my high school classes and presented a slideshow about what she had done in the Peace Corps. To this day, I can't remember if that slideshow was done in my social studies, English, or geography class. I just remember being inspired by the presentation.

Could this Coast Guard visit inspire some of the students at my school to think about a career path? Would that path lead to their joining the Coast Guard, working in solar technology, joining the merchant marines, or becoming a marine engineer? The students might not remember why the Coast Guard showed up at their school that warm spring day, but they might remember that visit because it got them thinking about a career and their future outside of school.

Being the Difference

I grew up in the era of Rev. Martin Luther King Jr., Cesar Chavez, and Mother Theresa. I grew up seeing these individuals create movements that focused on improving the lives of groups of people undervalued by mainstream society. What I learned from these great leaders was that to effect change, one person can't do it alone. Change requires working successfully with others and going out into the world.

The stories I have shared could not have happened without the support of my principal, superintendent, school board, parents, students, and school colleagues. This support has allowed me to become the type of teacher who doesn't teach in a vacuum. My students' learning doesn't just happen within the four walls of our classroom or in isolation from other students. The students get the opportunity to learn outside of their classroom and with other students. The love, understanding, and support that the teachers and other staff members at my school give me every time I come up with an idea or plan have given me the strength to continue to look for new learning opportunities, not only for my own students, but also for the rest of the students at my school. Looking for other types of learning opportunities requires a lot of extra work on my part. Yet, the support my fellow teachers and staff members give me when I implement new ideas or try new activities for the students at our school makes it worth going the extra mile in terms of my workload.

Even though I had wonderful support from within my school community, I also understood that I also needed support from others outside of my school. Making connections with individuals and organizations outside of my school has allowed me to look even further afield for learning opportunities for the students at my school. I learned very quickly that various individuals and organizations wanted to come into my school; they just needed a way into the school. I became that way into my school. Once I began connecting with individuals from organizations, I noticed that they used certain types of words when they spoke. They used words like *aligned, partnership, sustainability,* and *stakeholders* in ways that I didn't as a teacher. I realized that to successfully communicate with others outside the education field, I needed to become bilingual. I needed to learn how to speak "organization."

Just like schools, other organizations also need to document what they are doing in the communities they are serving and how their monies are being spent. I learned that embedding terms like *sustainability, stakeholders,* and *partnerships* in the grants I was applying for helped these organizations better understand the proposal for my project.

Another takeaway I learned from my interactions with individuals who worked with organizations is that these people had business cards. Whenever I would meet an individual from an organization, he or she would gladly hand me a business card. And I would then gladly scratch out my information on a scrap piece of paper. No one ever asked me for my business card or seemed to mind getting my contact information on a random piece of paper. Yet, it bothered me. If I was going to form partnerships with individuals and organizations, I too needed a business card. I needed to show them that even though I was just a kindergarten teacher, I too had value. Thus, I recently began creating my own business card that reflects who I am as a teacher. I can't wait to say to someone, "Let me give you my contact information. Here's my business card."

THE FINAL GRANT PROPOSAL FOR THE YEAR

A few weeks before school ended this year, I was feeling overwhelmed. I looked at what I still needed to teach my students in the short amount of school time remaining. I remember checking my email after school one day in early June and reading about a grant that was being offered by Maine Agriculture in the Classroom. The grants ranged from one thousand to three thousand dollars to support doing agricultural types of activities in the classroom for the following school year. As I read the email, I was tired, hungry, and thinking, "I don't have time to apply for one more grant." Yet, something caught my eye in the email. There was a link listing last year's grant winners. I clicked on the link and began reading about the winning grant projects. As I read each project, I began thinking about what I could do at my school for a project.

After I read the proposals for each winning project, I emailed my county's farm-to-school coordinator to tell her that I didn't have time to apply for this year's grant, but would be interested in applying for the grant next year. I briefly shared what my proposal would look like and wished her a great summer vacation. By the time I got home that day, my county's farm-to-school coordinator had emailed me back saying, "Suzen, what a wonderful idea! Let me do the legwork on my end, and you begin writing up your proposal. Remember, we only have ten days left to get your proposal written. Do your budget, and get three letters of recommendation. Good luck!" As I read the email I thought, "Oh, no! I am too tired and too overwhelmed now to begin working on a grant. I need to focus on getting through the last few weeks of school."

That night as I tried to go to sleep, I couldn't stop thinking about how to go about writing a proposal for the grant. My proposal would focus on having my kindergarten, along with the first- and second-grade students, visit six working farms in our county during the upcoming school year. My focus would be providing these students with the opportunity to experience what twenty-first-century farming looks like in our rural Maine county. I envisioned having the students bring iPads onto the farms, record interviews with the farmers, and take pictures of the various animals, crops, and buildings on each farm. The students could go back to the school and, in multiage groups, work together to create iBooks that they could share with others at the school. These same iBooks could also be downloaded on the iPads at our local town library.

The students would visit a cranberry farm, a blueberry farm, a cow and goat dairy farm, and a maple-sugar-producing farm. They would visit a farm in the winter time to learn about and experience planting seeds in a greenhouse, and they would go out in the spring and harvest one of the farm's crops from the field. Because these students would have had a full school year's experience learning about twenty-first-century farming in their area, they would then become farming ambassadors, promoting the idea that farming does have a positive impact on their local community.

Did I apply for the grant? Yes. Did my proposal get funded? Yes! Even though I had to really scramble to put the proposal together, I felt it was important that the students were given another opportunity to experience learning outside our school's walls. Again, I would be bringing our students to places they might never have seen before or could even imagine but that would nevertheless be so close to their home or school.

Sometimes as a teacher, I wonder if I will ever see firsthand whether what I am teaching has had an impact on my students if it isn't being assessed. Maybe my teacher who would always remind my class that we were in school to learn the three R's would think that my kind of opportunity learning for my kindergarten students has no value when it comes to student learning. She might even sit me down and say, "Suzen, why are you always having your students do things and go places? They need to be in their classroom, working and learning. Not traveling here, there, and everywhere to look at things."

While I was attending a local conference on poverty recently, I was talking with a health-care provider who works in the community where my school is located. She said, "Suzen, I need to tell you something. During this year's Fourth of July celebration, I saw one of the families from your school. The family was standing in front of a vegetable garden. As the mother spoke to her children about the importance of eating vegetables and the various types of vegetables that were being grown in the garden, one of her children turned to his mother and said, 'I already know all that. I learned all about gardening and vegetables in kindergarten.'"

CHAPTER TWO

Grade Four

Building Relationships with Whole-Heart Teaching

MARY GRAZIANO-GLYNN

School is about so much more than academics to me . . . and more about community . . . and how in my eyes, my students will always be my students.

LAYING THE FOUNDATION

The first day of school, he came strolling into the classroom with a bit of an apparently arrogant demeanor and an I-don't-care attitude. It didn't take long, though, to see that the attitude was a total cover-up. Brent was not a bad kid, but he certainly thought he was. He had no faith in himself whatsoever, and from what he perceived, no teacher had ever had any faith in him, either. I say *perceived* because he did have good teachers prior to this year. I know he did, and I know they cared. Sometimes, though, even great teachers don't make the right connections that are necessary to establish strong relationships with their students.

A colleague of mine once gave me a piece of advice: "Kids don't care unless they absolutely know and trust that you do." Brent was the perfect example of this observation. He needed a strong relationship with a teacher whom he trusted, someone who he felt truly cared about him and was interested in his life. Brent needed someone who did not stop trying to find a way to connect with him, no matter how many walls he had built around himself and no matter what type of reputation accompanied him at the start of the new school year.

Aside from the reputation, what I already knew about Brent was that he liked to run. I am part of a teacher running group that holds monthly 5K races for our students and their families, and I sometimes saw Brent at our races when he was in third grade. At those events, I discovered that he was actually quite a good little runner. Although he had never been to any other outside races before, he was fast, and he had amazing potential. He had no idea, however, what kind of potential he had, and for a child with low self-esteem and completely unsure of himself, I knew that I had found something to work with to build our connection.

I began to deepen that connection by getting to know him and by showing him that I was interested in his life. I couldn't accomplish this task by just giving him an interest survey at the start of the year. I had to make time every single day to reach out to him, not only to point out his successes and praise him when he was doing well, but also to talk to him about things other than academics: his interests, his family, or what he did over the weekend. All kids care about *something*. It's my job to figure out what that something is and run with it.

Of course, there were days when a question like, "So what did you do this weekend?" elicited a response like, "Not much," but my backup plan at first was to lead the conversation into something about running.

"Well, you know what I did? I ran in a five-K this weekend with some of my friends. It was so much fun. There was an obstacle course and mud and everything. I'm going to write about it later during writers' workshop," I told him.

His interest was suddenly piqued, and a conversation blossomed. Conversations like this one occurred every day. They took place when he first came into the classroom or while I sat with him at lunch when I was on cafeteria duty. They may have happened while I was in the hallway on the way to a classroom bathroom break or on the playground during my recess duty. They were authentic conversations that took place in those few spare moments outside of instructional time—spare moments that we all have. They didn't happen at the same time or in the same place, but they happened every day. I made sure of it. Brent and I were slowly connecting. The walls started to come down, and his behavior began to change. He was happier. He smiled more. He participated in class. He even began to put effort into his work and stay on task the majority of the time.

Brent was also becoming a runner right before my eyes. He attended our 5K races regularly. I shared with him my personal experiences with running: how I didn't become a runner until a few years prior, how I couldn't even run a mile when I did start running, and how I now had already run a whole marathon. I told him that with goals, plans, and hard work, I believed that I—or anyone else, for that matter—could accomplish anything.

As for academics, Brent was a struggling reader. He had been in Title I since kindergarten and was not making the growth that he should. Like most struggling readers, he hated to read. It is my belief, however, that a child who hates to read is most likely a child who hasn't found the right books yet. I knew from our conversations that some other hobbies Brent enjoyed outside of school involved the outdoors. He enjoyed learning about the woods and wildlife. He also liked to hunt. I found as many books as I possibly could on those topics, and I made sure they were around for him to "discover" in our classroom library while he picked out books for his book box. Also, when I went back and reread a parent survey his mom had filled out at the beginning of the year, I noticed that although he claimed to hate reading, he actually loved reading hunting and fishing magazines and catalogs. I called her up and told her to send them in, so that he could read them during independent reading.

Brent and I also came up with some reading goals. We started out by discussing everything *he thought* he did well, and then we talked about what *he felt* he needed to work on. We both agreed that his biggest hurdle was his fluency, so we decided to work on it. We made an official reading contract, signed it, and even shook on it. He and I met for ten minutes a day (aside from his regular twenty-minute guided reading time), and we worked on his fluency through repeated readings and other activities from *The Fluent Reader* by Timothy Rasinski.[1] Brent colored in his fluency graphs, and we tracked his progress every day. Each day, he was getting a little bit better. By December, Brent had gained over a year's reading growth, and he was released from Title I.

I don't credit Brent's growth to my being some kind of master reading teacher. I do, however, credit it to our relationship. If Brent didn't trust me, he wouldn't have tried.

My Brent story doesn't end on the last day of school of his fourth-grade year. *My* students will always be *my* students. Sometime in November of his fifth-grade year, I ran into Brent's mom at the grocery store. She shared with me some struggles he was having socially and behaviorally at middle school. I decided to write him a letter and send it to his new school. In the letter, I didn't share what I knew. I just asked him how his year was going and if he wanted to run with me one day a week after school and train for a 15K that I planned on running in the spring (I had already cleared this request with his mom). He eagerly accepted my offer, and we started training.

When race day finally came, his nerves took over. Two miles into it, his psyche started messing with him, and he didn't think he could do it. Phrases like "You can do this" and You've got this" came out of my mouth, just as they had in the classroom when he was frustrated with himself. An hour and a half later, he crossed the finish line. I looked into the eyes of this eleven-year old boy as he just accomplished one of his biggest goals: running a 15K race. Being eleven years old, Brent was by far the youngest kid entered in the race. The next oldest was sixteen. I was beyond proud of him.

The next day, my principal went up to the middle school to congratulate him. She said he proudly wore his finisher's medal, and he told her, "Next year, I'm running track, and when I'm old enough, I'm training for a marathon." A marathon! The boy who once had no confidence in himself whatsoever now believed that he could someday run a marathon—and you know what? I believe it, too!

Brent might be just one student, but I shared his story because he is just one example of what I do with all of my twenty-plus students each year. I build relationships first. Once the relationships are built, the academics fall into place. The reality is this: kids won't try or work hard for someone they don't like, and again, they won't care unless, as my colleague said, they know *you* care. They have to truly know it and *feel* it. It's not something you can just preach about to students or post on a wall.

Each year, I am lucky enough to have many Brents in my classroom. In fact, the Brents of the world make up the majority of my classroom population. I say "lucky," because these are the kids who have made me a better teacher. They've made me do research, try new techniques, step out of my comfort zone, take risks, develop serious compassion, and, yes, sometimes even fail. Not everything I try works, but that's okay. Mistakes are important, and as I tell my students, I learn from them.

Each year, the curriculum, the standards, and the standardized testing may or may not stay the same. Those variables are out of my hands. One thing I can be certain of is that my students will *always* be different. What works for one class of students might not work for another. What works from student to student within the same class might not even work. Each child is a story, one that I have to read and study and learn about. No story is the same, yet I am a character in each of them, a character that has many roles. I am a teacher, a coach, a role model, a cheerleader, and an advocate. I believe in all of my students. I push them to dream big, and I give them the assurance, the love, and the recognition that they need to reach those dreams. In the process, I build those critical relationships that are at the center of what I call *whole-heart teaching*.

How did I get here?

Eight years ago, I moved from southern to central Maine to be closer to my family. I had already taught at two different schools prior to my move. After taking a job in my current district, I discovered that many of my students did not have the same opportunities as the children in my past districts. Programs such as drama, swimming, and skiing were not available for elementary-age children; nor was there money for such programs. There was hardly any technology, and, again, no money for it. In fact, just two years ago, our budget was completely frozen, meaning we obtained nothing for our classrooms at the start of our new school year—not even a ream of paper. There were definite inequities between school districts, and I also noticed big differences in the kids.

Day after day, my "fun" lessons weren't working. Only a handful of kids actually seemed to care about school and appeared intrinsically motivated. Day after day, I also found myself becoming frustrated, angry, and upset. Although I did my best not to let the kids see my state of emotions, I'm pretty sure it came through. I kept students inside for recess every day. I took privileges away. There were all kinds of consequences, and I used positive reinforcement too. I even tried behavior plans. They seemed to work, but only as a short-term solution.

Miserable and extremely disappointed in myself, I searched for what I thought was the best solution; I looked for new teaching jobs. I looked in different areas—areas like those where I used to teach: places with less poverty, more parental involvement, and more opportunities and where parents valued education. Thank God I didn't find such an area.

Around the same time, I was working on polishing my philosophy of education (for the job applications), and I found a quote by Johann Goethe: "If we treat people as they ought to be, we help them become what they're capable of being."[2] It made me stop and think about my own students and the unfortunate reality of children living in poverty: many of them would walk into my classroom at the start of a new school year, already feeling defeated. Aside from any learning difficulties they were dealing with at school, many of them also had numerous external factors at home working against their educational success. These students doubted their competence so much that they had lacked the desire to try, to succeed, and maybe even to appear to the outside world (and me) as if they couldn't. These children weren't intentionally trying to be difficult; they were just in survival mode, and so were their parents. They didn't need labels. They needed someone to wholeheartedly believe in them.

It became apparent to me that as their teacher, I needed to teach my students *how* to compensate for all of their disadvantages. There isn't a curriculum for this lesson, by the way, and it certainly wasn't taught to me in college. Giving my students the skills that they needed went way beyond the realm of academics.

Engagement? Sure, it was critical, but *empowerment*—that's what these children needed. My new philosophy became something along the lines of this: Hook them with the fun and engagement, but then make sure to empower them. Don't just give them the content; give them the skills necessary to pursue their *own* dreams and to successfully navigate throughout life.

When I walk into my classroom each day, I want to see a community: a kind and caring community of learners all working together to accomplish their goals. If I don't see this community—if I see children who are talking badly to one another, who don't have good manners, who can't seem to work together because they can't stop fighting, or who don't seem to care, then unfortunately, it reflects on me. It's a tough pill to swallow, but it's the truth. Ultimately, I am the one who creates the weather in my classroom, and it is my job to teach my kids *how* to care and *how* to be part of a community. Keeping a positive attitude throughout all of it is essential. Building this kind of community is a fundamental part of whole-heart teaching.

There's no such thing as "I can't." There is only "I can't . . . *yet.*"

This year, like every year, on the first day of school, my classroom was bare. If I want to build a community of caring, responsible children and help each of them develop a sense of agency, I need to remember that I'm only one piece of the puzzle. There are still twenty-five-plus other pieces joining me, and *together*, we have to make the community our own. There are no premade posters or last year's anchor charts on the walls. There is only one sign hanging, and it says, "In this classroom, we don't do easy. We make easy happen through hard work and learning." We refer to it often, and it becomes a motto for us. My students need to know that when something isn't easy, they have to work even harder; they have to persevere. They also need to be equipped with the skills necessary to handle all the bumps in the road that life has in store. Whether it's not understanding fractions or failing their first driving exam, they will most certainly encounter bumps. It's how they deal with those bumps that truly matters.

On that first day, my students and I start off with a group activity where they answer the following questions:

Our classroom should be _____ every day.

What should kids in our class be doing to make sure our class runs as smoothly as possible?

What would you like to learn this year in fourth grade?

What do you need to do in order to be successful this year?

What does Mrs. G need to do to help you this year?

School is important because _____.

These questions are written on chart paper, and we hang them in different parts of the room. Students write their answers on sticky notes and post them on the chart, and then we talk about them. This year, as with all other years, their answers were extremely vague. I saw a lot of "Be good" for the question about what they need to be doing to be successful. My question to them was, "Well, what does it mean to be good?" I heard responses like "Listen," "Pay attention," and "Don't talk." I never heard anything about being proactive, making goals, persevering, using teamwork, or being problem solvers. When I probed a little more about what it meant to pay attention and listen, they really couldn't explain that, either. I received more vague answers like "Be respectful." It's as if they could say the terms, but they didn't actually grasp the meanings behind them.

Just knowing phrases like "Be good," "Be safe," "Be responsible," and "Be respectful" was not enough. If my students were to understand what being a real community meant, they needed to actually know what it looked like, sounded like, and felt like. They needed to learn the lifelong skills that would not only help build our community, but also help each of them develop a strong sense of agency, the belief that everything they do matters and that they are in control of themselves. To accomplish these tasks, I introduced them to *The 7 Habits of Happy Kids*, by Sean Covey.[3] These habits became embedded in virtually everything we did. Truthfully, they could have also been called the "seven habits of happy teachers," as they taught me a great deal about my own personal life as well. They changed the way I view others, myself, and life in general. The seven habits have also changed the way my classroom operates (see the sidebar "The Seven Happy Habits in Our Classroom").

THE SEVEN HAPPY HABITS IN OUR CLASSROOM

Be Proactive: I'm in Charge of Me

No matter what obstacles we're facing, we're still in control of our own lives. This is the habit we used when we talked about being responsible, a term that most of the kids knew, yet couldn't explain. We used this habit to talk about choosing our own attitudes and moods, not blaming others (or anything else) for our choices or actions, taking initiative, and doing the right thing even when no one is looking.

Begin with the End in Mind: Always Think Ahead and Have a Plan

One of the most critical things that children need to learn to do at a young age is to set goals. We had goals for everything in our classroom, from academics to a work ethic, citizenship, and personal goals we had for ourselves outside of school. We also used this habit to talk about thinking ahead. All actions will have an outcome. Outcomes can be good or bad. What kind of outcome will particular actions have? Thinking ahead is always a good idea. It's a great skill for children to acquire, especially for those who are impulsive.

Put First Things First: Work First; Then Play!

When you have goals, it is so important to stick to the plan to meet those goals. We used this habit to discuss setting priorities, being prepared and organized, spending time on the most important things, and saying no to things that we shouldn't do.

Think Win-Win: Everyone Can Win

All challenges are an opportunity for growth. I-can-do-this attitudes are important not only for ourselves, but also for those who are around us. My students needed to learn that in addition to gaining happiness from their own success, they could gain happiness from their classmates' success as well. Not everything had to be a competition to see who could go first, who had the better idea, or who was smarter.

Seek First to Understand, Then to Be Understood: Listen Before You Talk

Empathy and compassion are difficult things to teach, but it can be done. My students had a hard time seeing anything other than their own ways and had great difficulty understanding each other's differences. Communicating with one another posed a great challenge.

Synergize: Together Is Better

Two heads are better than one, but not if those heads are constantly fighting and if every head is only looking out for himself or herself (survival mode). Teaching my fourth-graders how to be a team was essential, not only for our community, but for each of them individually. Knowing how to collaborate is a critical life skill.

Sharpen the Saw: Balance Is Best

Learning could happen anywhere, and it should. I hoped that my students would eventually view learning as a wonderful opportunity, a means to find answers to all of their amazing questions (that they should always be asking). Learning did not have to be associated only with school, and it didn't have to stop when they walked out our classroom doors. Also, their minds and bodies needed to be ready to learn with the proper rest, nutrition, and movement.

IMPLEMENTING THE SEVEN HABITS

I started with the first habit: be proactive. I spent only about twenty minutes on Monday (during our morning meeting) introducing it. I talked about the word *proactive* and what it meant, and we all shared personal experiences (either positive or negative) that dealt with that habit. I modeled for them by sharing first, and then they turned and talked to their rug partners about one of their own experiences. The chart paper with the habit written on it then went up on the wall. We spent the rest of the week working on being proactive. My students each created a goal around this habit. The goal could be anything that fell within the boundaries of academics, work ethic, or citizenship, as long as it had to do with being proactive. At first, their goals were vague. I saw things like "Be proactive and get better at math," and I had to work with the students on being more specific. Eventually goals like "Be proactive by immediately practicing my math facts whenever I'm finished with other work" were created. For just a quick minute each morning, the students turned and talked to their table partners about the specific thing or things they were going to work on for the day in order to be proactive. At the end of the day, the students assessed themselves on a scale of "fist to five" on how well they did working on their particular goal. A fist meant they hadn't tried at all; five meant they had done their absolute best and had enjoyed all kinds of positive, proactive experiences throughout the day. They then shared their experiences with their table partners. Not only were students being introduced to a lifelong skill (being proactive), but they also practiced the skill daily and self-reflected on that practice as well.

Each week, I introduced a new habit, and we followed the same process. Most goals were completely different from one another, because students chose their *own* goals. But the goals always centered on that particular habit of the week. Of course, at the start of the year, kids sometimes used the same goal as a neighbor, but that was okay because we were a community, and a community *shares* ideas. The students weren't "stealing" ideas, as some of the kids tried to complain about. In time, once students started becoming comfortable with self-reflection, all the goals were different and truly unique to each individual child. Students even started helping one another come up with goals, in light of their observations.

After all of the habits were introduced and practiced, students self-reflected on the process. Which habits seemed easier than others? Which habits were still a struggle? Rather than work on the same habit, everyone chose a habit that was personally challenging, and the students created their own goals. I made goals, too. I expressed to my students how putting first things first was not always the easiest thing for me to do. When I arrived home after school, I had trouble exercising, because I put it off by doing all kinds of other things first. Before I knew it, it was really late, I was tired, and I didn't feel like exercising, so I didn't (my problem was much like their approach to homework). One of my goals would focus on the third habit (put first things first), and when I arrived home each night, I would make sure to run first and then do everything else after.

Students used the seven habits to make goals in four areas: academics, work ethic, citizenship, and personal choice. With guidance, they chose whichever area of academics that they were struggling with and came up with a specific goal. They did the same thing for work ethic and citizenship. Their personal-choice goal needed to be worked on outside school. One student wanted to shoot more baskets in basketball; another wanted to do more chores around the house. It didn't matter what the goal was, as long as it was unique to that student and what he or she truly needed and wanted to work on. We posted these goals on their desks, and the students reviewed and self-reflected on them daily and updated them as needed.

By giving my students ownership of their goals and letting them choose what they wanted and needed to improve on, I empowered them. Their intrinsic motivation skyrocketed. They felt good when they met their goals and wanted to keep feeling that way. They also started believing in themselves. The frustrated "I can't" that I heard so often turned into the motivated "I can't . . . *yet.*" Had I just given them their goals, they wouldn't have cared as much. In their eyes, I would have been just another teacher telling them what they were doing wrong.

The habits were integrated into everything we did. Each day, I made sure that every learning target for each lesson incorporated one of the habits. Targets such as "I can synergize with my partner to infer the meaning of unknown words in my *Titanic* article" were posted, talked about, and discussed at the start and end of every lesson. We always took the time to wrap up each lesson with more self-reflection. We called our learning targets *I-can statements.* The students used their fist-to-five self-assessment not only to assess how they did with the content, but also to assess how they did with the habits. We always discussed what went well and what didn't go well—a discussion that took only a few minutes during each lesson. Having those honest conversations with my kids was extremely valuable to their self-reflection. My students needed to be metacognitive, constantly thinking about their thinking and self-reflecting on their actions. If they didn't, their learning wasn't meaningful. They just went through the motions, not even thinking about the process and setting irrelevant goals.

Friday journals were another self-reflection tool that my students used. This tool was a choice on our "What should I do when I'm done?" board. (Early in the year, we had created a list of things we could do when we were done with an assignment. We called this our "What should I do when I'm done?" board.) By Friday, students were asked to have at least one written journal entry that told someone at home what they had worked on in school that week. Inside the journals were self-reflection forms. Students filled out their forms, stating what went well for them during the week and what they could have done better. They also set an informal goal for the next week, in light of their reflections. These journals went home every Friday, so that their parents could read them. Parents were encouraged to write back.

In our classroom, we constantly referred to our habits. They weren't just introduced, talked about for a week, thrown up on the wall, and forgotten about. Using the happy habits as our guidelines, my students helped create expectations for everything. Together, we decided how our classroom should operate in light of our habits. Every expectation was posted, modeled, and practiced. We came up with expectations for everything, from the most basic concepts, like how to move around the room during transitions (despite how crowded it was), to the more serious, such as how to have self-control, what to do when we become frustrated, and how to hold ourselves, as well as one another, accountable. My students and I used terms like *goals, self-control, accountability,* and *perseverance* every day. They also practiced their expectations every day at the beginning of the year and then less frequently as the year went on. I wore a timer around my neck, and they loved it. I timed them while they practiced. I said things like, "Let's see how long it will take all of us to transition carefully and safely during this next readers' workshop rotation," or "Let's see how long we can have the whole class working with each other following our accountable listener expectations" (*eyes on the speaker, gestures showing him/her that you're truly listening, awake body language—no slouching and looking bored—reciprocating the conversation by asking questions or sharing something you know).* Students loved the timer practice, and they wanted to beat their previous time goals.

Through our accountability discussions, we came up with consequences for poor actions. My fourth-graders learned that consequences did not mean punishment. Punishment happens out of anger. It involves things like having students sit with their heads down at recess. Consequences are different. Yes, consequences might happen at recess, but they are not punishments. They are opportunities to talk about poor choices and chances to fix them and discuss what we could do better next time. They are also a way to practice our expectations some more.

Early in the year, I saw a student throwing food during lunch in the cafeteria. I didn't call him out on it in front of everyone. I quietly walked over, bent down to his level, and I told him I needed to see him at recess. When it was time to see him, I didn't scold him.

"So tell me why I needed to see you today," I asked him.

"Because I wasn't being respectful."

"What do you mean by that? What exactly were you doing?"

"I was throwing food."

"Yes, you were. What should you have been doing?"

"I should have been acting good."

"How? What could you have done differently?"

"I could have kept my food on my tray."

"Yes, you're right. I noticed you had a hard time at lunch today. You threw food. That's not like you. Our custodians work hard to keep our cafeteria clean, and throwing food only creates more work for them. Plus, you could have hit someone with your food. I know you can do better than that. Let's use this recess to review lunchroom procedures. Grab a tray and show me how you *should* act during lunch."

I grabbed a tray too, and we sat down pretending to have lunch, following all of the lunchroom procedures. We talked, like anyone would talk while having lunch, and we used the time to practice. When we finished, I said, "Look at that. See, I knew you could do it. I know I won't see you throwing food anymore!"

By dealing with the situation in a productive way, my student did not feel threatened. I know from experience that when students feel threatened, particularly those dealing with so many life stressors outside of school, they shut down, or worse, they blow up. Neither of those scenarios work; nor do they help to build those critical, trusting relationships that I need to build with students.

Teachable moments like the one I had in the cafeteria were everywhere. It was so important for me to take advantage of those moments to model for my students how to deal with situations constructively. If I wanted my students to be honest with one another, positively critique one another, and solve problems together, I clearly had to model for them how to do so. They also needed to practice using constructive critiquing.

One way we started using constructive critiquing was during writers' workshop. Whenever my students shared their writing pieces, we all came up with an "I like" and an "I wonder" for them. The *like* was something they did well. The *wonder* was something that they questioned and that could help them make their piece better. We applied this approach to many other areas as well. My classroom became a place where students not only held themselves accountable, but held each other accountable (in a positive way) as well.

SUPPORTING EMOTIONAL GROWTH

Among my twenty-seven fourth-graders, seven were special services (with various learning and cognitive disabilities), seven were Title I, and a few had some serious behavioral or emotional disorders. Overall, the class lacked the compassion necessary to understand and accept one another. The way they all treated each other was far from acceptable. My mission was not only to educate their minds, but also to educate their hearts.

I quickly learned that it didn't matter how often I preached kindness to them. I read the books with the right messages, we discussed them and applied them to our lives, and I often gave them the "treat others the way you want to be treated" speech. I found, though, that just as the words *respectful* and *responsible* were hard for my students to grasp, the kids didn't actually think about what my messages about kindness meant. They could tell me on numerous occasions to "treat others the way we want to be treated," but their actions did not match their words.

In our classroom, a mystery reader visited us weekly. Mystery readers were guest readers who chose a book, came in on Friday mornings, and read to my students. The kids never knew who the mystery reader was going to be, and they prepared questions beforehand to ask me (to try to guess the mystery reader) and then the mystery reader when he or she had finished the reading.

In November, the special services director in our district took part in our mystery reader program. She read a story called "The Goodness Gorillas."[4] I had never heard the story before, and neither had my students. "The Goodness Gorillas" was about a group of children who decided to perform random acts of kindness for people in their community, particularly for one boy, considered the bully of the class. The children in the story decided that this bully needed some kindness because, most likely, he acted out because he felt so badly about himself. While she read the story, something inside of me clicked, and I had a new idea that could possibly promote more compassion in our classroom.

After she left, we talked more about the story. I asked my students about my idea. "How would you all feel about becoming goodness gorillas?" They excitedly cheered. We decided that we would be the goodness gorillas of the school, doing random acts of kindness for students and staff, as well as for the greater community. Students created lists of acts we could do and the people or groups that could be the recipients of those acts. They also came up with a twist—the recipient of our acts had to pay it forward and do an act of kindness for someone else. Would our school be able to create a ripple effect of kindness? How far could one act of kindness go? We couldn't wait to find out.

Together, we drafted a letter, explaining our goodness gorilla project, and each student colored in a copy of a paper gorilla. I laminated many copies of the letter, as well as each gorilla. Every time we did an act, we sent along a gorilla and a letter. We hoped that the recipient would pay it forward to a new recipient and pass on the letter and the gorilla with his or her act. In our letter, we also asked for pictures. We wanted the recipients to send us pictures with the gorilla and explain what they did for their acts of kindness.

My students and I created a goodness gorilla bulletin board. On it, we kept the pictures and letters from the recipients of our acts. Many people who sent letters were firsthand recipients, but others were recipients from the paying-it-forward acts. We also kept three maps: one of our state, one of our country, and one of our world. We wanted to see how far our project would go, and we kept track with pushpins. Most of the acts of kindness stayed in Maine, although some made it to California, North Carolina, New Jersey, and Tennessee. We also kept a large gorilla on the board and kept track of my students' daily small acts of kindness that they did for one another. Each time one of us caught someone being kind, that person received a small heart to pin to the gorilla.

Throughout the year, we had many conversations about how it felt to participate in these acts. We read the letters from our recipients and discussed the feelings we experienced after hearing about their happiness. We spoke often about "working for cause, not for applause." Although I recognized my students for their kind acts, I wanted them to understand that the recognition wasn't the point.

My favorite goodness gorilla act occurred in the spring. One of the groups on our list was a local animal shelter. I asked my students what they wanted to do for the shelter. They naturally wanted to donate toys and treats. My students didn't have the money to donate to such a project, so I made them a deal, which involved our classroom reward system. Through a reward scheme called *classroomopoly*, my students earned weekly salaries of fake money. They also earned bonuses for working extra hard, and of course, they had to pay fines for various things, like not picking up their desks at the end of the day or losing their pencils. Every couple of weeks, we had an auction, where they could "buy" items with their salaries and bonuses. For this deal, I told them that for every hundred dollars in fake money they donated back to the money bucket, I would donate a dollar of real money to our Humane Society project. My kids were extremely protective of their classroomopoly money. Most of them, being very poor, viewed our auctions as one of the few chances to buy toys and treats. I truthfully wasn't sure how many kids would give up their money, and I really didn't expect them to. To my surprise, though, every single one of my students donated *every* classroomopoly dollar in his or her possession. We ended up with a package that contained fifty dollars' worth of toys and gift cards to send to the Humane Society.

The goodness gorilla project enabled my students to give to homeless shelters, orphanages, other classrooms, the Humane Society, soldiers, and so many more. It wasn't long before my students were asking me if they could start their own fund-raisers for cancer patients or for other local animal shelters. As for those hearts that they pinned to the gorilla, at first there was a lot of working for applause. Students seemed to intentionally do kind things to obtain my attention. It wasn't as genuine as I had hoped, but as the months went by, things drastically changed.

In June, we placed on our gorilla over one hundred hearts, each of them coming from recognition the students in my class gave *one another*, rather than *themselves*. My kids came up to me and told me things like, "Travis bought me a pencil at the book fair because I didn't have any money. I think he deserves a heart." Teachers would come up to me and tell me about incidents they witnessed on the playground, incidents that involved my students acting like kind, compassionate leaders.

In time, all of my students started complimenting one another, sharing, helping, and looking out for one another. They started putting each other first, not only noticing when someone else did something kind for them, but showing appreciation for it too. When it was time to take turns, I often heard, "No, it's okay. You can go," instead of arguments over what was fair. When a deep freeze happened on our laptops and my students lost all of their How to Survive a Natural Disaster projects, they banded together to redo them. I watched students selflessly giving up laptops to let the slower typists work first or, even better, helping peers type before working on their own projects.

During my evaluation conference at the end of the school year, my principal opened with the following remarks:

> When I walk into your room, the culture of your classroom is phenomenal. Kids are working together; kids who didn't get along before are actually helping one another out. Your students jump up to hold the door open for me, and they politely ask me how my day is going. They say please and thank you. The biggest thing that I've noticed is that they're like that everywhere. I see it in the hallway, in the cafeteria, and on the playground, not just in your classroom. Your students are not the same group of children you had in September. When I walk into your classroom, I don't just see a community, I can *feel* it, and it's truly amazing.

I agreed with my principal. In fact, my kids amazed me more and more every single day. Establishing that culture of compassion was another crucial part of my whole-heart teaching.

"I WONDERS" AND CHOICE

One spring day, my class received an anonymous letter from a concerned community member asking the class for help.[5] The letter explained that the county was experiencing an obesity epidemic and that our class was known for being leaders. The letter asked the class to take on the mission of educating the community through a health and wellness fair in the school's gymnasium.[6] The kids were ecstatic. "I wonder who wrote it?" "Wow, I can't believe that they want *us* to do this." They saw this as something fun and meaningful, and they couldn't wait to get started.

We quickly got to work, coming up with all of our "I wonders." *I wonders* were what we called our questions. I encouraged questioning from the very start of our school year. What started out as a great reading comprehension strategy turned into a strategy we used for everything. I wanted my students to understand that asking questions meant that they were thinking. I even created something called a *wonder wall*. As students read or talked—or did anything, for that matter—I encouraged them to keep track of their questions on sticky notes and hang them on our wonder wall. I also encouraged them to find the answers to their questions. The wonder wall served a second purpose as well. Sometimes, I could use their wonders to plan lessons based on what *they wanted to know*.

At this moment, though, our wonders revolved around our letter. We first acted as inference detectives and tried to figure out some of the words that confused us in the letter. We then listed all of our wonders, from words we were unsure of, to questions we had about the human body in general. After all of our questions were listed, my students perused all kinds of books about the different human body systems. Using those books, they decided which systems they each wanted to learn more about. They each picked an organ and decided what they wanted their specific topic to be. Topics ranged from how smoking affects the lungs to how we control our blood pressure, what our kidneys do for us, how we can keep them healthy, how exercise helps the heart, why bones break, how we can make bones strong, and so many more. Some students even picked topics close to their hearts because they had family members who suffered from particular diseases like diabetes or glaucoma.

Once the students chose their topics, they created lists of more I-wonders in their research journals. Over the next two months, they conducted research during our literacy block. During this two-hour readers' workshop, students had a lesson and then rotated through four centers, one of which was guided reading with me. The other centers were based on choice, but there were always centers that offered various activities within the following areas: comprehension, accuracy, fluency, and vocabulary. I made research one of their comprehension centers. Students used laptops and various books to answer their I-wonders and to take notes on their topics during this rotation.

My fourth-graders used skills that we worked on all year: questioning, thinking, determining important information, and paraphrasing, and they gathered all the information they needed. I even brought in some guest medical speakers to share what they knew about health and wellness. Students eagerly took notes and explored x-rays, ambulances, and surgery prep kits.

When all their notes were gathered, they had more choices—choices on how they wanted to present their information. There were PowerPoint presentations, brochures, informational two-sided pamphlets, and posters. Despite the different media the kids used, all students included key components of informational text. The students also created additional projects to go along with their information. On the day of the wellness fair, there were jump-rope stations that demonstrated how exercise increases the heart rate. There was a blood pressure station where the school nurse helped a student take willing participants' blood pressures. There were several experiments that showed different human body functions such as how the brain sends messages through the body, how the kidneys filter waste, and how yoga and stress balls alleviate stress chemicals released in the brain. Twenty-seven stations took up occupancy in our gym!

The gym was filled with students, staff, and parents. Former mystery readers joined us. Even the superintendent and assistant superintendent accepted our invitations. My students beamed with pride and couldn't wait to share what they had learned with our community. They even took turns walking around, sharing and learning from one another.

When the health and wellness fair was over, I continuously heard the same thing from every adult: "Wow, not only did they have amazing information and projects, but they could also truly articulate their topic. They did so well answering questions. It was clear that they took this project seriously, and it was so impressive."

"It was impressive," I agreed.

My students' health and wellness fair was a meaningful project, full of choices. Students had a real, authentic purpose—to educate our community.

They also had many choices along the way. When students have choices, their interests guide them and they become more invested and more excited. They want to keep learning, and they take ownership of their work. Again, it's all about empowering them.

GETTING ON THEIR LEVEL

"I have a secret," I told my students.

Their eyes lit up. I suddenly had everyone's undivided attention. "But before I tell you, you have to promise to not tell." They eagerly nodded, calling out, "We won't tell, we promise."

"When I was your age, I hated to write."

I still had their interest. In fact, I think I had their interest even more, because most of them could relate. Writers' workshop was a mess that year. My students hated writing, and I knew I had to be creative and do something drastic to change it.

"I hated to write," I said, "because I never knew what to write about. My teachers had me come up with different interests and topics and ideas, but I didn't want to write about them. Do you know what, though? Now, I *love* to write."

"Why? What happened?" they all asked.

"I decided to look for stories everywhere and to write on my own at home. I asked my mom to buy me a journal. I kept track of all the things I could write a story about. Sometimes it was something really silly, like how my brother knocked the head off the snowman that I just built. I wrote all about that moment and how it made me feel. Sometimes I didn't even write stories. I would just write lists of words that maybe described an object in front of me. I wrote songs too. Once, I even wrote a whole story about the Christmas lights on my tree.

"How did you write a whole story about lights?" one student asked.

"I just described them: everything I saw, how they made me feel, and then I just used my imagination and added to it. The funny thing is, I love to write now, but I hardly ever write anymore."

"Why?" one of them asked.

"Because, you guys know how busy I am. I can hardly find the time. I think I've come up with a solution, though."

My students couldn't wait to hear how I was about to solve one of my own life problems.

"Well, I thought that maybe you could write for ten to fifteen minutes a day, completely uninterrupted. That time could be all yours to write about anything at all that you wanted to write about."

"Even about zombies?" a student excitedly interrupted.

"Yes, even zombies," I stated.

"What about Pokémon?" another asked.

"Yes, I mean it, anything you want. But here's the deal, instead of me walking around like I usually do, checking in and conferencing, this time will be our sacred writing time where that's *all* we do. You will write the whole time, and I will write too. I'll even take turns sitting with different groups each day, but I won't conference. I want this time to write myself! When we're finished, I will even share my writing with you! Should we try it today?"

My students, who thoroughly disliked writing, couldn't wait to get started. I had no idea if it had to do with the news that their teacher, like them, had once hated writing too. Or maybe they wanted to help me out with my problem, or maybe they wanted to hear what I wrote about. Perhaps now they felt that they had total choice over their writing. My guess, however, was that it had something to do with all four factors.

Like everything else, I set the timer, and we started writing. Some kids just sat, but that was okay. They were thinking, which was a start. Others wrote a couple of sentences. Some wrote a whole page. When the timer went off, I directed them to the gathering area. I asked if anyone had any writing shares. As usual, no one wanted to share his or her writing piece, so I asked the kids if they wanted to hear my story. I told them it was about a roller coaster ride. They all nodded. I held my paper out in front of me, but then I stopped and put it down at my side.

"I hate sharing my writing in front of people," I told them. "It scares me. What if you guys think it's stupid and I get embarrassed?"

All of a sudden I had twenty-seven children coaching me, just as I coached them. They were telling me they wouldn't think it was stupid and to not be scared. My tactic was working.

"Okay, I'm going to be brave. Are you sure you want to hear it?

The loudest yeahs and yeses came bellowing out of their mouths. I started reading. The whole time I read, they were each smiling from ear to ear and laughing at different parts, like the part about how terrified I was and how I thought my husband was insane because he let go and put his hands in the air.

When I finished, I asked if anybody had any writing shares. Slowly, a few hands went up into the air. As each child shared, more and more wanted to share. Some kids didn't write a bit during those fifteen minutes, but they asked if they could go into their writing folders and share pieces they previously wrote. At this point, the time allotted for writers' workshop was almost over, but I couldn't stop. This moment was far too important. By the time we finished, twenty-two out of twenty-seven students had shared their writing.

From that day on, no matter what type of writing I taught—persuasive, procedural, informational, or personal narrative—and regardless of the lesson or the genre that we worked on, my students and I had those free-choice minutes. During those minutes, they wrote about anything they wanted to and were challenged to complete a whole-class goal (e.g., "I can use transition words when I write"). Students also worked on individual writing goals, tailored to their needs. I always wrote with them, even when I had absolutely nothing to write about. After all, I was their model, and they needed to see me write. I shared with them too. We had many laughs over my mischievous dog's antics and my silly running stories. My kids not only saw me as a writer, but as a real person who had experiences just like them—experiences that could so easily be turned into writing pieces.

The more I wrote and shared, the more my students tried to mimic the strategies I used. The more they wrote, the more their writing improved. Best of all, my students developed a love of writing, something their parents witnessed at our big year-end event, A Night for the Stars: A Celebration of Writing. The students transformed the lobby and the gymnasium into "Hollywood" for the celebration, including a Walk of Fame: individual stars with sets of decorated, traced handprints for each of my twenty-seven students.

One by one, each of my students, proudly and confidently, walked the red carpet, up the stairs of the stage, and took a seat in the "author's chair," which had been strategically placed in front of the Hollywood sign. They read their writing pieces into real, working microphones, a big deal to them for sure. The pieces ranged from personal narratives to realistic fiction to fantasy—yes, some were even about zombies and mysterious plane crashes. Despite the different topics and genres, some things were consistently the same: enticing leads, exciting word choice, great voice, fabulous organization, and smooth sentence fluency, to name a few. Of course, I cannot leave out what else was most apparent: their enthusiasm for writing and their excitement to share as they took their author's seat. Even my two nonreaders eagerly made their way up on stage, without any hesitation, peer helpers at their sides, whispering in their ears the words that they had written, but couldn't remember how to read. There was no embarrassment, just pride, and of course, acceptance for the differences among our community, a community of writers.

Proud parents, grandparents, siblings, and former teachers filled all seventy chairs that we set up earlier in the day. I'm sure that through those beaming, happy smiles and proud faces, our audience could never imagine the tears, the crumpled-up papers, the struggles, the bed-to-bed stories, the sighs, the moans and groans of, "Do we have to write? I hate to write. I have nothing to write about, and I'm bad at writing" that I once experienced with all of them.[7] It was hard even for me to imagine it these days, when students who once begged to skip writing were now begging at the end of writers' workshop, "Can we *please* keep writing?"

At the end of the evening, I was approached by a set of parents who eagerly exclaimed, "This is our third child going through elementary school. We've been to many author's teas, but we've never seen children so confident and excited to get up on stage and share their own writing. Plus, their writing was actually really good. What's your secret?"

My response? "There's no secret. They owned it. It was *their* night. They created it. I just facilitated it. As for their confidence, well, that's simple, I believe in them as authors, and now they believe in themselves too."

You see, nights like this one don't just magically come together. Nor is there any kind of secret when it comes to being a teacher. Nights like this are the result of a long journey, one that involves so much more than academics—the journey that I call whole-heart teaching.

EVIDENCE OF READING ACHIEVEMENT GAINS

Last year, according to Fountas and Pinnell benchmarking data, only 46 percent of my students started the school year reading on grade level, and 25 percent of my class were at least two to four years behind.[8] My student learning objective at the start of the year was for each child to achieve *at least* one year's growth (to close those gaps) in reading. This was a difficult task, considering how far behind my students were. The children who were two to four years behind hadn't made a whole year's growth within one grade level—ever—in all four years of their elementary school experience.

By the end of the year, 92 percent of my students met their growth targets for their student learning objectives. This meant that every child in my classroom, except for two, met his or her growth targets. Five students actually exceeded their targets (gaining one and a half to almost three years of growth). The child who grew almost three years had actually plateaued in third grade. She was reading at a mid-first-grade level during her whole third-grade year and when she entered grade four. By the end of fourth grade, she was reading at a beginning fourth-grade level. The two students who hadn't met their one-year growth target missed it by only *one* benchmark, which means they were just a few months shy of one year's growth. The class's overall improvement brought the percentage of students whose reading levels met the standards from 46 percent at the beginning of the year to 71 percent at the end of the year.

My students made tremendous growth, after years of little or no growth during their key windows of opportunity. They grew socially, they grew emotionally, and they grew academically. I know that they were being taught all the necessary reading skills and strategies in their prior years, but for most of them, school had become a place they hated, a place they associated with failure, a place where they thought reading was work and not pleasure, and a place where they couldn't see the value in what they were doing. Their attitudes about school drastically changed when they reached fourth grade, and so did their academic success.

Being a teacher means I am always learning: from books, from colleagues, and even from my students. I use everything I know about my students to take them where they *need* to go, despite any obstacles. When I come across those obstacles, I see them as opportunities—opportunities to learn something new and then use what I've learned to help my students overcome the challenges. I am always searching for new ways to make learning meaningful and relevant to each of my kids. I view each student as a whole child, and I understand that not only do they have academic needs but they have social and emotional needs as well. I know that if any of them is struggling socially or emotionally, then an academic struggle is inevitable. I can't possibly teach my students every fact there is to know, but I can show them just how much potential they possess and how very valuable that potential is.

CHAPTER THREE

Grade Four/Five Multiage

A Journey of Transformation: Redesigning the Classroom for Students

SHELLY MOODY

The most important thing we can do as educators is to help students discover the power of the word *yet*.

MY BEGINNINGS

Mrs. Wakem, Mr. Cosgrove, Mrs. Rushton, Mrs. Gauer. These are a few of the names that come to mind when I think of the teachers who helped shape the way I approach my own classroom. What makes them stand out from the rest? Maya Angelou said it best. "I've learned that people will forget what you said, people will forget what you did, but people will never forget how you made them feel."[1]

I remember when Mrs. Wakem let me make the sign for our classroom library in fourth grade. I can even recall how she delicately offered feedback when I incorrectly wrote "libary" in large, colorful letters. Even though I had to redo my original design to correct my mistake, I walked into our classroom every day feeling at home when I noticed my sign proudly hanging above our bookshelves. I was not a visitor in this classroom; I was a member of a community.

I remember how Mr. Cosgrove created silly nicknames for each student in his social studies class. Seventh grade was such a difficult year for me after moving to a new city and a new school. I started the year feeling a bit lost, desperate to find peers with similar interests. Sitting in the back of the room, he knew how to draw me in and make me feel like part of the class. I knew that he was rooting for me to be happy at school, and even though I never went to him in tears, I felt that I could, and that was enough.

I remember the way Mrs. Rushton, my middle school math teacher, made me feel like a rock star. My mind was always like a knotted rope when it came to math, all tangled. In her classroom, I felt successful for the first time with algebraic equations and concepts that had puzzled me for years. It was her patience and her silly antics at the chalkboard that transformed me from a reluctant, frustrated mathematician to a more confident learner.

I remember Mrs. Gauer, my high school French teacher, who always greeted us with a smile in the hallway before class and a friendly "Bonjour!" I can still see the picture frames filled with wallet-sized senior pictures that lined her walls. After two years of French class together, I couldn't wait to hand her a copy of my senior portrait for her Class of 1994 frame. Walking into her classroom every day, I felt important, and I knew our faces would grace the walls of her classroom for years to come. We would not be forgotten.

As I've approached my own classroom, I've kept these teachers and the lessons they taught me close to my heart.

Each child is valuable.

Be present.

Strive to make every learner feel like a rock star.

Create a classroom that centers on your students.

MY JOURNEY OF TRANSFORMATION

I've always viewed myself as a student-centered teacher. Every day, I lead a morning meeting where the students and I greet one another and share moments from our lives. I create projects, such as our autobiographical timelines, where students design a creative representation highlighting special moments from their lives. I love reading to my class under the shady tree behind our school. I teach with laughter. I believe in connecting with the community through our giving tree donations at the local library at Christmas. I know my students as people outside our classroom. I learn about their passions. I attend their sporting events and ask about their weekend games on a Monday morning. I celebrate their accomplishments. But after attending a workshop in the summer of 2010, I had to ask myself, Is my instruction student-centered enough?

In 2010, my school district, along with the Maine Department of Education and five other cohort schools, began a partnership with RISC (Reinventing Schools Coalition) to transform our schools to a more proficiency-based, student-centered model.[2] As a district, we found that according to our achievement levels on the annual state assessment, we were not meeting the needs of all students. Our district administrators gathered a group of stakeholders to create a strategic plan and vision for our schools that led to the goal of moving from a time-driven system to a performance-based one. Part of the vision included allowing students to own their learning and have a voice in their education—a goal that aligned with the work of RISC. During the summer, I attended the Classroom Design and Delivery workshop led by RISC trainers, who encouraged me to reflect on my student-centered environment. This training caused me to transform how I create my classroom environment and how I approach my student-centered instruction.

In the past, I spent hours, days, even weeks, decorating my classroom before the students arrived on the first day. As we participated in this three-day training, my colleagues and I started to ask each other why:

Why do *we* decorate our classrooms if this is a shared space?

Why do we create our procedures for routines without the students' participation?

Why do we list rules or agreements for behavior before the students arrive?

It was time for a new approach. After this three-day training, I went back to my classroom invigorated, inspired, and ready to put new ideas into practice.

As a staff, we spent many meetings brainstorming how our practices could reflect that students learn in different ways and different time frames. We closely examined our instructional practices and how they aligned with our district's new guiding principles. The sidebar "China & Messalonskee School District Guiding Principles of Learning" outlines the principles that we came up with.

CHINA & MESSALONSKEE SCHOOL DISTRICT GUIDING PRINCIPLES OF LEARNING

Our assumptions about learners and learning are grounded in research and guide our work with all learners. Learners are individuals, children or adults, pursuing new knowledge.

Learners

- Learners learn in different ways and in different time frames.
- Learners do best in an environment that is welcoming, orderly, accepting, and safe.
- People can learn, like to learn, and want to be successful in their learning.
- Learners have unique interests that heighten motivation for learning.

Learning

- Learning and curiosity are basic human drives.
- Styles of learning differ, and learners demonstrate their intelligence in many ways.
- Learning is enhanced when connected to real-world contexts and challenges.
- It is enhanced when learners are encouraged to take risks, understanding that mistakes are inherent in the learning process.
- The rates of learning vary, and prior knowledge helps a learner acquire new knowledge.
- Learning is enhanced with frequent feedback specific to a learning goal.
- Successes encourage future successes and influence esteem, attitude, and motivation.

Source: Adapted from China & Messalonskee School District, Regional School Unit 18, home page, www.rsu18.org.

One day during a professional development session, I remember turning to my colleagues, Valerie and Jody, and saying, "I feel like I should write an apology to my former students!" It would go something like this:

Dear Students,

I'm sorry for always giving all of you an assessment on the same day. I'm sure there were times you were ready to take the test before I gave it, or sometimes you may have felt like you needed more time. I should have allowed you to take the test when you were ready, not when I thought it was the right time for most of you.

I want to apologize for asking all of you to complete the same assignment or project. I think you may have felt more engaged at school if you were allowed some choice in how you demonstrated your learning. I know that there were certain units of study, like the solar system, where I gave you a menu of project choices to choose from, but I should have allowed you to create your own ideas. I'm sure you would have thought of examples that never crossed my mind.

Please forgive me for not always honoring what you already knew about a topic when I started teaching. In math, we followed the same pages in the journal, and in science, we all participated in the same experiments and activities related to rocks and minerals. I know now that I should have given you a chance to show me what you knew before we got started with our learning. I should have honored your prior knowledge and started teaching what *you* needed to know. Instead of teaching you the learning goals for your grade level, I should have focused on your individual goals and needs.

The most refreshing part of this reflection is that I can never go back to those practices. I may have started my career as a teacher focused on the best interests of my students, but through this process of self-reflection and continuous improvement, I've discovered that I can always do better. I am continuing to discover new ways to center my instruction on my students while honoring their passions, interests, prior knowledge, and talents.

CREATING THE CLASSROOM CULTURE

How I Used to Start the Year

Each learner is an important part of my classroom community. When I first started teaching, I would begin the first day of school with an activity that set the tone for our entire year together. I gave every student a chunk of one color of clay, so the students had a variety of colors. The goal was to create a rainbow-colored ball that could be baked into a bead representing each student in our classroom. After receiving a small bit of clay, students walked around the room asking each other questions to learn more about one another and exchanging a pinch of colored clay. A student might have started out with a piece of red, but twenty minutes later, the student would have a handful of pieces representing all colors of the rainbow and all the students in our community. I loved watching them return to their seats to create a design with their twenty pieces of clay. After baking the balls, each child would create a necklace with his or her bead. Each year, some students were still wearing their necklaces to school at the end of September, or a child might even bring the bead back to school on the last day as we reminisced about our favorite moments of the year. When my students look back, they may simply remember the bead itself, but I remember how twenty individuals became one community through this simple activity.

How I Now Start the Year

After the RISC training, I continued with the bead activity. But in addition, I start the first day of school by creating a shared vision with my students. I pose the question "What does the ideal classroom look like, sound like, and feel like?" Individually, they reflect on this question, creating lists of ideas. At first, students often focus on the physical space, their desire for a class pet, and the materials they wanted to have available. I encourage them to think deeper. If someone walked into our classroom, what would we be doing in an ideal classroom? What would they see? What would they hear? How would you feel every day being in school? As I continue to pose questions, the list of ideas grows and grows, but I can always tell that some students are unsure of how we will use their thoughts. After a few minutes, students pass their papers to one another in small groups, underlining the ideas that they agree are important.

Finally, it's time to gather in the meeting area to collect all of our underlined ideas on chart paper.

In the past, I would have posed a similar question and gathered everyone in the meeting area immediately to share ideas. A few students would likely have dominated the conversation by sharing their ideas, while others would have listened to the brainstorming session without ever raising their hand or offering a thought to the group. By asking students to brainstorm their ideas individually before gathering together, I'm giving each child a voice in our classroom. Now, when we gather in the meeting area, everyone has a thought to share. I make sure that each underlined idea from every child's paper is represented on our chart. Starting from day one, students understand that their ideas are welcomed, appreciated, and validated in our classroom.

Our chart always includes words like *safe*, *calm*, *respected*, and *fun*. Even though the concepts seem to be the same each year, every class creates a vision that is unique and represents the students' thinking as a community. The goal for this process is for students to be able to articulate to anyone who walks through our door the vision for learning and growing in our classroom.

That first post-RISC year, my students and I wrote an acrostic that included our key ideas. Each day, we would read the vision by saying, "We are GREAT!"

*G*ood listeners
*R*espected
*E*veryone is safe
*A*lways try your best
*T*reat others the way you want to be treated

The next year, I handed over the task to my fourth-graders. I allowed them to work in small groups or individually to create an idea for our shared vision. Some students wrote poems and songs, while others created images that represented our classroom. Every idea was accepted, including the acrostic PARTY, which I honored, even though I hoped our vision for the year would not be to party! We hung each proposal on the wall as students presented their ideas for our shared vision. Finally, each child voted by placing a sticky dot on the vision he or she felt best represented our classroom. One year, after the students had read the book *Oh, the Places You'll Go,* by Dr. Seuss, they selected a hot-air balloon with the acrostic SOAR as our vision for the year.[3] In 2012, the Olympics were fresh on our minds, so the vision that was selected was the Olympic rings with our key words represented in each circle. Our goal for the year was to be Olympic learners. Each year, a new group of students enters my classroom, so naturally the vision changes slightly to represent their voices, their ideas, and their goals for our year. After our vision is posted, we all sign it as an agreement that we are striving to follow. I've found that the vision helps to unite us as a community. By reading it daily at our morning meeting, it becomes a living document rather than a piece of chart paper hanging on the wall.

Creating Our Code of Cooperation

Once we have a vision for our year, our next step is to create a list of agreements for how we will meet our shared vision. Using a process called the *affinity diagram,* each student starts with a small stack of sticky notes. Individually, students write one behavior on each sticky note. The goal is for each child to have three sticky notes that can be added to our class chart. With notes in hand, students gather in small groups to post their squares on chart paper by grouping similar ideas. For example, a category could be labeled "be kind" if it included sticky notes with ideas of helping others and sharing materials. I love watching this process unfold as the children move notes together as they notice common concepts. It's impossible for a student to sit back in this process, as each child arrives at the group with ideas to be included on the poster. Again, each voice and idea is valued, honored, and represented on our chart. If we have a long list of behaviors, I give each child two sticky dots to vote for the targets that are most important. My goal is to have a list of five to eight behaviors that we agree to use at school. In previous years, I started the school year by brainstorming with my students about agreements for our behavior. By handing over the entire process to the class, our agreements have become fully student-centered, as they were created, sorted, and selected by the students.

Because of the high level of engagement and ownership in the creation of our shared vision and code of cooperation, the students hold one another accountable for their actions. And because the students and I are creating these documents together, I see in the students a greater sense of belonging. It takes time, but by October, even challenging students feel more included, as they were part of the creation of our vision for learning together.

For example, Meghan was known as a challenging student who, in previous years, had spent more than her share of time in the principal's office. By October, she was visibly softening. She smiled. She laughed. She completed her work and was open to feedback. One day in late autumn, as she was getting ready to leave, she handed me a note. "Don't read it until after I'm gone," she directed me. As I sat at my table later unfolding the paper, I read, "I'm sorry for the second week of school because that Monday I wasn't being very kind or following the code of cooperation or our classroom shared vision." I had to chuckle. I couldn't remember what she had done on the second Monday in September, but this note was her olive branch. She was recognizing that her behavior had an impact on others and that I cared about her. From that moment on, Meghan was a part of something; she was a part of our classroom family. Of course, there were difficult moments, but we had fewer difficult days. If she became upset, we were usually able to work through her frustrations after she was able to cool down. Meghan saw herself as someone who mattered to me and to our class. As a result, she was willing to follow our vision, because she knew she had a voice in our decisions.

Student-Led Routines

Organized chaos. I can't think of a better way to describe our classroom when we are hard at work. Students may be found working at tables or spread out on the floor. There may be papers covering a table, books cracked open, or folders stacked beside a chair. We are busy learning.

Visitors to my classroom often ask, "How do they know what to do when everyone seems to be doing something different?" The routines we create together at the beginning of the year lay the foundation for the students to be self-guided and engaged during our work times all through the year. In the past, before the children even arrived on the first day, I established the procedures for our morning routine, our literacy workshops, and what to do when your work is complete. Now, these routines are created side by side with my students. I've found that a process that seemed logical for me didn't always flow for them. This collaborative approach led to the creation of processes that have more meaning for my learners, which allows them to internalize our routines even in the latter months of the year. I also learned the importance of making our routines visible by posting flow charts of the procedures to help students remember the steps in each process. Because the students are the authors of our routines, I've found the children to be far more independent and productive.

Implementing a Feedback Loop

Teachers naturally give feedback. "Remember to show your work." "Here is a place where you can add more details." "I love the way you read that part with expression!"

As part of the Classroom Design and Delivery RISC training, the presenters encouraged us to give students feedback through a tool called the *parking lot*. They asked us to share what went well, what we would change, the questions we had, or our ideas for improving the training. This was a novel idea; I've never been part of a training where the presenters are willing to check with the participants and adjust the schedule to reflect the feedback and suggestions of the participants. Throughout the day, our trainers took the time to read the notes posted on the parking lot and address our concerns, questions, or suggestions. As teachers, we appreciated that our voices were acknowledged and our ideas validated.

How often did I ask students for feedback on my classroom or my teaching? I couldn't think of a single example. I knew that I was open to feedback, but I didn't have a specific process for students to share their opinions. After our RISC training, I immediately went back to school and created my own four-quadrant parking lot that offered space for students to post things that were going well at school, things they wanted to change, ideas, and questions. As I introduced this tool and welcomed the students' feedback on the first day, I thought they would be excited to add a note to the board. But at the end of the day, it remained blank. Didn't anyone have something to offer me for feedback? I went home a bit puzzled. After reflecting, I realized that maybe students didn't know what to say, because they had never been asked to give the teacher feedback before. I wondered if they thought I would be mad if they gave suggestions for improvement. How could I show them that I would welcome their opinions and ideas?

At the end of the week, I asked everyone to post something on the parking lot for feedback on our week. As the sticky notes began to fill the chart, I shared each one with the class and addressed any suggestions. One student wrote, "Can we get a class pet?" I explained that because of allergies, we were not allowed to have classroom pets with hair, but that I would be open to having a class fish, if the students were willing to care for it. Instant cheers of excitement! A few days later, a red beta fish became a member of our classroom community. In this moment, students recognized that I took their ideas seriously. Students posted positive comments after science experiments or a great read-aloud book, but they were also willing to post proposals such as "We should have math in the afternoon instead of the morning." Whenever possible, I honored their requests, even changing our schedule if they had a rationale for why a change would help their learning, to show them that I valued their input. At times their suggestions led to deeper discussions around ideas that might previously have gone unshared. As an equal member of our classroom community, I considered it important that decisions were made as a collective unit whenever possible.

The parking lot is just one way that I encourage students to provide regular feedback. I also use quick-writes and surveys for students to share their thoughts and suggestions. It's not the format of the feedback that's important. It's the feeling that their teacher is willing to listen and values their ideas. I want them to have ownership of our classroom and know that I am not the lone decision maker. When my students enter my classroom each day, I want them to feel valued and excited to be part of our classroom community.

ORGANIZING THE INSTRUCTION

Individual Learning Plans

"Isn't every child deserving of an IEP [individualized education plan]?"

This was the question Kathy posed to us during her first year as principal of Williams Elementary. Of course, I wanted every child to make at least a year's growth in reading, writing, and math, but I didn't take the time to create a plan that outlined measurable goals for each child. In the past, only students who had been identified with a learning disability were given an individualized plan with learning targets and measurable evidence. Although I could articulate our goals and instructional approach for each student and believed every student was deserving of an individual plan, it was time to put my vision on paper.

As a staff, we learned how to dig into our assessment data for each child to create individual education plans that included at least two goals for reading, writing, and math for the year. These plans are a road map for success and growth, as they communicate both to parents and to students the current achievement level on a variety of assessments and measurable standards that I want each learner to meet by the end of the year. Because children are in different places in their development, the goals are not the same for every child. If I set the finish line at the same place for all students, I am not challenging them to reach their full potential. I review and include grade-level-based expectations in my plans, but I've discovered it's not about the grade I teach; what's most important is to articulate for each child the next learning steps that foster her or his growth and achievement.

Implementing individual learning plans has created a stronger culture of reflection at our school. At our staff or Response to Intervention meetings, we periodically review our goals and the evidence of student growth with an eye on the targets we set in the fall. Creating a goal-based plan for each child affects the achievement of *all* students: the special education students, Title 1 students, students who began the year on grade level, and students in our enrichment program.

In sharing these plans with students and parents, I found that when children understand that the purpose of their work is to help them attain their goals, their work becomes more meaningful to them. Every student needs to believe that he or she can be successful at school. This message comes from me, their teacher, every day. By providing each child with a personal learning plan, I believe I am putting the student at the center of my classroom and demonstrating that I have rigorous expectations for each child within my care.

Honoring Prior Knowledge and Passions

At times in my career, I have participated in a training session and felt overwhelmed with new information. At other times, I was quite familiar with the content and felt that my prior knowledge was not being recognized. One of my greatest revelations during the past four years as a teacher is the importance of taking into consideration what our learners bring to a lesson or have experienced. Instead of teaching to the middle or focusing on what *most* students know, I strive always to understand the prior knowledge of my learners through formative assessments. I can determine what a child brings to a new topic through a paper-and-pencil task, a conference, an interactive class activity, or a hands-on center. By determining where my students belong in a learning progression related to any subject area, I can tailor small-group instruction to my students' needs.

Last year, I created a formative assessment covering concepts such as perimeter, area, volume, and measuring angles. Using the information from this assessment, I assembled into small groups students who were working on a similar learning goal. In my classroom, students are not grouped by ability; rather, they are grouped with others who are working on a similar standard. As students demonstrate proficiency through lessons, tasks, games, or activity centers, they can move to a new group focusing on a different topic. Students know that our groups are flexible and that I will not hold them back from moving to a new topic as soon as they are ready.

For example, Reid shared with me that he feels frustrated when teachers ask him to complete multiple worksheets on a topic when he already knows the concept and can demonstrate his proficiency in a single assignment. "Why do I have to keep showing her?" he asked. Lauren explained to me that sometimes she is overwhelmed when a teacher moves on to something new and she doesn't feel ready. Although these students feel differently, they are both frustrated by the pace of their learning. It's important for me to find just the right pace for instruction for each student, not too fast and not too slow. One of the pillars of my work in a learner-centered classroom is that I must design my instruction to meet the individual needs of each learner in the room by recognizing their prior knowledge and their learning pace.

Empowering Our Learners

When I first started shifting away from giving the same assignment to all learners, I started by creating menus. During our study of the environment, we explore a number of learning goals related to biomes, biodiversity, and animal food chains. I designed a menu that offered students choices of projects, including anything from comic strips to demonstrating food chains using cups, to designing a picture book or even a slideshow presentation. After reviewing the menu together, I thought the students would dig right in, but a number of them immediately approached me and asked, "What should I do?" They were overwhelmed by choice. They wanted me to tell them what to do because being compliant felt comfortable to them. Had I simply told them to go off and start working on a picture book, these students would have happily followed my direction, but I wanted them to make the decision.

"What do *you* want to do?" I asked them.

Shrugs. Silence. I offered to sit down with this small group of girls and review their interests and choices. As we processed the options, they decided they wanted to work on comparing two biomes. Instead of focusing on their choices, I next asked their activity preference. "Would you rather work on a computer or use poster paper and markers? You can even create your own way to compare the two ecosystems!" The girls explained that they were excited about using technology but knew that they would need help getting started. Once I provided them with a little guidance on the computer, they were off and running. And they never looked back. I've found that once students get a taste of choice, they usually don't want to go back to being told what to do. Choice is powerful, and it should belong to our students.

Learners can also be empowered through opportunities to lead. Ryan, for example, found reading and writing to be a big challenge, and he did not like to leave our classroom for extra help. But Ryan was amazing with his hands. He could take anything apart and put it back together. He was always the first student to rush to help if something was broken or if I couldn't seem to connect my Smart Board correctly. I watched him grow to become a leader and valued member of our classroom team in the eyes of his classmates when we worked on our roller coaster simulation project.

As part of our unit on force and motion, we focused on working toward team goals as well as our science learning goals. Our targeted reasoning process was *invention reasoning*, as students experienced the importance of revision in improving a design. Ryan was an engaged member of his team as the group worked to design a compartment to protect an egg dropped from our second-floor balcony. But he really shined when it was time for his team to design a roller coaster using paper tubes. He became a leader, calmly explaining the principles of design to his team as they struggled to design a coaster with enough speed for a marble to complete a full loop. He was patient, always willing to try again and make adjustments. After the four teams had designed their coasters, we gathered to observe and celebrate our success. "We couldn't have done it without you," Sarah told Ryan as they dismantled their design.

In the past, a child like Ryan might have been overlooked in a group activity, but because his strengths were honored and recognized, he had something to offer to others. The highlight of the unit for me was watching this boy shine. He was empowered, not by me, but by his peers, which can make all the difference for students. This experience with Ryan reminds me that every child can be a leader when given the right opportunity to use his or her talents. Success breeds success, so it was not surprising to me that after this project, Ryan walked a little taller and finally viewed himself as valuable and successful.

Now, when I plan a unit, it's not just about determining the content area standards. I also think about ways that I will provide voice and choice to my students. I've discovered that after giving students a few experiences with choice, they gain a better understanding of how they learn best. Empowering the students in my classroom to choose how they will demonstrate their understanding has the potential to increase engagement and achievement for all students.

Transparent Instruction

My plan book has always included standards and our daily goals for instruction. I understood what I wanted each child to know and be able to do, but I don't think I ever clearly communicated our targets to my students or posted this information in our classroom. I'm sure I shared it orally at the beginning of our lessons, but was this enough?

During the last four years, I have watched my students transform into more engaged learners who strive to meet our learning goals because our targets are transparent. When we start any new unit of study or lesson, I begin by discussing the standard or learning goal with my students. After I post the target on chart paper, we work together to highlight what we need to know (content knowledge and key words in the standard) and what we need to be able to do (verbs). For example, if the learning goal states "compare the similarities and differences between two-dimensional and three-dimensional shapes," we would highlight the word *compare* as what we need to do and *similarities, differences, two-dimensional,* and *three-dimensional* as what we need to know. Our next step is to discuss what this learning goal looks like. A common conversation in our classroom includes questions such as "How can you show me that you understand the similarities and differences between two-dimensional and three-dimensional shapes?" As a class, we might discuss a few examples before brainstorming on our chart paper how students can demonstrate their understanding, such as through teacher-created tasks, learning stations, creating a video, or designing their own project that compares sets of figures.

By late fall, the exploration of a learning goal becomes natural for students. I can hand an individual student or a small group a new learning goal and ask the student or students to examine the target. Adam told us that because we thoroughly examine the standards, he now knows what he's working on at school. He said, "I can meet my goals more quickly because I know what's expected." I have watched my students, like Adam, transform into engaged learners who strive to meet our learning goals, because the expectations are clear and visible.

After the learning goals are explored, I post them on a wall in my classroom, where we can refer to them daily. I try to organize standards in a particular concept, like geometry, in a progression so that students can see the learning goals they may have already accomplished, as well as their next steps. Last year, when Matt was working on multidigit addition and subtraction, he noticed that the next standard in the progression was solving word problems. "I'm ready to move on!" he confidently told me one day. Because our targets were transparent and the expectations for proficiency were clear, he knew that he had evidence to show that he could add and subtract and he was ready to apply his understanding to word problems. It's powerful to hear a student advocate for his learning, which is a direct result of examining the standards together and making our targets transparent.

When my principal visits our classroom, she takes the time to ask students, "What is your learning goal? How will you know when you meet it? What will you work on next?" How students answer these questions is my most valuable feedback. If a student is unable to articulate a learning goal, how can he or she focus on meeting the target? When a student cannot explain how he or she will meet a standard, then I know I need to reflect on my practice. Student-centered instruction no longer means to me only that I am singularly focused on the individual needs of each student. I want the learner to be at the heart of my teaching, but I also want each child to truly understand the goals that we are working together to accomplish.

A perfect example of the power of transparency took place in my son Jacob's kindergarten classroom. In our district, students are scored on a standard using a four-point scale. A score of a three means that a child is proficient at the learning goal, while a two means that the learner has the foundational knowledge of the concept or skill. At the time, Jacob's teacher defined a score of a four as advanced, meaning that the child was able to teach other students or understood the concept in a more complex way. At the beginning of kindergarten, she chose to demonstrate this four-point scale with a concept all children could understand, coloring. Before any explanation of the four-point scale, she simply asked the students to color a rhombus. She defined proficient coloring (a score of three) as fully inside the lines, while a score of a two meant the coloring went outside the lines and was incomplete. Finally, she showed the sample for the score of a four, which was decorated with colorful stripes and dots. Before asking the students to rate their coloring, she let them examine and improve their work. Jacob quickly went back to his table to add stripes and dots to his rhombus before showing it to his teacher. When she asked him how he would rate his work, he proudly said, "A five!" Rather than telling him there was no such thing as a score of five, she simply asked him why. Jacob explained that his rhombus included many colors, stripes, and dots and went beyond the coloring for a four-point score. When I think of students aiming for a target whose goals are transparent, I always think of Jacob and his rhombus.

Engaging Students

Two years ago, I worked with a group of learners with a wide variety of needs and interests. Although I valued voice and choice, I still controlled the outline of our daily schedule. After much reflection, I decided to dedicate thirty minutes a day to a new routine we called *target time*. During this block of time, students were allowed to choose a learning goal in any subject area and decide how they were going to work toward proficiency. If this sounds daunting for a group of fourth-graders, it was—at first.

It took time for us to create a routine for what target time should look like in our classroom. In the beginning, I started each Monday by asking students to select a target that they wanted to focus on during the week. I didn't want students to change topics every day and never bring anything to completion, so we decided that each week, every learner would declare a goal and decide what he or she would work on during the week to demonstrate proficiency. At first, we sat together as each student shared his or her goal for the week. I charted the students' targets or recorded them on a clipboard for my planning purposes.

During target time, I sat with small groups of learners to complete assessments or provide targeted instruction related to their learning goals. I gathered students into small groups working on the same content area, but with different learning goals. As the year progressed, I often found that there were small groups of students working on the same learning goal. I wasn't sitting at my desk during this time or circulating the room, making sure everyone was on task. Because students were in control of deciding how they were going to use their time during the week, they were engaged and focused. If a child wanted to change a learning goal in the middle of the week, the student just needed to have a conference with me so that we could decide if there was a way to solve the roadblock or if it was truly in his or her best interests to change to a new topic. My learners were empowered and in control of their learning.

A month into our implementation, the students had a deeper understanding of their goals and how they could meet the expectations of a target. Students investigated content topics, such as Egypt or World War II, which were not part of our fourth-grade curriculum, but the children were motivated and interested to learn more about these topics through reading nonfiction books and designing projects rooted in our informational writing goals that demonstrated their understanding. Students chose to work on math goals where they identified that they needed more time, more instruction, or a new approach.

If I ever considered not having target time during the day because of a change in our schedule, the students immediately advocated for preserving this learning block. When asked to explain the strengths and challenges of target time, Olivia said it best in her reflection: "I love that I get to choose what I do. I am working on a pilgrim project. I want a goal to be to develop creativity." She signed her note "The one who learned 2 by 1 division today. Squeal!"

As I look to the future, I hope to place some sort of target time in my schedule first, as I've seen the power of giving students time each day when they are completely in the driver's seat. Although this time is valuable, a teacher can become overwhelmed planning instruction for this block. I found that after goals were declared on Monday, I was able to gather materials for the week for small-group instruction related to the targets that were selected. Even if I met with a student individually or in a small group one day a week for instruction, the remainder of the week was devoted to the child's learning choices. There will always be scheduling challenges, but if I make voice and choice a priority for my students, I believe I can provide the time for students to be more in control of their learning.

MORE THAN ACADEMIC LEARNING

Developing Habits of Mind

My school district is part of the Maine Cohort for Customized Learning, which works with a model of instruction containing three connected parts: content knowledge, reasoning processes, and habits of mind.[4] As part of our curriculum, teachers work to help students understand the traits of successful learners.

My favorite habit is developing a growth mind-set, because I feel it has the most profound influence on the academic growth of my students. Carol Dweck defines a *growth mind-set* as the belief that basic abilities can be developed through dedication and hard work.[5] A *fixed mind-set*, on the other hand, is the belief that abilities such as intelligence and talent are fixed traits. People with a fixed mind-set presume that talent, without effort, creates success. When I introduce these mind-sets to my students, I share that I have a fixed mind-set about my ability as an artist and often avoid tasks that require drawing or painting. If I had a growth mind-set, I would adhere to the belief that my art ability would improve with lessons, perseverance, and effort.

For years, I've watched some of my students identified in the gifted and talented program battle with their fixed mind-set as they meet a new challenge. When these students encounter a problem that challenges their thinking, they may respond by thinking that they are not smart enough or can't do it because it doesn't come to them quickly or naturally. Students in our Title I reading program sometimes feel that they will always be a struggling reader, rather than feeling that their reading ability can improve and they may not always need help. Students who exceed standards or who struggle are not the only ones who battle a fixed mind-set. Educators also struggle with this fixed attitude. The most important thing we can do as educators is to help students discover the power of the word *yet*. This three-letter word encapsulates the message of a growth mind-set and can change everything about how a student views his or her learning and potential.

One day as part of a Habits of Mind activity, I had students work in small groups to sort statements into two categories: fixed mind-set and growth mind-set. One of the most difficult statements for them to categorize was, "I can't solve a long-division problem yet." At first, students focused on the word "can't," which we easily associate with the fixed mind-set. My learners know that the growth mind-set is rooted in the belief that anyone can achieve a goal with hard work, effort, and dedication. A few students recognized the word *yet* as the most important word in the statement. As a class, we started a discussion about the power of this small word. The lives of our students are filled with *yet* moments: learning to ride a bike, memorizing multiplication facts, or striving for any other goal that needs time and effort to achieve. I believe that when we create a classroom culture based on the words *can* and *yet*, our learners will believe that anything is possible.

WORKING WITH COLLEAGUES

Collaborating to Group and Regroup Learners

For twelve years, I was the primary teacher of the approximately twenty students assigned to my class each year. I was their learning coach for every subject, as well as their main advocate. Three years ago, as a result of our district vision and strategic plan, I had an opportunity to implement a model of team teaching with my colleague, Valerie. The goal of our collaborative instruction was to group and regroup students between our classrooms to best meet the needs of each learner.

Valerie and I started the year by creating a shared vision, a code of cooperation, and standard operating procedures with our two classes together as one community. After our culture and routines were established, we used formative assessments and work samples to determine the academic needs of our students in each content area. Students were not grouped according to ability; rather, we looked at each child's learning goals in math, reading, or writing to group students who had similar learning targets. For example, during one of our writing units, I worked with all the students who were focusing on developing ideas and improving organization in their writing, while Valerie worked with writers who were revising for word choice and voice. During our ecosystems unit, Valerie and I grouped students around their interest in persuasive or expository writing. For our reading instruction, we created groups according to learning goals, reading levels, or student interests. While investigating historical fiction, I led discussion groups and lessons for students who were interested in the Revolutionary War, while Valerie worked with readers curious about World War II. During our content area time, we often taught different units and grouped students according to their interests. Our various grouping arrangements allowed us to design lessons connected to the content, as well as the learning styles of our students. Valerie and I focused on the needs and interests of our students when making any decisions. If we were combining students from both classrooms into a group, we always felt there needed to be a clear purpose for our collaboration.

My work with Valerie allowed me to sit side by side with another educator not only planning, but also analyzing my instruction and the needs of my students. This experience helped me to grow professionally as I learned the value of collaboration. The role of an elementary teacher can be overwhelming when you are planning differentiated instruction for a minimum of four content areas every day. Our team-teaching model allowed us to better meet our students' needs as we shared the responsibilities of implementation. Valerie reminded me that less is often more. I often take a topic for instruction and plan big investigations, simulations, or creative projects to engage my students. Valerie would laugh when I would start a conversation with "I was thinking . . ." She encouraged me to reflect on my purpose and always to keep in mind our learning goals. Was my great idea going to enrich the understanding of our students? Did it really connect to our targets, or was it beyond the essential understanding? Was it worth our time? Occasionally, I had to admit that I had gone too far. I appreciated her ability to realign my compass.

Although Valerie and I are now in positions supporting other teachers, we continue to turn to one another to analyze data or provide feedback on our plans. I now appreciate that my elementary classroom does not need to be a solitary place where I am the only teacher my students have. After my experience working with Valerie, I discovered that I am a better teacher when I can collaborate and instruct side by side with educators who share my passion for student-centered teaching.

When our district began its journey of transformation, we found that we were not meeting all kids where they were and moving them forward from there. Although the kids were growing, not all of them were achieving a year's growth. Furthermore, we were not closing the gap for our struggling learners. One of our measures of academic progress is the Northwest Evaluation Association (NWEA) assessments (www.nwea.org). Using the NWEA measures, we assess students in reading and math in the fall, winter, and spring of each school year in grades two through eleven. We focus on the percentage of our students who meet the standard, and we examine the number of students who meet their annual target growth.

Our instruction now has a greater focus on proficiency. For example, the use of target time in my schedule allows students to learn in different ways and time frames and aligns with our district guiding principles (see the sidebar "China & Messalonskee School District Guiding Principles of Learning" at the beginning of the chapter). Finally, as our school has shifted to a more collaborative model of instruction, my students worked with two other teachers in math so that we were better able to target the individual learning goals of the approximately sixty students on our team. This past year, 100 percent of my homeroom students met or exceeded their target growth for the year in math, and 88 percent met or exceeded their growth in reading. Of the three students who did not meet the fall-to-spring target in reading, one student did meet the spring-to-spring target for a year's growth as determined by NWEA. The other two students received services through special education and showed at least a year's growth on their developmental reading assessment.[6]

Although the data shows significant progress, there is so much more to our learners than these numbers reveal. I believe in educating the whole child by focusing not only on the child's academic needs, but also on his or her social and emotional well-being. The positive outcomes show themselves over time and cannot be easily expressed as a number. Of course, I want my learners to progress academically, but I take pride in their personal, emotional, and social growth after a year in our classroom community. My role as a teacher is to help my students fall in love with learning—an attitude that should last well beyond the year spent with me.

FINAL THOUGHTS: PIECE BY PIECE

My daughter and I love to work together to assemble jigsaw puzzles. Now that Grace is six, she proudly tackles puzzles with up to one hundred pieces. I must admit that as we put our heads together, we keep a close eye on the cover of the box, as it provides us with a view of the complete picture. Striving to be a student-centered teacher reminds me of assembling a puzzle with Grace.

In 2010, when my principal nominated me as Maine's Teacher of the Year, she captured what I believe is my philosophy and the heart of student-centered teaching: "Shelly really looks at the whole child. She welcomes any child in her classroom. She is going to respect and love that child and pull out any potential she has. She is a very reflective teacher. She's constantly refining or looking at what she can do to improve both herself and her instructional process. She genuinely cares for each and every one of her students and works tirelessly to ensure their academic, social, and emotional success. Once a child is placed in her class, she becomes that child's greatest advocate."

I haven't figured out yet all the pieces required to be a student-centered teacher, just as it takes time and patience for Grace to assemble a more complex puzzle. What I do know in my heart is that each child comes to school open to learning. Student-centered teaching isn't only about instruction; it's the willingness to look at the whole child. A child's understanding of content is just one piece. For the picture to be complete, I must foster their emotional and social well-being as I help them to grow not only as learners, but also as people. It's my job to put each piece in the right spot so that each child's picture is complete.

CHAPTER FOUR

Grade Five

Modeling a Passion for Learning

SUSAN CARPENTER O'BRIEN

> As I reflect on why I teach, I come full circle to the intrinsic rewards I
> receive every day. I am rewarded when I witness the moment a stu-
> dent grasps the essence of a new idea. That moment can surprise and
> delight a student at any level, from how to master division in math class
> to the recognition of both saltwater and freshwater in an estuary. This
> is why I teach and why I love to come to school each day.

Becoming an elementary school teacher was always my calling. In my primary
years, I adored my teachers in the little Birch Street School. We had three grades
and three teachers, all of whom instilled in me curiosity and confidence in
learning. From cozy read-alouds to correcting my math paper with a soft smile,
Mrs. Sutton was a nurturing, grandmotherly figure. I learned that school was a
safe place, with many hugs from my teachers with their soft, reassuring voices.
I never worried about very much as I learned to read, write, and do math. I
learned because I was surrounded by their love and passion. Our days were
filled with very traditional teaching and learning. I remember math worksheets,
copying over birthday cards off the chalk board, and sitting in small reading
groups named the Blue Birds, the Cardinals, and the Sparrows.

   In fourth grade, I switched to the Asa Adams School. This was the big
school in town. I was overwhelmed with all the teachers and a cafetorium,
where we had gym class, assemblies, and lunch.

I vividly remember the first day of fifth grade. I waited in line for the bell to ring with my friends Pam and Sarah as we entered fifth grade for the first time. We looked across the courtyard into the window of room 18, our new classroom. We had been assigned to the room with the new teacher. Through the glass, we could see a man—an old man with gray hair that circled a big shiny bald spot. We had never had a man teacher before, to say nothing of an old man. We didn't know whether to laugh or to cry—so we giggled all the way down the hallway to room 18. Little did I know that fifth grade would be the most memorable year of school ever.

Mr. Edinger was an eccentric man who loved to teach. He cared about us. He wanted to meet our families. I remember when my mom came home from the grocery store one day. She said, "Mr. Edinger was there, but I didn't have time to talk, so I cut through the frozen foods." My mom was right. If you started talking with Mr. E, you just couldn't get away. He had story after story. Only later would I know how much I was learning from all these stories.

Mr. Edinger was a household name. Each night at dinner as we sat around the table, the meal would begin with my latest "Mr. Edinger said . . ." story. To this day, my dad often quotes that line—"Mr. Edinger said"—at our now grown-up family dinners.

In Mr. Edinger's class, we learned by doing. We sang boisterous songs about John Henry and the Erie Canal. He told passionate stories, and history came alive. Last summer, my husband and I traveled to upstate New York to participate in a one-hundred-mile bike ride. As we sped along, I realized we were on the Erie Canal. That song from fifth grade jumped into my head and stayed there for days. Suddenly, American history, which I had learned in 1968, was fresh in my brain all over again—all because of Mr. Edinger's engaging teaching.

I got me a mule and her name is Sal; fifteen miles on the Erie Canal.
She's a good ol' worker and a good ol' pal; fifteen miles on the Erie Canal.

That year, I learned math through sessions of crunching numbers through-out the baseball World Series. I learned the names of famous baseball players like Carl Yastrzemski and Tony Conigliaro. We made tables and graphs with their statistics. We all were having a grand time learning math through base-ball. I must admit, I never liked baseball before that year and have little interest in it now, but that year, baseball was very important. My teacher was so engaging that we became captive learners. I learned because I was actively involved.

MY EARLY YEARS OF TEACHING

Fast-forward to when I started teaching. My goal was simple: to have a quiet, well-organized classroom where students behaved correctly and completed their work neatly and accurately. Cute bulletin boards would be of the utmost importance. It didn't take me long to realize my vision of being a great teacher had something missing. Teaching encompasses the whole child; I hadn't yet realized I needed to be part of their whole lives to make thinking and learning happen. My relationship with each child was the key. I thought back to my own years in school and what made me want to come to school and what made me a good learner. Thinking back to Mr. Edinger, I decided that I needed to connect with my students on a personal level. Students needed more than a teacher; they needed someone who cared, someone who taught them about life, someone whom they trusted and wanted to please.

This personal approach worked for a while, but after a few successful years, I was beginning to feel stale. I thought that getting a master's degree would help perk up my teaching. It did help. After earning my degree in middle-level literature, I came back to the classroom with great books for my students to read, and we loved to talk books. This was all very good, but not great. I wanted and needed great!

THE TURNING POINT

The year after I received my master's, as my husband and I were building our house, a neighbor stopped in to figure out who we were and to welcome us to the neighborhood. "Oh, you are teachers," she said. "I used to be a science teacher. I'm Elaine, and I'm the education director for the Maine Department of Marine Resources. I know what you need to do! I'm teaching a night class, and you can get recertification credits for it. Every teacher needs recertification credits. You don't even need to travel. It's right here in town!" The next thing I knew, I was taking the course The Sea Comes to the Classroom.

This single course changed student learning in my classroom forever! I have never been so inspired. After the first class, I returned to school the next day excited to share a horseshoe crab I had in a cooler. We set that horseshoe crab on the floor, and I taught all I had learned the night before. I suddenly had a passion, and so did my students. Marine studies opened doors for my students and me. The course led me to plan large units on the ocean for science, and I borrowed a saltwater tank to share among all fifth-grade classes. I started teaching professional development courses for my fellow fifth-grade teachers on how to use the tank to teach marine science topics. Later, I wrote grants to obtain our very own fifty-five-gallon refrigerated saltwater tank.

Suddenly, I felt once again how much fun it was to come to school every day. My enthusiasm became contagious, spreading to the students. One day, we had a huge snowstorm and school was canceled. The following day a mother contacted me to tell me how disappointed Shawna was to stay home during the snowstorm when we were supposed to have a scallop lab that day. She just didn't want to wait!

Once I had my own saltwater tank, the connection with Elaine didn't end. It had only just begun. As the years went by, Elaine's children grew older and entered elementary school. I eventually had all three of Elaine's children in my classroom. The first two participated in the hands-on science, and we also built lighthouses and colonial villages and took a field trip at the end of the year to search for marine life in tide pools.

THE SALTWATER TANK: OUR IN-CLASS PERPETUAL TIDE POOL

The tank is where my students observe, hold, and experience the Gulf of Maine ocean critters. By the end of each school day, the desks are covered with a film of saltwater, the floor has the remains of a big puddle, and the custodians enter with a smirk: "Mrs. O'Brien is at it again!" True life experiences help engage my students to think deeply and have a passion for learning, just as I did in fifth grade in Mr. Edinger's class.

THE SQUID DISSECTION: A RITE OF PASSAGE

Coming to fifth grade has several rites of passage, one of which is the squid dissection. My students love getting face to face with their squid. I found a local seafood distributor who donates these unusual creatures. Students explore the squid during this in-depth experience, which is their very first dissection lab ever. They learn proper lab procedures while they wrestle with the tentacles of their squid.

I give students the option of working solo or with a partner. Today, Riley and Courtney decide to pair up. Armed with scissors, a ruler, hand lenses, and tweezers, they listen carefully as I give the first set of directions. Their eyes are wide, and the excitement is rising.

Students begin by measuring the length, width, and girth of their squid. They count the tentacles and record the color of the flesh. Riley and Courtney whisper quietly as they work together filling out the lab sheet. They are amazed when we begin learning how a squid camouflages itself. The girls gently remove a thin layer of clear skin that looks like ultrathin clear plastic wrap. This is when they discover with amazement the camouflage layer. I overhear the girls speculating about the environment this squid was in to be a brown-reddish color when it was caught. Of course, the curious girls need to check out the colors of several other squid in their group to properly compare and contrast for their lab sheets.

Courtney is a bit timid when we start the lab and is concerned with the sticky feel and the fishy smell, hence taking the option to pair up with Riley, who tends to be a bit more assertive and daring. As the lab progresses, I notice their roles changing. Courtney is up to her elbows in squid, and Riley is looking for a paper towel to wipe her hands.

As we move toward the dissection of the eye, the girls are again tentative. On the document camera, using the magnification feature, I show them the internal anatomy of a squid's eye and how it has a lens just like we do. Once we get deeper into the scientific discussion, their interest goes from "yuck" to "neat!" to "Wow, they can be nearsighted and farsighted just like people. It all depends on the lens." At this point, I set the students off to discover the hard little ball in the center of the eye. Without any hesitation, the girls explore the eye until they find the lens. After a quick rinse, they are in awe that it is just like a tiny clear marble.

Our next move is to find the *pen*, the backbone-like structure that defines this animal as a mollusk. Slipping the structure out, the girls are curious about why it is called a pen. I help the class find the ink sac. Benny knows immediately why it is called the ink sac: "It's the sac that holds the ink that the squid squirts when in danger. It makes a cloud in the water so predators don't see them!"

Benny's prior knowledge helps the class understand this squid's adaptation, and soon Sarah raises her hand very excitedly. "I get it! If you put the pen in the ink, you can write!" Excitement suddenly mounts as the lab groups return to their squid to find the ink sac and then use the pen to write their names with the ink.

EXAMINING THE SEA STARS

Another favorite event in my fifth-grade classroom is sea-star week. My students have been looking forward to this since the tank was filled with Gulf of Maine saltwater. Dylan has been asking daily about the sea stars because they were his favorite. When the animals first arrived, Dylan called them "starfish." But when Elaine delivered the saltwater to our classroom, he soon discovered that this was a less accurate term, since the creatures aren't fish. Right away, being the scientific-minded child he was, Dylan gathered his classmates, telling them he'd make a big X with his arms every time someone said "starfish" instead of "sea star."

Before we distribute the sea stars, I start out having a little fun with the students by pulling a toilet plunger and a turkey baster out of a bag. "What do these have to do with a sea star?" I ask. They make a few guesses, to which I do not respond; later I will ask that question again.

The lab begins with quiet excitement in the classroom as one student from each group carefully tiptoes across the classroom with a dish brimming full of cold saltwater and a single sea star. Another student from each group gathers the lab trays that hold a timer, a few hand lenses, a ruler, lab sheets, and the always-important paper towels.

The day before this lab, we learned that sea stars are echinoderms, and the students have brainstormed what they wonder about sea stars. Now they are going to answer the question "How long does it take for a sea star to flip over?" We review the attributes of an echinoderm, and the students begin to predict what will happen when we time their flips.

In their lab group, Lani, Amanda, and Jake begin their data collection. Lani is in charge of timing, while Amanda flips the sea star upside down. Jake is recording the data. The students stare quietly at the motionless sea star, or is it motionless? Lani picks up the hand lens and studies the sea star. "Look," she says, "I can see its little round things moving!" "What are those called?"

Jake asks. Amanda quietly takes the information sheet from the lab tray. After quickly studying the information sheet, she explains to the group that the round things are called tube feet: "Tube feet function in locomotion, feeding, and respiration." Jake asks, "Locomotion? Like a train?" Lani cuts in: "I think it means moving, which makes sense with a sea star."

The group continues and finds that the first time the sea star flips over, it takes four minutes and thirteen seconds. Lani turns it over again, the group watches, times, and becomes excited when the second flip takes only three minutes and two seconds. The group discusses why it could speed up so quickly. Each time the sea star flips and the scientific data is recorded, the students become a bit more confident in their results.

Once the sea star investigation is complete, the students compile data in the front of the room on chart paper to compare and contrast the outcomes of each group's experiment. Students look for patterns in the data and discuss their observations as a class. "Look, the smaller sea star flipped quicker," Sam notices. But then Benny quickly responds, "I am not sure that is the reason, because the biggest sea star was the second-fastest a few times!"

When the students share their findings, I use scientific vocabulary, like *rate*, to talk about their findings and to raise the academic level of the experience. Using vocabulary appropriately within the lesson helps my students understand the meaning and correct use of these terms better than using traditional vocabulary lessons of memorizing a list of words and definitions.

The students record their observations and their data in their science notebooks. They have the basic information once they've done the investigation; they just have to fill in the gaps.

Only after the students share observations do I present additional content. As a whole group, we look over the internal anatomy chart and I show the students how the water vascular system of a sea star works. On the document camera, I have a sea star projected and magnified. We watch the tube feet slowly move, like a rhythmic dance. I pull out the toilet plunger and the turkey baster again and ask the students, "What does this have to do with a sea star?"

Right away Sam raises his hand. "The turkey baster is the tube foot, and the plunger is the suction cup at the bottom of the tube foot." The content is more meaningful once the students have experienced the phenomenon. I used to teach the content first, and then we did the lab, but using the inquiry model, we're doing the investigation first and then sharing and discussing content. This way the students can visualize and think back to their investigation when I give the content information, which helps them remember better.

I often find it difficult to hold back information until the end of an inquiry investigation. I try to sit back and see what they figure out, but I must admit that sometimes I can't help but share a few content-specific facts as I move around the room taking notes. It is certainly a challenge!

These activities work well with a wide range of ability levels. Inquiry-based lessons can be easily adapted for different levels of students and for different learning styles. Visual and kinesthetic learners respond to the hands-on activity, while students with auditory strengths learn from the group discussions.

Our class ends with a flip chart full of data ready for math class later in the day, science notebooks filled with sea star observations, and puddles everywhere!

A SUCCESSFUL INQUIRY MODEL

Early in the year, I provide a research question for the labs. But by the end of the year, students are writing their own research questions. In this model of gradual research instruction, the students practice lab skills early in the year but soon become independent and, by the last investigation, are shaping their own research questions and designing the entire investigation. Thus, their efforts become closer to true inquiry.

As I described earlier, I don't tell the students what results I expect from their investigations. I allow them to make their own predictions and observations. I save the content for last when we do a lab. While the students are working, I walk around the classroom taking notes on their procedures and conversations. When the groups reassemble as a class for discussion, I share some of the particularly perceptive observations I overheard. By doing this, I instill a sense of pride in my students. They'll say, "Oh, that was my comment; that was me!"

The inquiry model that I use is based on Roger Bybee's five-step learning cycle that he called the five E's. Later, Arthur Eisenkraft expanded this to the Seven E's model, shown below.[1]

These are the five (or seven) steps:

1. Engage (and elicit)
2. Explore
3. Explain (students explain)
4. Elaborate (and extend)
5. Evaluate

BURNT ISLAND LIGHTHOUSE

By the time Elaine's third child was in my fifth-grade classroom, my friend had a new mission. She had procured a lighthouse for the Maine Department of Marine Resources, and she thought I should bring my class to visit. That year, Elaine and I took on another project as a team: we developed a three-day curriculum on Burnt Island off the coast of Maine. We spent many evenings on her living room floor brainstorming ideas with notepads on our knees. What should we teach? How should we teach it? How could we incorporate my classroom labs into lessons about lighthouse life on a Maine island?

The Early Years

"All aboard," the captain of the *Novelty* yells as I walk my excited students down the long ramp to the Maine Department of Marine Resources pier to load the charter boat taking us to Burnt Island for three days and two nights. Each child carries a bulky life jacket and a small daypack with a lunch and extra warm clothes, and some kids have a camera.

I scan the excited smiles of my students as we embark on this adventure. Slowly the captain backs the boat off the pier and crosses the harbor. The salty breeze is cool, and the mist hits my students' faces, making their smiles a little bit brighter. It's near the end of the school year, and we have been looking forward to this adventure since the very beginning of the school year many months ago.

Our annual three-day classroom trip to Burnt Island is the ultimate learning-by-doing experience. Each year, students learn about tide pools while getting their hands and feet sopping wet in the saltwater, as they turn over rocks to discover the actual habitat of the ocean animals that inhabit our classroom saltwater tank. The children participate in a living-history reenactment, eagerly learning about the life of a lighthouse keeper. Later, they tackle survival skills while building a personal survival hut. Lobstering is no longer a vicarious experience through a storybook but an experience that creates a vivid memory. The ride with lobsterman Clyde in his small lobster boat while he pulled some traps was a memorable experience.

That first year and for several years thereafter, my students were the only student guests on the island. Each year, we would pack up our tents, sleeping bags, and plenty of food and travel for two and a half hours on the yellow school bus to the pier. There, Elaine and her friend Jean waited with great energy to guide our group through the educational experiences.

My students made fish prints of the mackerel they had caught. They learned how families on lighthouse islands lived. Suddenly they were transformed back into the 1950s, experiencing a wringer washing machine and lot of artifacts like green stamps, flour sifters, and potato ricers. The children played kickball in the field before dinner and slept soundly in their tents each night, thanks to all the fresh salt air and exercise.

Burnt Island Now

After a few years, Elaine was able to build an educational center on the island to house school groups just like ours. This beautiful educational center has two bunk rooms upstairs. Long tables and chairs are neatly lined up downstairs for rainy-day activities and dinners. The center took learning to a new level. Because we aren't spending time teaching the art of pitching tents and drying out wet sleeping bags, we are able to create more learning experiences. The students now are learning not just about lighthouse history and ocean animals, but they are also involved in compass hikes, GPS studies, nautical signals, and reading navigational charts.

Weaving our classroom studies in with this outdoor experience is seamless. My students are successfully thinking and acting like scientists as they wander about this little island world. Throughout the year, the children have studied in depth many of our Gulf of Maine marine critters, including lobsters, crabs, mussels, clams, and sea cucumbers. Holding these on their desks, collecting data on the animals' behaviors, and learning additional content information were all successful learning experiences, but now the ultimate learning takes place. The students will be visiting these animals in the wild, in the animals' own habitat. While searching the tide pools, my students turn over seaweed and rocks to find animals just like the sea stars, sea urchins, and crabs they know from our classroom tank.

This Year's Experience

Leading twenty-three students, ten parents, Elaine, and Jean down the steep rocks toward the shore of Burnt Island, I hear waves thunder onto the shore and smell that crisp salt air. I pull my hood up a bit tighter around my face for warmth and to model a behavior that I hope my students will follow before we venture even closer to water's edge. Before heading on to the slippery seaweed, I ask everyone to sit down for directions. I look across the rocks at my students sitting patiently, each with a raincoat, rain pants, and big rubber boots. I must say, this is the moment I have been waiting for all year long. My students are going tide-pooling!

Elaine now takes over to ensure safety and to get a feel for my students' prior knowledge. "Welcome to the heart of Burnt Island. Tide-pooling is an experience that most students never get; you are lucky to be here!" She continues, "Who can tell me how scientists organize animals?"

Claire's hand is up a split second before everyone else's. "Scientists divide animals into phylums," she responds with great confidence.

Elaine then asks the excited students which phyla they already know. Every hand is up, and the students are eager to impress Elaine with their knowledge. Poor Elaine doesn't want to leave anyone out, so she says, "Let recite them together in the order you studied them!"

"Mollusks, echinoderms, and arthropods," my students chant.

"Wow, you really learned a lot this year!" Elaine says. Now the students are ready to be good listeners as she goes over the rules of tide-pooling. "You must stay between that big gray rock and the line of rocks over there," she explains. "Please stay with your group parent leader at all times. You may step into the water, but be careful; it is only fifty-eight degrees, and the waves can pull you right out. The surf is forceful. Seaweed is slippery! Students—wait for the adults while they walk across the seaweed; it will take them longer."

We all laugh, but we know it is so true. The students can scamper right across the slippery seaweed while the adults are sitting down sliding across the rocks at a snail's pace. This is a greater learning experience for many of the parents, who haven't studied these phyla like the students have. The students take great pride in teaching the parent volunteers about each animal they discover.

Once the groups set out and slowly move to the various tide pools left when the tide moves out, I hear the students chatter. "I want to find a crab!" says Amanda. "Mrs. O'Brien said we can find them under the rocks, but if we turn over a rock, we have to turn it back over because that is their home."

Each group has a clear collection tray with several inches of cold saltwater. I notice that the parent is carrying the tray in most groups, while the children are busy lifting seaweed, peeking under rocks, and chattering away. I love seeing my students so excited about learning and so excited about sharing their knowledge.

"*Look, look, look!*" yells Neville. "I found a baby lobster!" Carefully he sets the tiny crustacean in the tray, and all the groups venture over to take a look.

"Great find, Neville!" I say. "I wonder who can find a sea cucumber?" I challenge the students, hoping this question resets their focus to get back to the search.

Sure enough, about five minutes later, Riley screams, "I have one!" as she holds up a medium-sized sea cucumber. She becomes the hero of the moment.

By the time an hour passes, every group has found many crabs and sea stars. Each group has a fistful of gunnels, a few crumb-of-bread sponges, and, of course, the famous lobster and sea cucumber.

I blow our signal horn, and we regroup around a big blue tarp set between several rocks to make an imitation tide pool. While we were out searching, Elaine and Jean had set up the tide pool and filled the tarp with seawater. With tender loving care, each group empties its tray into the blue tarp and excitedly displays each animal found.

As I do in the classroom, we save the content for the end. Elaine and I take turns picking up animals and asking who found it. I let the group briefly tell where they found it and what they know about it, and then Elaine gives several interesting content facts about that animal. Tide-pooling is the ultimate assessment for my students' winter of learning.

Each year, my students return home from this experience more mature and better learners without even realizing their accomplishments. They thought they were just having fun!

EXTENDING THE CLASSROOM

Burnt Island is not the only way I extend my students' learning and that of all fifth-graders in our school. My grant-writing initiatives have created opportunities for hundreds of students to become involved in rich learning experiences. Loads of Weatherbee fifth-graders depart for active field trips like the Northern Maine Children's Water Festival or the Gulf of Maine Research Institute in Portland.

Many nonprofit educational centers understand that schools can't pay admission fees or, in some cases, even provide busing. More and more of these educational facilities are funding their programs through grants, and some grants even pay for transportation.

Northern Maine Children's Water Festival

At the Northern Maine Children's Water Festival, my students actively participate in hands-on learning activities dealing with water issues. At the festival, my students learn from water resource professionals from across Maine as these adults conduct presentations and lead activities about water, wetlands, human health, and aquatic life. My students participate in water trivia quiz shows hosted by local radio and television personalities. They enjoy and learn from activities using music and art. All these experiences are provided at no cost to our school. In fact, the festival provides funding to help us pay for transportation. My goal for the festival experience is for my students to learn the value of clean water and healthy habitats. Our school was chosen to attend in light of our application, which showed that we currently teach about water and which explained how the festival experiences fit in with our curriculum.

Gulf of Maine Research Institute

Another exciting learning experience is when I load up a lobster-themed coach bus to go to the "big city" of Portland, the largest city in Maine. To my students, the trip is an exciting opportunity that they rarely, if ever, experience. The Gulf of Maine Research Institute is funded through large grants from very generous people who support the learning center, the technology, and the staffing, as well as a coach bus to transport students to the facility on the Portland waterfront.

The institute staff immerses my students in many perspectives to understand the interconnectedness of the Gulf of Maine ecosystem. From scientific, fisheries, and species points of view, the students make connections between humans, herring, cod, and lobster. As scientists, my students peer through microscopes at zooplankton and measure live lobsters. The students role-play as lobsters and make survival decisions in the presence of their predators, cod. As fishermen, my students make fishing gear choices for a responsible and profitable harvest. Moving from station to station, the students plan and record video reports about their scientific findings. They actively learn as they work together during a scientific conference to share their personal findings, make deeper connections, and learn from each other.

WHERE IN THE WORLD IS . . . MR. EDINGER?

Mr. Edinger taught at the Asa Adams School until the early 1980s. He had moved there in the mid-1960s; I am guessing it was 1967. He must not have been as old as I thought he was, since he taught for another twenty years. He then transferred to Weatherbee School in Hampden, where he taught for several more years. Meanwhile, I had graduated from college and was teaching eighth-grade literature at the Weatherbee School. Patiently, I waited for an elementary position to open up. Finally, and truly ironically, my dream came true! In 1986, I had the privilege of replacing Mr. Edinger as one of Weatherbee School's fifth-grade teachers when he retired. I continue to honor his legacy by committing my career to actively involving students in their education just as Mr. E engaged me in his fifth-grade classroom so many years ago.

MORE THAN SCIENCE IN MY CLASSROOM

From what you've read so far, it may appear that all we do in room 212 is science. That's not quite true, but science is the hub around which other curriculums revolve. I love science, and I use science to teach all day long. I also understand there is so much more that ten- and eleven-year-olds need to learn, so of course, I need to fit all those lessons in as well. I joke with my students, "When science happens in our tank, we stop everything else!" Well, that is not entirely true, or is it?

Writing Through Science

Recess was over, and the students returned to the classroom. They were excited about our first snowfall of the winter, yet disappointed that the recess seemed so short. Little did they know that the excitement would get even greater back in the classroom. Dylan walked by our saltwater tank as he does a dozen times each day. He stopped; something was different! Unlike it was before lunch, a scallop shell sat in the bottom of the tank, now wide open. Oh no! Where was "Oliver"? (The students had named all the creatures in our tank.)

Suddenly the whole class was gathered around the tank, all eyes wide and surprised. Questions were flying.

"What happened?"

"Where did he go?"

And then the theories came next.

"Maybe the lobster ate him."

"Mrs. O'Brien said she loved scallops just yesterday! Where was she during lunch?"

"We learned that sea stars eat scallops!"

"The sea star didn't have enough time to eat him!"

It was time for writing class, not science, so my students all returned to their seats with their writing notebooks. I knew that nothing would be accomplished with the writing lesson I had so carefully planned on alliteration. Or could it? A new topic appeared on the board: "Who Scarfed the Scallop?"

I led a brief class discussion on alliteration with a few examples using *scallop*. The students turned and talked, sharing ideas, and the next thing I knew, pencils were flying across their papers as the students reflected on and wrote about what could have happened to our scallop during recess. Walking around the classroom, I understood the sudden excitement as I peeked over their shoulders. Did Mrs. O'Brien eat it? Was the lobster the culprit? How about the sea star? Some students gave humorous twists to their stories; others were emotional, since "Oliver" was a class favorite. Other students wrote from a purely scientific standpoint.

I could see my students' skills with alliteration shining through in addition to the science content. Max wrote a fictional story about the scallop's hundreds of eyes looking around the tank as the daytime custodian made a lunchtime visit to our ocean tank: "Hungry, Mr. Clements quickly slipped his arm into the tank. At the same time Oliver saw a shadow moving quickly in his direction. Oliver knew he had to take action, using his super strong abdominal muscle he slapped and snapped, but Mr. Clements was faster than Oliver. Oliver was cornered!"

In the classroom, my students wrote. It was so quiet that the hum of the saltwater tank seemed loud, as the students wrote a variety of hypotheses, fictional stories, and theories. Science, writing, and imagination were clearly evident as the students wrote their rendition of "Who Scarfed the Scallop?"

FOSTERING DIFFERENT PERSPECTIVES IN SOCIAL STUDIES

Declaration of Independence and Brown v. Board of Education

Teaching current events side by side with history is a way for us to reflect on our mistakes as a classroom, as a community, and as a country. This year was the sixtieth anniversary of school desegregation, an event I taught alongside the study of the Declaration of Independence. Because my students have very limited knowledge of what goes on outside our state, it is a challenge to help them understand why other regions of the country have different viewpoints. When they travel, they see little of local communities; instead they see mostly resorts or family homes. Each week I use *Scholastic News* magazine to bring current events and social issues into our reading and social studies lessons. My students need to understand perspectives and events from other periods and places in our world.

We begin our study of the American Revolution by reading Jean Fritz's book, *Can't You Make Them Behave, King George?*, which gives the perspective of King George on the cause of the revolution.[2] Later, the topic changes to the Sons of Liberty and why they felt they needed their independence. From there, we tackle the writing of the Declaration of Independence, where students learn about the phrase "all men are created equal." We have many productive discussions about the issue of who these men were that were created equal. Who wasn't equal, and why? Was this discrimination and prejudice? As these discussions evolve, we fast-forward through time. During the Civil War, what did "all men are created equal" mean? That led us into the current-events lesson, where the students read about the sixtieth anniversary of *Brown v. Board of Education*, the famous US Supreme Court case deliberated in 1954, when schools were still segregated in some states. After learning about some of the events showcased in *Scholastic News*, the students not only discuss the events of desegregation, but also look deeper to see why our nation had different laws, rights, and perspectives during those times.[3]

The topic is engaging because students are putting themselves in the shoes of other students on this anniversary of the Supreme Court decision. My students come with a range of prior knowledge, skills, beliefs, and concepts that significantly influence what they notice about their world and how they organize and interpret it. Students become empathic by thinking about students like themselves. Building on this prior knowledge also has a flip side; it can be the root of misconceptions that need to be processed. My students do have misconceptions. For example, they thought Maine has greater racial diversity than the Southern states. Cultural and generational values are a key to helping them understand this lesson. As a result, I challenge students' comments to encourage the children to assume responsibility for their thoughts and actions. For example, I often play devil's advocate to keep them thinking deeply. I ask questions that provoke my students' thinking. "Let's think critically," I might say. "Why would all the white children go to one school, while all the black children go to another?"

Students in fifth grade are able to begin to understand how upbringing, social influences, and economic status are variables that influence people's perspectives. This is important for my students to understand because times change, as do people. This change has happened historically and will continue to do so, which is why I help them see that it's important to study history. For these reasons, I create opportunities for my student to engage in compelling instructional activities to become informed, questioning citizens in our global society. This perspective helps establish a foundation for future social studies instruction.

Malala

The week after the *Brown v. Board of Education* unit, the class reads another *Scholastic News* article about Malala Yousafzai, the schoolgirl from Pakistan who fought for the right to go to school and was shot.[4] Discussion on the article focuses on what other countries think about "all men are created equal," making students aware that current issues are often still based on freedom, justice, and equality. My students showed empathy as they thought carefully about the privilege of going to school, which gave the students pride for our school.

Later, during our computer lab, several students chose to use their free time to research Malala's biography. Others found maps and discovered where Pakistan is located, and still others found news broadcasts to extend their multicultural awareness. All the while, they were reflecting on the question "Are all men created equal?" Bart was thoughtful as we were leaving the computer lab. "It seems like this was right back in the time of slavery," he said. Once we returned to the classroom I decided to return to Bart's comment.

"Bart, tell the class your thoughts on Malala's situation and our Declaration of Independence."

"I was thinking that Malala was treated almost like a slave during the time of the Civil War. They didn't want slaves to learn or become educated. Isn't that what happened this year with women in Pakistan?"

I asked the class to turn and talk with their table mates about Bart's statement. Suddenly, there was a hum of excitement across the classroom as they students reflected and shared ideas. Once we came back together, Sam summed it up nicely: "History seems to repeat itself. We need to do a better job of learning from our mistakes."

I realize my students are leading very sheltered lives when they don't have prior knowledge on racial diversity. Seldom do they travel to places that aren't populated by all white, middle-class families. Lacking these experiences does limit my students, but in the classroom, I need to continue to have my students read and reflect to develop empathy for situations outside their small world. In spite of this, they are caring and they do try to be sympathetic to others, which makes lessons like this so important. Reading, talking, and processing their thinking leads to greater understanding and helps students learn to approach change with expectation, understanding, and an open mind.

MY PHILOSOPHY

I have witnessed many educational approaches come and go. But one thing I have learned—the steadfast and absolutely essential element to successful learning is student and teacher engagement. My daily goal in the classroom is to present engaging lessons that involve my students with their learning. At times, struggling students might not know that they like science, math, or writing. However, when I present a lesson with passion, my students suddenly develop new interests and become excited. The next thing I know, students are putting their heart and soul into what they are doing. When students take this interest home, their parents and siblings join in the learning. My students enjoy an interactive learning experience when they go home with confidence and the command of new knowledge.

The hours fly by in my classroom as students continuously interact. My role as the teacher is to create enthusiasm and to promote critical problem-solving. During a forty-five-minute math lesson, children are actively involved with direct instruction, cooperative work, and guided practice. When I notice that my students are ready to practice the skills learned in class, we engage in cooperative math games with manipulatives such as dice, cards, or game templates. Science is always interactive and engaging in room 212, as you've already seen. When we study electricity, we use light bulbs, wires, and batteries instead of textbooks as we create learning by building simple and complex circuits.

Students who are intrinsically motivated enjoy challenging work and may think in greater depth about ideas. As a teacher, I encourage the development of intrinsic motivation by having students work on projects, labs, and writing that allow them to see how the information is relevant to their lives. On the flip side, as I reflect on why I teach, I come full circle to the intrinsic rewards I receive each day. I am rewarded when I witness the moment a student grasps the essence of a new idea. That moment can surprise and delight a student at any level, from how to master division in math class to the recognition of both saltwater and freshwater in an estuary. This is why I teach and why I love to come to school each day.

Find a Passion, and Fly with It!

I want to inspire my students and help them find their passion, so I first show them my own passions. Mr. Edinger loved baseball and American history. Right from my first day of fifth grade, I too loved both baseball and American history. Modeling passion and the love of learning is a quiet, subtle way to excite and motivate my students. I found my passion through science. For me, science is a perfect conduit to all learning. I influence my students while guiding their learning through science. Science is what makes me want to tromp into school early on cold winter mornings, organize the materials for the day, and join my students in becoming the best thinkers and learners while solving inquiry-based problems. Inquiry-based thinking, learned through science, spreads throughout all subject areas to guide my students into higher-level thinking and greater learning.

Relationships

I want my students to feel cared for and valued by all the important people in their world. As their teacher, I consider it critical to establish a strong relationship with every student and her or his family. Family relationships and communication are important ways to improve student learning. When families respect and trust the teacher, they become equal partners in a child's education. I develop this rapport by establishing and maintaining open lines of communication. I open this communication long before the school year even begins. I start with the usual "Welcome to our class" letter on move-up day in the spring, send a summer postcard, and continue with our weekly student-generated newsletter.

Once school begins, I send out several short group emails each week. I now can reach every family by email. These emails update parents on what is going on in the classroom or provide a quick reminder of an upcoming math test. I sometimes simply mention something funny that happened that day, building positive, consistent communication with parents. Parents often mention that they appreciate the great communication. The continuous group communication encourages individual communication. Parents get used to hearing from me, and as a result, they become comfortable in emailing me back to let me know of a problem, concern, or even a happy moment. Once the families are comfortable, I learn so much about each student and her or his family. Parents will write to me explaining that a family pet is sick, a grandmother is visiting, or there are financial stresses in the family. All of these situations affect the child when he or she comes to school, and my knowing about these situations helps me be compassionate and understanding.

Transparent communication is the key to trust, comfort, and great student learning. An example of the importance of constant communication happened last fall, when a student was out of school for the day. I emailed the mom to give the math assignment, as I usually do. The mom replied, saying that I must be mistaken because Katie was in school that day. I quickly called the mother, and we got to the bottom of the story after several phone calls between us and to our office staff. It turned out that when the school called to check, Katie's older sister had answered the phone and explained that they were all "home sick." Yet, the mother knew nothing about this. Because we have an open line of communication, we prevented this from happening again.

Another example of the productive use of email is with a parent of a child with anxiety. His mother emails often with issues that concern both the child and the mom. Because I email right back, the child's worries (and the mother's) don't have time to build. Nipping the problems in the bud keeps problems small.

PARENT MEETINGS

Parent meetings are also important to our classroom. We have the usual conferences, open houses, and curriculum meetings throughout the year, but I meet the parents several more times because of our end-of-the-year field trip. We have fund-raising meetings, the actual fund-raising events, and several pre-trip meetings, and about ten parents join us on the trip to help keep students safe and to help with instruction. Parents truly become partners on this trip. Getting parents active in the classroom builds a bond. They begin to feel at home in the classroom, knowing all the other students by name. I am fortunate to have this time to develop relationships with them. This team spirit helps student learning. Community building is important to student learning because it has an impact on how students value their education.

QUARTERLY REFLECTION

At the end of each quarter, I take time to reflect on my students' progress. I take this opportunity to ask the parents to also reflect. I send home a very quick online survey to find out how the families are feeling about the school year. This communication asks parents what excites their child about school, what successes they want to see, and asks how they feel the year is going. I purposefully word the questions in a positive way to get constructive feedback with a proactive twist. The results help guide the direction of my teaching.

CREATING A POSITIVE CLASSROOM CULTURE

Fairness, equity, and access for all students are norms in our classroom. My students and I are vigilant to make sure these norms are followed. I start each morning outside the classroom greeting students as they arrive. I do this to ensure a personal, daily conversation and to check in with every individual student, creating a caring atmosphere where I listen and they share events, feelings, or excitement. This greeting sets the tone for the entire day as the students reset their minds and focus on the transition from home to school, and it strengthens my relationship with each child. *Morning meeting* follows as we move from individual greetings to whole-group conversations, which builds a bond of classroom community. As a group, we make sure that all are heard and all voices valued. For example, when students say, "I am just going to take a wild guess on this," the students felt it was safe to do so. Another example of student risk taking is when we were discussing desegregation and a student said, "I think there are more black people in Maine." The student took a risk with this statement because he was not sure of his answers. Risk taking is evidence of a safe community environment. All students in our class were involved in these discussions, regardless of ability.

My strategies to promote student learning and to encourage students to present their ideas while respecting others include working in small groups to encourage student engagement, building on prior knowledge, and clearing up misconceptions. Small-group work is an important strategy, both to support in-depth conversations and to practice being respectful of others when they are sharing ideas. Compared will full-class discussions, there is less competition and students have significantly more opportunity to speak. When I was working with one small group, the other groups were self-guided. This is an example of how this small-group strategy engages students and helps them develop independence. As I look around my classroom, I see some groups quietly reading and then discussing, while other groups read together and stop to discuss as they move down the page. Each group chooses how to manage the work and follows through with the approach that fits their needs. All groups are quiet and productive because of the classroom atmosphere I have created, promoting high-quality, independent learning.

Each group has a balanced mixture of challenges, some academic, some behavioral, and some emotional. A low-level child has full access, as do all students, to the materials. Because his group takes the time to read to him, they are all successful. All students have full access to me. When I set up groups like this, I am mindful of how much time I spend with each group. The advanced students have opportunities to think deeper with my open-ended questions as I rotate around to groups. An example of deeper thinking arose in the desegregation lesson. A high level student, Annie, mentioned that currently, schools in New York City are not segregated by law, but because of the neighborhoods, they are segregated. This statement got all the students thinking deeper and talking emotionally as they discussed if busing students away from their own neighborhoods is appropriate in 2014. This young lady advanced not only her own thinking, but also the thinking of her classmates from a concrete to an abstract level. Small groups help all students to learn at their own level and to move beyond that level as the children work to become questioning citizens in our global society.

EVIDENCE OF ACHIEVEMENT

Yes, I teach my passion and we have a grand time in the classroom while being actively engaged in learning, but I am very careful to follow our state standards while preparing my students for our state and national standardized tests. In a portfolio with a divider for each subject, each child tracks his or her own progress. The first page of each section contains a list of the year-long standards. The students record the date as they make each "hit" on a standard. They also record their assessments. When students become responsible for tracking their own progress, they have a better understanding of what, why, and how they are learning.

Helping the students take responsibility for their learning may be responsible, at least in part, for the increase of our science scores on the state test from a mean of 547 in 2008 to a mean of 554 in 2014. The state mean in 2014 was 547. Student engagement leads to student achievement. When children are excited about learning, the high test scores follow.

LEARNING FROM MY VIDEO FOR THE NATIONAL BOARD FOR PROFESSIONAL TEACHING STANDARDS

I spent this year working on my portfolio for the National Board for Professional Teaching Standards, and one of the requirements was to create video recordings of my class while I was teaching. I then viewed the recordings and critiqued my teaching. It was a powerful lesson! For example, I observed that when I was not sitting with a small group, the group worked well together and supported each other's learning, but when I pulled up a chair to join a group, the attention immediately focused on me. My students and I discussed this during morning meeting, and the students devised some guidelines for themselves to follow when I was sitting with their group, such as turning to the person speaking, then replying using their name. Using these student-driven strategies worked well; both the students and I noticed an improvement with eye contact and the level of student engagement. Our classroom community became more respectful, and student listening skills improved.

In the videos, I also noticed that although the room felt like it was mostly filled with boys, with a few very quiet girls scattered among them, in fact I had more girls in the classroom. Because my boys had great ideas and were so enthusiastic, I gave less attention to the girls without realizing it. I saw myself in the classroom calling on boy after boy. In many videos, Bailey would quickly raise his hand and give it a little shake while sitting on the edge of his seat. I would see myself looking around the room, and Bailey's excitement seemed to be spreading to others. What was I supposed to do? Call on Bailey, of course! We all wanted to share his passion and rich background. At first, my repeated calling on Bailey didn't seem to be a problem, but then I continued to watch video after video of our class, especially in science. My singling out Bailey repeated itself in most classes. As the videos progressed, I saw fewer and fewer hands being raised from other students, especially from the girls.

When I realized what I was doing, I made certain to call on the girls much more often than I called on the boys, even when the girls didn't raise their hands. Bailey and Bruce, another strong personality, were called on only once per class. Often I would assign all-girl groups in the class so that the boys wouldn't take over with the lab work. Slowly but surely, I saw a gradual change in the behavior and confidence from the girls. These young ladies had such valuable ideas and added to the rich discussion in the classroom. I will be much more aware of these behaviors—mine and the students'—next school year, and I will work to instill confidence in all my students, especially my girls.

MY COMMITMENT TO IMPROVE

I have done a lot of reading to prepare a strategy for the first day of school. One twenty-year study showed that, remarkably, elementary and middle school boys received eight times more classroom attention than girls. When boys called out, teachers listened. But when girls called out, they were told to raise their hands if they wanted to speak. When boys did not volunteer responses, the teachers were more likely to encourage boys over the girls to give an answer or an opinion.[5]

My plan for the first day of school is to be aware of the classroom tone. Boys tend to enjoy discussions that are more matter-of-fact, loud, and direct; this approach needs to be balanced with emotional, thoughtful discussions that are often more comfortable for the girls. I will seat more of the girls in the front of the classroom, which would afford them more chances for attention and recognition. I find that girls work best when sitting in a circle facing each other and find it more comfortable to learn in a group setting. A study by David Sortino showed that girls are sensitive to the emotions of peers, especially when the discussion involves problem solving; the girls become more passive in a class discussion and choose to wait their turn.[6] I will be sure to ask higher-level questions to the girls as well as the boys.

Often, girls do not like to take risks and frequently underestimate their abilities. Girls may react to stress as a threat, which drives blood to their gut, not their brain, causing a physical and emotional reaction. However, for boys, it's often the opposite. They love to actively take risks and often overestimate their skills, according to Sortino. Certainly these statements do overgeneralize and stereotype boys and girls, but I need to keep these in mind as I work with individuals. Being aware of the biological learning differences between boys and girls should help all children in my classroom learn as I create greater opportunities for both genders. Being cognizant of this research along with the research on attitudes in science and math will help address this area of concern and will change my classroom next year.

In their study of single-sex and coed high schools, Valerie Lee, Helen Marks, and Tina Byrd assert that classrooms "should be free of gender social definitions—those ideologies, norms, and stereotypes that impose limits on students." Teachers "have the major responsibility for creating equitable conditions in their classrooms; in their procedures; and what is most important, in their interactions with students."[7] After watching the videos of my students and me in the classroom, I have decided that fair does not always mean equal. As a result, my focus on, say, that quiet girl in science class will not only enrich her own learning but will also enrich the other students' learning, as they hear a new viewpoint and recognize that quieter students might have much to offer, given the chance.

Additionally next year, I will encourage girls to participate in extracurricular math and science activities. Our local university has a wonderful girls' summer engineering program that I need to promote. To do this, I will invite the director as a guest speaker. In retrospect, all my guest scientists were men over the last year. The only women have been interns to these speakers. It is time to change that. Girls need role models to imagine themselves in those same roles.

What else can I do? Whenever I see a technical job in the classroom with a computer or other electronic equipment, I will ask a girl to set up the equipment the first time; later, a boy will have a turn. I certainly won't make this into a girls-only classroom, but I do need to be sure I am creating equitable conditions for all students. I will use wait time for answers to all students. If they become uncomfortable with this, I can simply explain what wait time is, and why I am doing it. I will be extra careful not to have gender-specific jobs. When we haul saltwater jugs of water around the classroom for our tank, one day the girls will do it, another day the boys, and, finally, a girl-and-boy day.

Over the years, I haven't separated the girls from the boys, but now I see advantages in dividing our days into those with all gender-specific groups and those with mixed groups. Variety will be the spice of life in our classroom.

CHAPTER FIVE

Grades Six and Seven Looping

Real-World Tasks for an Authentic Audience

KAREN MacDONALD

THE SPRING EXPEDITION: RIGOR, RELEVANCE, AND RELATIONSHIPS

In late January 2014, I stand at the doorway as students enter the cafetorium, each child taking a small piece of colored construction paper from the box I'm holding. They proceed to the section of the room that matches their paper's color. Some walk to the set of milk crates, each of which has a crayon and a single sticky note attached. Others gather at the old metal folding chairs in another section of the room. On each chair, they find a pencil and a single piece of paper. Yet others drift toward the set of newer and nicer chairs, where they find a pen and some writing paper waiting for them. The rest of the students find themselves in the section of the room with very comfortable chairs, and there they discover a brand-new notebook and an expensive pen. Giggling is rampant as the students make their way to their color-assigned places. "Oh, what do you think we're doing?" "What color do you have?"

"Welcome to King Middle School in 1988," announces Mr. McCarthy, the principal. The room is suddenly silent, with a few students glancing around at their friends, looking slightly uncomfortable with what might be coming. Mr. McCarthy tells the students he's turning on the time machine and taking them back twenty-six years, and he proceeds to hand out comment cards to each group of students.

After all the comment cards have been distributed, Mr. McCarthy invites students from each group, in turn, to read their cards, beginning with the students sitting on the milk crates. The seventh-graders on the milk crates read statements that describe spending their classes coloring, never making the honor roll, feeling that no one really knows them, and getting sent home for behavior issues. One student stands, shoulders slumped and head down, and reads his statement: "Our field trip was to the jail to see our future."

A mix of giggles and sounds of disgust from the entire group follow this comment.

Mr. McCarthy interrupts to remind the group that the time machine is reflecting the truth. "Everything written on these cards was true at King in 1988." The room is quieter now, and most of the sounds are those of concern and dismay.

Students continue with this activity. A student in the section with comfortable chairs stands with his pen, writing paper, and notecard and reads: "We get along with our teachers as long as we are quiet. Our teachers don't expect much."

Students sitting in the most comfortable chairs read cards that describe always being on the honor roll, playing on all the sports teams, and going on field trips to museums. These students describe getting a ride home from the guidance counselor if they are involved in an altercation, but students in the group sitting on the milk crates are suspended if they exhibit similar behavior.

By the time all the cards are read, the students figure out that the milk-crate group represents students who are academically challenged, the metal-folding-chair students are below average, the comfortable-chair group includes average students, and the last group represents the academically advanced students, as all the students were labeled back in 1988.

Mr. McCarthy asks, "What are your thoughts about King Middle School in 1988?"

A student in the average group stands. "It's not fair that those kids go to the museum and those kids go to the jail," he says.

An advanced student stands and describes how the unique pen and notebook and very comfortable chair make her feel special, but her body language reveals her discomfort in this role.

A milk-crate student stands, crayon and sticky note in hand, and says, "I feel depressed that I don't have any future at all."

After about fifteen minutes of student reflections similar to these, Mr. McCarthy tells the seventh-graders that this is exactly what King was like when he arrived to lead the school back in 1988. The students at that time were actually divided into seven groups, or tracks, and they traveled as a group to all their classes.

"Is this what segregation is?" one student inquires, reluctantly.

Bingo! This student makes the connection between this opening activity, or kickoff, and our next learning expedition focusing on the Civil Rights Movement. King is currently a very diverse school with an ELL (English language learners) population of 26 percent speaking twenty-nine languages. Our students work well together every day, but we wanted them to get a small glimpse into what it feels like to be segregated. For the next ten minutes, the room is silent as the students write their reflections about this experience. They scatter across the big room, at the lunch tables, on the floor, on the steps to the stage—wherever they find a place that's comfortable for them to write. Here are some examples of the students' reflections:

"I was in the challenged group. It made me feel bad about myself that I had no future. I felt this way because we were treated like we were stupid and didn't know anything. For all they knew, the challenged group could be smarter. We were treated like idiots."

"I was in the below-average group. It made me feel like everyone is better than me. It's not a good feeling. And I'm thankful that Mr. McCarthy came to this school. I couldn't imagine King being separated by how smart you are, and it's amazing what Mr. McCarthy has done to this school. Without Mr. McCarthy I wouldn't be as smart as I am, as self-confident or as happy."

"I was in the advanced group. It made me feel powerful and better than everyone else. I had my future planned out. I was different, special."

"I was in the average group. Being in the average group, I felt like it was in the middle of being the best and being the worst. The challenged group failed all of their classes and the advanced group got all As and Bs. It made me feel kind of sick by the way people were treated."

This day marks the beginning of our learning journey, an expedition called Small Acts of Courage. At King Middle School, we deliver the majority of our instruction through a project-based approach, where students study an issue or topic in depth, complete original research, and create high-quality products for audiences beyond the classroom. The teachers design the expedition around standards, both state standards and the Common Core, and we select topics that are engaging for students. Through Small Acts, the students focus on six major events during the Civil Rights Movement: *Brown v. Board of Education*, the Little Rock Nine, the Montgomery Bus Boycott, the Children's March, the March on Washington, and the Selma to Montgomery marches in their social studies and language arts classes. Then the students interview a local citizen who had a connection to the movement in some way and write the citizen's story to capture this point in history. These biographical narratives are bound into four volumes and donated to our local university, which houses a special collection for diversity.

After the students' kickoff experience with the time machine in the cafetorium, we return to our classroom, where I invite the students to describe how they are feeling as we begin this particular learning journey. Here are some of their thoughts:

> "I do not know much about the Civil Rights Movement, so I am curious to learn about the subject."

> "I think the next expedition is going to be intense and depressing."

> "I think the next expedition is going to be exciting and fun considering we will be interviewing someone who was actually in the Civil Rights Movement."

> "I am saddened and a bit mad of how my ancestors were being treated. I am also proud of the hard work they did for me not to be segregated as much as they did."

> "I feel like we are going to be focused and there is going to be a lot of work."

> "I really love Expeditionary Learning because I love working together with a team to get something done. I also love building up to a final product. I would have liked it to be another science expedition because I love science, but I'm actually pretty excited to do this expedition."

I now know from this quick check what the students are feeling and think-ing, and this is important to me. I understand that some students are nervous about the intensity of the content, while others may feel anger as they see video clips and read selections about how African Americans were treated. I can also see that the interviews of citizens are an important hook for many students. The more information I have from my students, the more I can personalize this learning journey.

My school is an Expeditionary Learning school, a school reform model we adopted in 1991, three years after Mr. McCarthy became King's principal. We deliver content according to standards, but we do it through integrated instruc-tion and active learning. At King, the focus is on both academics and habits of work. We have strategically divided our school into six separate teams of about ninety students each, and each team creates a community that supports one another throughout the learning journey. Students loop with the same teach-ers from grade six to seven, and the students continue as a group to their new eighth-grade teachers. It might be hard to imagine that a school so focused on community would also balance that philosophy of community with a student-centered approach. But our success, in fact, comes from that balance.

King Middle School has the largest percentage of minority students of any middle school in the state (table 5.1). King is approaching a majority minority school, and about a quarter of our students are foreign-born English language learners.

TABLE 5.1   Demographic snapshot of students at King Middle School, Portland, Maine, 2012–2013 school year*

Demographic category	King	State
Percentage of students receiving free or reduced-price lunch	55	31
Percentage of minority students	48	7
Percentage of students classified as English language learners	26	1

*Among King's 540 students, 70 percent live in single-parent homes, and 23 percent were foreign-born.

INTENTIONALLY BUILDING THE LEARNING COMMUNITY

At King Middle School, we are deliberate about building a learning community. Every interaction with students, parents, and colleagues helps establish a positive culture. Specifically, four structures within my year build a respectful learning community for all:

- Crew groups
- Home visits
- Looping
- Community meetings

Crew Groups

Every child deserves a caring adult to mentor her or him throughout the child's education. That is where a crew teacher comes in. Crew allows us to build personalized relationships with a small group of students. We divide our school into homerooms of ten to eleven students called crews, and we can do this because *all* teachers are involved in this work—the gym teacher, the guidance counselors, the special education teachers, and the related arts teachers. This total commitment from the staff allows us to create groups that are an ideal size.

Each morning, the crew group reports to the crew teacher. We take the attendance and make announcements, but most importantly, we are able to see how each student is starting his or her day. If there was a problem the night before or that morning, we can deal with it before the child begins his or her academic work, or we can have the student start the day with the appropriate resource person within the school. In addition, each week, we spend approximately one hundred minutes with these students through crew time and targeted learning time. During crew time, we provide instruction and activities aimed at twenty-first-century skills such as collaboration, problem solving, and communication. Crew teachers also use this time to monitor the academic progress of their students. We discuss course summative assessment results and habits of work scores and set goals for the upcoming week, using crew time for follow-up.

Most teachers remain with their crew for two years, during which time we build strong bonds between the family and the teacher. When something is up at home, the first call is often to the child's crew teacher, and conversely, the crew teacher contacts the family when the student is beginning to struggle at school.

Home Visits

About eight years ago, I decided to visit the homes of my crew students. Because my own children were older, I had time in my schedule to try this approach. I worked with another crew teacher, and we drafted a letter to parents. It shared our belief that parents are the most important teacher in a child's life and asked if we could get together at the home, or somewhere else, to discuss goals for the upcoming year. The response was overwhelmingly positive. The first year, I visited with all my families by the fifth week of school. Parents appreciate that I reach out to them immediately, students are excited for their teacher and family to connect, and I am able to focus on goals for the students from the start—not waiting until the first conference held before Thanksgiving.

While not yet the norm in my school, home visits have become an important strategy for me, one that I have repeated in subsequent years and that will continue throughout my classroom career. Providing a student-centered classroom, I believe, starts with building strong connections with families.

Looping

When we adopted the Expeditionary Learning model at our school, we were strongly encouraged to loop with our students. Sixth and seventh grade core subject teachers follow the same group of students for two years of academic instruction. Looping relates to our crew structures in that both are designed to build long-term relationships with students. At our school, the sixth- and seventh-grade teachers make a two-year commitment to the students. This investment builds strong bonds with students and families and allows us to improve learning for all. We don't need time at the beginning of seventh grade to get to know the students. The summer between sixth and seventh grade allows us to advise students and parents on extended learning opportunities, and we don't have any moments at the end of sixth grade where we are tempted to say, "Well, I just have to get through six more weeks with this student." Over the course of two years, we invest deeply in these young people.

Community Meetings

Once a week, our school team (core teachers and about ninety students) gets together for a community meeting. We structure this time so that everyone hears the same message. Often the information is quite mundane: what to wear on the field trip, a change in schedule for the coming day, or ways we could improve the behavior in the lunchroom. But we also make sure to honor our students each week. We do this to publicly acknowledge the habits of work we want everyone to build: respect, perseverance, and responsibility. Each teacher has four raffle tickets, and as we place the name of a student in the raffle bin, we describe a positive action we have observed during the previous week. Everyone applauds. At the end, our student of the month selects four names out of the raffle box, and they get a small prize from the team prize box. So at each community meeting, twenty to twenty-five students are positively acknowledged while we review the type of behavior and actions that build strong habits of work.

I use these four strategies—crew, looping, home visits, and community meetings—to build strong relationships with my students and their families. When I invest in this part of teaching, I am better positioned to ask students to reach high academically. These structures allow me to deliberately build a culture of caring and learning. It is hard work, requiring a consistency that is demanding and purposeful. But these efforts allow me to provide the type of challenging, authentic learning experiences that have been important at our school in fostering student success. They also give me the necessary information and support structures to move each child individually forward. Yes, I am working with a team of students. But I need to nurture the team as a whole *and* each individual on that team. Home visits, crew groups, community meetings, and looping all help me learn about my students and nudge them forward in ways that match their individual needs.

THE HEART OF THE LEARNING JOURNEY

As I work to build strong personal relationships with students, I also strive to create engaging learning experiences. Selecting compelling topics for our expeditions, which are long-term, integrated units of study ending with an authentic final project, is a critical component of the work. As we, the four core content teachers, were planning for the second year of our loop, seventh grade, we felt that the topic of the Civil Rights Movement would capture the interest of our students while providing them with rigorous historical work. In the course of this expedition, the students found themselves connecting with both ordinary and extraordinary men and women of the time—people who stepped up to make a difference.

To start an expedition, which generally lasts about twelve to fourteen weeks, we design a kickoff experience that builds a connection to the content. The kickoff with Mr. McCarthy, described earlier, got the students talking about labeling and separating people. Through collaborative planning, the social studies teacher and I now need to begin weaving instruction and critical learning experiences to build a knowledge base about this time period. While the social studies teacher starts to dig into events such as the Children's March, the Montgomery Bus Boycott, and the March on Washington, I support students in learning about the Civil Rights Movement through student book clubs. I always start the book club experience by using a book-pass strategy to introduce the choices. During the book pass, the students quietly look at each book, evaluate it on personal readability and interest, and then let me know their first and second choices. I do everything I can to give students their first choice, because choice is such a critical component of student-centered learning. But I also keep an eye on the appropriateness of the student decision. If I don't feel that the choice is right, we discuss it. Often, the students can convince me of their choice, and sometimes, I can gently push them toward a different path. But we decide together. At the end of this process, we have four or five book groups, each with about five members. Each group will collaboratively explore and analyze the book the students have selected in common.

This time, all the books are nonfiction selections. They include some texts that build on what the students are learning in social studies, such as a Rosa Parks biography and *Warriors Don't Cry*, about one of the Little Rock Nine.[1] Some book choices also fill in content gaps, such as *Malcolm X* and *Muhammad Ali*, both by Walter Dean Myers.[2]

Once the book clubs are organized, the students are in charge. They plan the sessions, decide how much to read each week, select who will facilitate the groups, and develop questions for the discussions. About once a week, the students arrive in class with their books in hand, often with sticky notes pouring out of the book. They also have the teacher-designed page with targeted questions, overflowing with their thoughts and analysis. They sit in groups and work together to make meaning out of their nonfiction text. I sit back. I listen. I jot down observations. If a group appears to be stuck, I pull up a chair and offer some gentle assistance. But this is *their* learning time. Their targets, developed from the Common Core State Standards, include engaging effectively in a collaborative small-group discussion about a nonfiction text.[3] I structure the learning opportunity and then stay out of their way.

These book clubs are an example of how I plan on multiple levels. I plan in a way that allows me to keep an eye on groups of students, small or large, while simultaneously planning with every individual student in mind. For example, one of my students has selective mutism. Although she speaks some in class now, it is at a low volume, and I literally have to put my ear right beside her to hear what she is saying.

Her book group consisted of students that I knew would carefully support her participation. When it came her turn to facilitate, I wasn't sure how it would go. However, I was confident that I had set her up for success, so I asked her to facilitate the third discussion in her group after she had observed two of her classmates facilitate the group. As I moved from group to group around the room, I kept an eye out. She took control of the discussion. Everyone in her group leaned in to hear her speak. If her question was difficult to hear, the boy sitting next to her would repeat her question. The group supported her, respected her, and accommodated for her needs. That group discussed their book for over forty-five minutes as she facilitated. Her group had a valuable exchange of ideas, and she made strides in her comfort with speaking.

It doesn't always end with this type of success in any classroom. I make hundreds of decisions each day. The facilitator in another group that day was completely unprepared. She had been struggling emotionally, and her attendance had been spotty. I wondered, how do I balance my concern for her academic progress with my understanding that her emotional health is also critical? As teachers, we face situations like this daily, but there is never an easy answer. In this case, I did not intervene in the group's discussion, as other students took the lead, but instead I talked with the girl later in private, discussing how to be fully present the next day, when she was in class. I did what all good teachers do. I used my knowledge of her as an individual learner and person to guide my decision making. Did I make the right decision? I don't know.

Book groups are one strategy I use to develop content and the twenty-first-century skills of collaboration and communication. Placements in book groups are individualized, but book choices are limited because of my content goal. Student reflection is always a way for me to collect anecdotal data on my instruction and modify my approach in the future.

THE AUTHENTIC WORK

Now that the students had built some content knowledge about the Civil Rights Movement, they were ready to begin the real work of interviewing a local citizen who had been involved in the movement in some way.

Student choice is a critical component of student-centered learning. However, as the teacher, I need to frame and circumscribe students' choices and provide structures within which those choices can operate so that every student can succeed. For example, for this expedition, our team of teachers did the background work to recruit twenty-two local citizens who were somehow involved in the Civil Rights Movement to be the interviewees for the students. Then we proceeded to match the students to the citizens.

Why match students and citizens? you might ask. Shouldn't students be able to pick their own interviewee? Where is student choice in this practice? It's a fair question. As a professional educator, I have specific goals in mind. One is that I want each small group (three or four students) to work together as a team in planning for and conducting the interview. They need to be from the same class to allow time for this collaboration. Also, I match the students to the interviewee strategically. I know the people coming to be interviewed, and I know our students. Students who are more politically engaged I might match with someone from government. Those who will succeed with a clearly defined story with a beginning, a middle, and an end will get matched with interviewees with such a story, and students who can dig out a story where it is not as clear are matched accordingly. All of the groups are heterogeneous, just like our classrooms, and one goal is to have students collaborate with a diverse group, something that is another twenty-first-century skill.

Heading into the interview week, there was excitement in the air. Charts in the hallway listed the name of each interviewee, the students in that group, and the date and time of the interview. There was some juggling ahead of time. We had to make adjustments for students who had a previously scheduled dental appointment or family trip. One student had received a five-day suspension for fighting, and he quickly found me to tell me that one of his days was the day of his interview. While I expressed my disappointment in his actions, I also noted the responsibility he was showing around his interview. It was a message to me that he felt the weight of the task ahead. I negotiated an in-house suspension with the assistant principal so that the boy could attend the interview.

On Monday morning, about halfway through the expedition, the interviews started. As the students filed into the hallway for homeroom, the energy was electric. The students were dressed up, looking professional but a bit anxious. Two groups gathered in the hallway to do a quick review of the questions. Passes to leave class and to head to the library for their interview were pulled out of their expedition folder.

As a teacher, I am continually reflecting. One thing that is clear to me is that the act of interviewing a local citizen creates engagement and connection with the content. As a middle school teacher, I need to be mindful of the national research on declining engagement as students progress through middle school and to proactively provide compelling learning experiences to counter this trend.

Everyone returned to class excited after the interview. They now have a story and the beginning of a relationship with a community member. And these adults were incredibly special. One interviewee was a Tuskegee airman; one founded the local chapter of the National Association for the Advancement of Colored People (NAACP) in Portland, Maine, in 1960; and another interviewee is currently serving as our US senator. But everyone had a compelling story. Besides the connection to the content, all our students got another important lesson, one that will probably not be covered on the next standardized test—how one person *can* make a difference.

While the interviews were taking place in the library over a ten-day period, regular classes were happening upstairs. All the students had passes to attend their interview and needed to check in with teachers about what they missed, but just as we encourage a collaborative model with our students, we work together as educators. At team meetings, all the teachers in the house knew what was happening. Not only that, but they supported the work. Every teacher on our team attended at least one of the interviews, sitting back to take notes as a backup and making sure everything ran smoothly. Over the next few weeks, the students were hard at work in social studies, language arts, and art class to work on their final product, a biographical narrative and an accompanying illustration. In science and math, they continue to focus on their curriculum.

But if some extra help or time was needed, we knew our team would work together to adjust the schedule so that all students could reach the goal of telling the story of these courageous citizens.

AN AUTHENTIC PRODUCT FOR AN AUTHENTIC AUDIENCE

In my language arts class, we spent time focusing on the rubric for the biographical narrative they would be writing. I frequently use rubrics with students, who are now quite familiar with them. However, I felt that they were still struggling with digging into the rubric, owning it, and making it the guidepost for their work. I designed an activity where we looked at exemplars of stories from previous years and scored them on various sections of the rubric. This exercise allowed them to read these stories and get a gist of what they would be doing, but also forced them to carefully examine the rubric, decide on a score for the story they were reading, and justify their score with evidence from the story.

A full-class discussion of the rubric and how they scored the pieces followed. When the groups reported their findings, I felt that the groups had analyzed the rubric effectively to score the pieces. Listening back to this discussion, which I recorded, I could see that some aspects of the rubric still needed further explanation. It's a delicate balance between creating student-friendly rubrics on the one hand and using academic language with students on the other hand. I decided to keep the academic language in the rubric as a way of teaching and reinforcing the academic language of language arts.

At the end of the class, I used exit tickets for students to let me know which area of the writing would be the most challenging for them: organization, the writing process, language use, or ideas. Later that day, I reviewed the responses and could now plan mini-lessons based on the thoughts from individual students. This feedback is important for planning. I don't do this often enough. I too often wait until the students are well into something and problems emerge. But students know up front what is hard for them. With a clear sense of the project and the rubric, which detailed the expectations, they were able to give me a road map of focus areas for my writing instruction before they traveled too far down the writing path.

As in any other classroom, things don't always move along as planned. As we entered the second week of interviews, our school was working to eliminate our pull-out classroom for beginning ELL students. All ELL students would now be mainstreamed, with support from a certified ELL teacher floating among several rooms. Two days before the interviews ended, two new students who had missed the background-knowledge phase of our work joined us. The plan? Set them up for success, as well. We scrambled to meet with the ELL teacher in the early morning two days before the last interview. She got up-to-speed on the expedition and learned some background information on the final interviewee. Could she work with these students and get them ready for the interview? Could they each develop one or two questions for this African American musician who had traveled the country during the 1960s, facing discrimination and segregation? Could she attend the interview and provide them with support? Yes was the answer to all these questions. So these two students, one from Iraq and one from Angola, dove headfirst into the work with a lot of support, accommodations, and personalized attention.

At this point, everyone had his or her information from the interview recorded on an iPad. After time spent with exemplars and rubrics, and with tablets charged up and headphones in hand, the students started the arduous work of piecing together a story from their recorded interview. In social studies and in my language arts class, each student had a note-catcher/planning sheet/graphic organizer. First, they brainstormed major topics they remembered from the interview. Next, they put the topics on their planning sheet, which was divided into four-by-four-inch squares. After the tentative topics were placed, the headphones went on and the work of collecting the evidence began. Some of the students explored the recording app we had used to record the interviews and noticed that they could actually put labels on sections of the recording, a great tool for returning to the interview later to confirm a detail. They shared this technology information with others. There was intense focus in both classrooms (social studies and language arts) as the students worked to capture evidence for the story.

We grouped students back into their interview groups to review their notes. Yes, the students were writing their own story, but they could also support each other in the work. The students reviewed their notes and added any details they were missing. No one balked at this collaboration. They didn't own the material themselves; they were a group all working to accurately capture this story of history.

Once the note-catcher was complete, the students began writing. Individually, students checked in with one of their teachers to make sure they were progressing. This was a chance for us to review their notes and assess whether they needed additional support with this task.

Check-in points help us keep everyone on the learning train. It is important to have lists going and check in on each student. When students slip behind or are struggling with understanding, we lose them. We are structuring this project for everyone's success, so we don't lose anyone.

As the writing progressed, we moved to a workshop model in my room. Classes started with about twenty minutes of instruction and practice on a skill they needed for their writing: transitions, writing an introduction, how to create a hook, and the inclusion of strong verbs.

I tried to time the instruction carefully, just when they would need it. Of course, not everyone needed this at the same time, but I could always review the instruction with individuals later when they were ready. Students who felt they didn't need the lesson were free to get going on their individual work. Once the instruction was done, I spent my time conferencing individually with students. This allowed me to personalize the instruction for students and get a sense of areas that needed more attention.

When the students were finishing their first draft, they took it through the writing process of editing, revising, peer feedback, and teacher feedback. There was a hum of intention in the room—much like any workshop environment. Everyone had specific needs for his or her own product. Resources and support were available for all. Special education teachers worked with us to provide necessary support for students. I put out an "all call" to support staff. If they had any available time, I needed them in my room. The revision stage of a first draft is when the need to know can drive individual instruction, and I didn't want students sitting and waiting for one adult to make it around to all twenty-two of them.

Collaboration continued to be critical. Groups met and read their drafts aloud. They gave feedback and corrected faulty information, and the authors uncovered their own errors as they shared. The process of collaborating, working on your own, and going back to collaborating was the rhythm in the classroom. The informal audience of their group was an important warm-up for the authentic audience, their interviewee, who would soon receive the story.

Honestly, I didn't fully comprehend the power of the collaborative nature of the work until I heard directly from the students at the end of the expedition:

> We had to work with people that we may not always work with and also may not always agree with. I personally think that this exposed us to different ideas and ways of thinking, that we may not have experienced if we had chosen the groups ourselves. It also drew W7 closer because our groups got to know each other and had to learn to persevere together, respect one another, and carry on our responsibility as one. The knowledge we received was a knowledge of one another.

April 18 was an important day on our team calendar. It was the day we were sending our stories to the interviewees. Energy and tension filled the air. The students were putting the finishing touches on the writing and sending it off to the interviewees with a letter outlining our expectations. We did *not* want our interviewees to edit the piece for conventions, but we *absolutely* wanted their feedback on the content of the story. Are the facts correct? Did the student do your story justice? Do you have any suggestions? At 1:30 p.m. on Friday, April 18, ten students marched the envelopes down to the office to be mailed. The story was temporarily out of their hands. They were now requesting that the citizens give them feedback, within a week if possible. That gave the students April break to relax and leave the story behind before opening the emails and letters that might suggest additional revision.

The feedback from the interviewees arrived in the form of emails, letters, and phone calls. After a week's break, it was back to work for every seventh-grader. Each student had a unique experience with this phase.

GETTING FEEDBACK FROM THE INTERVIEWEE

Back to workshop mode again. The students read the suggestions, reworked their pieces, collaborated with their peers, and had conferences with teachers. Now was the time to edit, polish, reedit, and do whatever wordsmithery they could to make this a high-quality work because the culminating event, a showcase of their work, was now looming and the work would soon be very public.

We had invited the interviewees back to King Middle for a final celebration and to receive the stories, which would be gathered into a four-volume collection of oral histories. The students would honor their interviewee and give them a copy of our oral history collection—four volumes of writing about local citizens involved in the Civil Rights Movement. There was pressure on all of us, but a positive real-life pressure. The books needed a final edit and had to be assembled on the computer before heading to the printer. Invitations needed to be sent out. Special committees had to be formed. Four students volunteered to be the editors and work with our technology teacher. Eleven students stepped forward to take on additional speaking roles at the presentation. This would involve extra writing and speaking rehearsal. Some of our musicians volunteered to pull together a performance of a civil rights song to end the celebration.

We teachers initiated a few strategic invitations for students to step up. It has been our experience that when a teacher approaches a student and suggests that his or her talent would be a good match for a situation, the student usually shines. We are always looking to provide opportunities for all students to show their strengths. Over the two years we have with these students, we can spread the leadership roles to all students. We actually keep a list of which students took on additional responsibility so that we can build these skills with all students. I approached one young man, a student who was emotionally engaged with the topic, and asked him to be one of the emcees at the final event.

All of the students would be on stage speaking briefly about their interviewee. Actually, all but one would speak. The student with selective mutism met with me after class one day. She decided that she could not speak on stage, but would run the technical side for the performance. We figured it out together. While I wanted all the students on the stage, many of whom would be completely out of their comfort zone, this was a unique situation. I always wanted what was best for that particular child, and in my professional judgment, overseeing the technical side of the action was the right call.

Finally the day was here to share this authentic work with the distinguished audience of civil rights activists, their peers, their parents, and other school community guests.

CULMINATING AND CELEBRATING

Why do we end each expedition with a culminating event? In our school, we believe that sharing a high-quality final product with an authentic audience provides motivation and purpose for the learning and work. This is a big show for these young people. They have practiced, rehearsed, revised, and refined, and now they are ready to share their learning. And they got to this end point, this celebration, together. *Everyone* had a story in the four-volume collection of oral histories. *Everyone* was contributing to the final presentation on the stage, but individual plans and preparation were in place to make sure each student was successful. The seventh-graders had met deadlines and taken responsibility for their own learning to get to this point. The hard work was complete. Now it was time to share the result with significant adults.

May 21. We had set the date at the beginning of the expedition, and here we were, ready to celebrate. The first student I saw was at 7:20 a.m., when the young man I had asked to speak arrived with suit bag in hand. "Can you store this for me?" he asked. He was to be the emcee in our culminating presentation and was ready.

"Is your dad coming?" I inquired.

"Of course, he wouldn't miss it!" So this proud young man followed me to the teachers' room, and we hung up his suit so that it would be wrinkle-free until he was ready.

As the homeroom bell sounded, all the other students came in. Everyone looked great. *Professional* was the word we had used to describe how the students should dress for the day, and most students had followed through. They were smiling, but nervous. After homeroom, all the students headed to one class before we lined up for the cafetorium. As the homerooms ended, I checked on attendance. One hundred percent of our students were here. Maybe not a big deal in some schools, but huge for us, especially since we were asking students to do a very risky thing today—present a section of their writing, out loud, in front of an audience of 225 people. But these seventh-graders felt a responsibility to their group and their interviewee, and hopefully to themselves, to see this project to the end and celebrate all of the hard work.

One of our interviewees was spending the day at King, and he got a lot of attention that morning from some of the males in our house. He knew how to tie a tie! When the word spread, he had a small line ready to get instructions. During the first class, the math teacher tried to have a normal class, but he said that about forty-five minutes into the class, one of the students raised his hand and said, "Can't we *please* just practice our speeches a couple more times?" So the teacher graciously accommodated their request.

The clock hit 9:30. Three young ladies made their way down to the lobby to greet the guests. Name tags with HONOREE written on them were ready to go. At 9:40, the tech crew headed down. They were completely responsible for the audio and slide system for the event. At exactly 9:48, the remainder of the group lined up and arrived in the cafetorium. Everyone had note cards for his or her speech.

At 10:02, the students presented their work. The event started with a strong, poised but passionate voice from the student I had encouraged to speak. And then the others followed. They gave presentations about major aspects of the movement: youth activists, school and housing integration, the March on Washington, the Selma to Montgomery marches, and the national scene. One by one, the students approached the microphone and shared a bit of the story of their interviewee while a picture of the adult flashed on a screen. Some students were relaxed and confident, making eye contact with their interviewee. Others had to dig deep to deliver their words in a clear, audible manner. But they all did it!

Celebrating the learning is important. These students had worked hard over the last fourteen weeks. They wrote many, many drafts of their story. They had to balance the feedback from their interviewee with their own writing voice. They had deadlines to meet.

Yes, there were a few glitches that day. One student found me at 9:15 to tell me he had left his speech at home because he was practicing with his parents. We printed another one. One student told the special ed assistant that he wasn't going to go on stage. I asked him to come down to my room and we talked outside. He was firm. "I am not going up on that stage," he said. But as we talked, I realized it was more about his concern for his appearance, since he forgot to dress up, than the actual speaking. Once he was assured that his appearance was great and his group needed him to tell the entire story, he agreed to step onto the stage. And he nailed it! These are the kinds of decisions we make as teachers every day. When do I push, and when do I back off with students? When do I ask them to be responsible, and when am I standing right behind them making sure they do not fall? Yes, part of teaching is an art, one that develops every day.

A reception followed the presentation. It was time to share the written oral histories, celebrate the work, pose for pictures, and bring this specific learning journey to a satisfactory conclusion. The students will all continue to move forward but will be changed by this experience. Many students wrote more than they have ever written in their lives; they understand a difficult and emotional period in our nation's history. Others have pushed through their personal fear of public speaking, and some have made personal connections with an adult in their community that will continue. The teachers simultaneously brought students through a learning journey together as a group and as individual students with unique needs.

King Middle School has a culture of reflection for students and teachers. The students returned to class after this amazing morning to contemplate their experiences. I asked them to write about six topics related to their fourteen-week journey, including the culminating event. Here is a sample of students' reflections and a reflection from a parent:

> *Student 1:* Our culminating event for Small Acts of Courage was highly successful and played an important role in the overall expedition. Personally, I think that this was one of our best, or the best, of all our culminating events with this house. While watching the presentation, I realized how professional it was and [how] very informative of our work. I think it was good that all of the students were able to play a part in the culmination, and that it made an impact on the interviewees and the audience that each and every one of us helped in the presentation of our project. If I had to change anything about it, though, I might make the reception afterwards in a bigger space if possible, or make the reception more straightforward for ushers, other students, and parents to enjoy. All in all, though, this event was very professional and well put together.

> *Student 2:* In my eyes, I thought that the culminating event went really well; everyone was focused as well as I was. There was no fooling around and no horseplay (as there was in practice). I think that people got serious into thinking, "This is it. After so much hard work, this is the moment to show that hard work does make us smarter." I thought personally that my volume, eye contact, posture, and eye contact went very well. One thing I could have worked on was my pace. Sometimes when I get nervous I go really fast, to avoid reading. Although there were things I could have worked on, I thought overall that the culminating event and my presentation were great.

> *Student 3:* The project is a positive project overall because it talks about what people did, how people overcome struggles, and [how] if you persevere,

you can achieve great things. It is a positive project because it helps our generation understand what they did and not to take what they did for granted. It's letting the public know that there is more than the people who are well known. Martin Luther King and John Lewis are well known, but it is not only them that made the movement. There are other people and we should actually inform the nation that people did small things that contributed and I feel like that's what we are doing. We are bringing that small story out into the public and letting people know that no matter how small things are, it can be a great thing.

Parent: I was very impressed with the content and thoroughness of the presentations during the culminating event. But what really struck me was the full participation of all the students who bravely got up on stage to address a sizable audience. I know firsthand how intimidating a prospect like that can be—and I'm relatively practiced. But for many young people, this is not a usual role, being in front of a crowd. Even more impressive, as with any large group, a good number of the speakers weren't polished. Many were obviously English learners; others had common speech issues, such as lisps, stutters, and other articulation issues. But every one of them—everyone—got up and spoke calmly, proudly, and without fear. And I think that speaks volumes to the safe environment that has been created at King. That these kids could stand in front of a crowd, work through a presentation, and do so without fear really means that they feel safe: safe with their teachers, their audience and—most importantly, I think—with their peers. It hasn't always been that way in schools, and I'm guessing it still isn't that way in many places. Sometimes the most important thing you teach isn't the stuff that's in the lesson plans.

A few weeks after the completion of the expedition, the teachers met to reflect and make recommendations for refinement. We debriefed the work. We took notes on our suggestions for our next time around.

For me, our Small Acts of Courage expedition offers long-lasting, important learning. It is community centered and student centered. The content and skill building were deep and purposeful. The work was real and meaningful. Not once did I hear a student say, "Why are we learning this? What is this for?" The connections between the learning and practice time in the classroom and the final product were clear.

FINAL THOUGHTS

Schools are challenging places to work, and teaching is a complex profession. But the challenge, complexity, and relationships keep me professionally engaged and energized. As I enter my thirty-sixth year of teaching, I can see that schools are on the cusp of major change. But for me, it comes down to a few core beliefs that guide me throughout these shifts and that helped me guide these students through Small Acts of Courage.

It's All About Relationships

My job is to build relationships with students, parents, colleagues, administrators, and community members, all in an effort to support student learning. Above all, students must trust the teacher. If they know I will support and nurture them, they are willing to come along with me on the journey. Getting up on stage in front of two hundred people was a new challenge for most of the students. But the message from me is clear: I believe in you. You can do it. I can help you. In addition, when I have strong relationships with other adults in the building and community, I improve my ability to support students. If I need to make specific accommodations for a child, such as a change in schedule, the relationships I have built with my colleagues help me successfully provide those accommodations.

Everyone Gets to the Top of the Mountain

Feeling success is a wonderful thing. It gives students the confidence to face the next challenge. Many of the students who arrive in my classroom are not feeling confident. My job is to give them that experience of success. I believe that everyone gets to the top of the mountain. We all get there by working to the best of our ability, supporting each other, and celebrating our achievements. We are in this learning journey together. In this expedition, all the students completed a biographic narrative about a local citizen, and all participated in some way in the culminating event.

Make Sure the Learning Is Rigorous and Relevant

Students need to be challenged. Creating learning experiences that are engaging and relevant helps students persevere through rigorous content. By teaching through long-term learning expeditions, or interdisciplinary units, I help students build a connection between their learning and the world around them. Each student works toward creating a final product that showcases the learning, in this case, the biographical narrative. These products are based on real-world professional products and are shared with an authentic audience. All along the way, the students are clear about the learning map. They are interested in the content, they understand what is expected of them during the journey, they realize that each step in the learning process is critical for success, and they share and celebrate in the completion of the journey with a community audience and their classmates. There is a spirit of adventure and challenge in my classroom.

What About Test Scores?

From my descriptions of the students' work and performance during the Small Acts of Courage expedition, it should be clear that their academic work matched the rigorous expectations of seventh grade. But does the academic learning from these expeditions show up in standardized test scores? It's a fair question. Table 5.2 shows how our students at King Middle School compare with other middle school students in Portland and with all middle school students in Maine. (As noted earlier in table 5.1, a quarter of our students are ELL, and over half are eligible for free or reduced-price lunch.) During the era of the time machine in the kickoff described above, King students' reading and math scores lagged behind those of other district middle school students and students across the state. However, during the recent 2009–2011 loop, King students scored higher than both district and state middle school students.

Additionally, I look forward to the day when schools can effectively disseminate data on the twenty-first-century skills that were the focus of this work and when the public can consider these skills an additional piece of the education puzzle. These skills are critical to the students' future, but are often ignored because of the intense focus on standardized testing, which is limited in scope.

Be a Reflective Learner

Students are constantly reflecting in my room. They assess their work throughout the process. They expect a clear picture of the assessment criteria, which I provide through rubrics. My job is to help students develop a picture of quality.

TABLE 5.2   Achievement test scores for students at King Middle School,
Portland, Maine, 1987–1989 and 2009–2011

	King	District	State
Grade 8 three-year cumulative average MEA scores, 1987–1989*			
Reading	235	260	255
Math	280	320	285
Grade 8 three-year cumulative average NECAP scores, 2009–2011[†]			
Reading	851	848	847
Math	843	841	842
Grade 7 three-year cumulative average NECAP scores, 2009–2011[†]			
Reading	751	747	745
Math	743	741	742

*During these years, the Maine Education Assessment (MEA) was not given to grades 6 or 7.
[†]Maine changed its annual assessment to the New England Common Assessment Program (NECAP).

This ability to self-assess is a critical life skill. They also set goals and reflect weekly on their progress. The thoughtful cycle of learning, reflecting, adjusting, and learning is a constant feature of my room.

Culture Matters

Along with my colleagues, my job is to create and nurture a classroom culture that encourages all of us to treat each other with respect. When we emphasize kindness and understanding, we create an atmosphere where all can do their best work. It builds a safe place where we can all dig into the learning, make mistakes, and finally master the content. Such an atmosphere provides the backbone for a classroom where feedback is respectfully given and received as it was throughout our Small Acts of Courage expedition. The culture of respect permeates the hallways, the lunchroom, the ball field, and everywhere else in the community and follows the students into the future.

It is important that I consistently match my classroom practice with my philosophy. Every year, I strive to improve by learning from other educators. When educators share their practice publicly, they allow other professionals the opportunity to ponder and question. Unfortunately, unlike many other professionals, we don't get enough time to observe each other in action. My hope is that this glimpse into my practice allows fellow educators to continue their own learning journey as a reflective practitioner. I invite you to reflect deeply.

CHAPTER SIX

Grade Seven

Transparency, Efficiency, and Acceleration

CYNTHIA RAYMOND

OUR DISTRICT SHARED VISION: TO BE A SYSTEM OF STUDENT-CENTERED LEARNING

I like to think of April as the month of optimal learning for my students. I am amazed and incredibly proud of my students' commitment to and responsibility for their own learning. When they enter my classroom, my students are immediately engaged in work with their individual learning targets, ranging from opinion writing, to determining the central idea in informational texts, to writing an informative piece, or to conducting research on their chosen topic. Today, in mid-April, however, we are returning to an organizational tool I taught them to use earlier in the school year: the daily goal-setting template. It seems that some of the students have become lax recently in meeting their deadlines, or due dates. The template is a five-by-five matrix of squares with the days of the week (Monday through Friday) written across the top. Students write the date in the upper right-hand corner of each square. When I first introduced this tool during the fall, it took some practice, but the students were soon using the tool to plan and monitor their progress on their individual learning targets week by week and day by day. I passed out the blank calendars and briefly reminded my students how we had been using them up until just a few weeks ago, and I asked them to fill in their learning target goals for this week, both for the whole week and for each day. As I circulated around the room, I noted that all the students were on task and all their calendars were filled out for the week. When I asked several students to share their plans for the week, each was able to articulate exactly what she or he needed to do this week and why it was important to complete the particular set of tasks for the week.

FIGURE 6.1   Daily goal sheet

NAME:		CLASS NAME:	DATE:
Today's goal:	*Did I meet my goal (yes or no)?*	*Do I need to check my work with a peer or teacher (yes or no)?*	*Do I need to adjust: replan or redo? If so, what?*

Today (circle one):	
4	I was on task and quiet, working to complete my goal, 100 percent of the time.
3	I was mostly on task. I kept my conversation limited, showed positive behaviors, and worked to complete my goal.
2	I strayed from my task on occasion, had some slip-ups in behavior or noise level, and didn't get as much work done as I could have
1	I was rarely on task, struggled with my behaviors, and got little done.
Today (circle one):	
4	The class was 100 percent on task and worked hard to complete goals.
3	The class was mostly on task, maintained a low noise level, exhibited mostly positive behaviors, and worked productively.
2	The noise level and off-task behavior limited the class's ability to get work done.
1	The class spent too much time off task, noise levels were too high, and our behavior consistently limited the class's ability to get work done.

We also reinstated the daily goal sheet, which provides a template for students to monitor their learning on a day-by-day basis (figure 6.1).

The growth my students have made since September in becoming self-directed learners is remarkable, as I described above. Just how did we get to this place where I am the learning facilitator guiding my students to be fully engaged in their own active learning process? The following sections describe the process of self-empowerment for my students.

BUILDING A CLASSROOM CULTURE

Establishing a positive and supportive classroom culture is a necessary first step in creating a student-centered classroom. My district's shared vision, "to be a system of student-centered learning," guides every decision I make in my classroom. I work hard to structure and organize classroom time and space to meet the learning needs of every student. For example, one of my whole-class mini-lessons at the beginning of the year invites the students to talk about what they think our classroom code of cooperation (respect, responsibility, and commitment) should look like. Figure 6.2 summarizes the large wall poster that we

FIGURE 6.2   Student-centered code of cooperation at Hall-Dale Middle School, Farmingdale, Maine

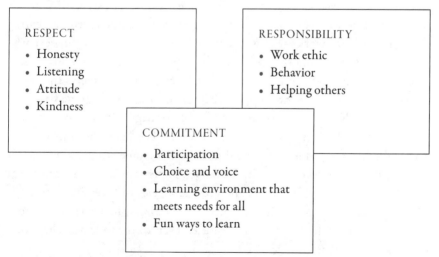

RESPECT
- Honesty
- Listening
- Attitude
- Kindness

RESPONSIBILITY
- Work ethic
- Behavior
- Helping others

COMMITMENT
- Participation
- Choice and voice
- Learning environment that meets needs for all
- Fun ways to learn

made to describe what we think the code of cooperation should look like in our classroom.

My next whole-class mini-lesson invites the students to contribute their ideas about what kinds of specific day-to-day classroom procedures they think would help create an environment that could support learning for every one of us. The students brainstorm, discuss, and eventually come to consensus. During this time, I keep referring to our code of cooperation poster, modeling, for example, how to show respect (listening), how to assume responsibility (behavior), and how to demonstrate commitment (participation). This demonstrates to the students that the poster is a living document, not just a pretty wall hanging that we designed.

Eventually, we do manage to agree on what the classroom should look like when we are working independently, in pairs, in other small groups, and as a whole class. On a large bulletin board, we posted our consensus lists of what we'll see happening when we're working in any of these four conditions (figure 6.3).

TESTING MY BELIEF SYSTEM

The steps to building the classroom culture I described above were embedded in a much deeper struggle than might be evident in these descriptions. The transformation was not exactly as Pollyannaish as it might seem. This group of students tested every ounce of my beliefs, which I had developed over thirty years, about what works with students. I knew that these fifteen seventh-graders, twelve boys and three girls, had not made nearly enough progress in sixth grade to be ready to jump into grade seven learning targets. Therefore, I needed to begin the year to support their completion of the grade six learning targets so they would have the foundation for beginning seventh grade. I also knew that they carried the label of "the bad class," and they knew it too. Some of them seemed almost proud of the label. Some students refused to follow rules and procedures from the outset. Some constantly exhibited distractible behaviors, while others allowed themselves to be easily distracted. Many had apparently lost sight of their potential and had succumbed to a feeling of defeat, which meant they refused even to try to learn. They were obviously testing me.

FIGURE 6.3   Standard operating procedures in Cynthia Raymond's classroom at Hall-Dale Middle School, Farmingdale, Maine

WHAT DOES IT LOOK LIKE TO WORK IN A WHOLE GROUP?	WHAT DOES IT LOOK LIKE TO WORK IN A SMALL GROUP?
• Don't talk while a person is talking • Sitting, looking, listening to teacher or peer and interacting by asking questions • Good eye contact on person speaking • Raise hand to ask a question • Inside voice, not yelling • Cooperation • Respectful comments and feedback	• Talk quietly with your small group • Share ideas and opinions • Be respectful of one another's comments • Compromise; meet in the middle • One person talking at a time
WHAT DOES IT LOOK LIKE TO WORK INDIVIDUALLY?	WHAT DOES IT LOOK LIKE TO WORK WITH A PARTNER?
• Quietly working • OK to ask others for help • Not distracting others • Focused on your own work • Staying on task; don't talk with others about nonrelated subjects • No wandering around the classroom	• Each partner doing an equal amount of work • Partners are quietly talking and sitting together • Cooperating • Sharing ideas • Focused on your partner when talking

I knew that I needed to take charge of this class to put the students' learning in order. Consequently, the classroom would need to be more teacher-directed at the beginning, with a gradual release of responsibility to the students as they became more independent learners. They needed modeling. They needed praise, praise, and praise. They needed to persevere when the learning task was difficult, not by giving up but instead by working through the difficulty. They needed to know that they could do anything and everything. They needed to feel success. They needed me.

The first week of school, I met with my principal to explain (justify, really) why I felt I needed to be more teacher-directed with this class. After describing the students to my administrator, he said he had full confidence in my ability to meet their needs: "Student-centered learning can look different for each child. If you are meeting that child's needs from where he or she is, then you are student-centered." He gave me his approval to trust my instincts and rely on what I knew to be best practices to meet my students' needs.

The them-versus-me mentality was evident from the very first day. They clearly distrusted teachers, including me. I had never experienced such a resistant, angry group of learners. They would be a hard nut to crack. Instinctively, I knew what I must do. This class needed structure. I had to establish a tone of respect among them and show that I cared about and believed in them. Beneath their hurt faces were kids who perceived themselves as failures. Behind their hostility were feelings of fear and sadness. I just had to help them get past their facades.

In addition to working with them to create the code of cooperation and standard operating procedure documents, I asked the students what they thought would be the ideal learning environment for them. They listed what they needed to be successful learners in an English language arts class. Like other middle school students, they wanted to interact with their peers and work together on mastering new knowledge. In order for this to happen, the classroom first needed a tone of respect (which I was not seeing). I had to teach them *I* messages (i.e., first-person statements about how the speaker was feeling, instead of accusations about another person) and how their tone and phrasing affected others in the class. Additionally, these learners wanted resources to be readily available and wanted to receive help from the teacher as needed—two very reasonable requests. The setup of my classroom easily allowed for these things to happen. Interestingly enough, the students identified that they were easily distracted and needed a fairly quiet learning environment. These needs they shared were, not surprisingly, all closely aligned with my own expectations for the class.

From September to December, I witnessed students taking one step forward, then two steps back. Change did not happen overnight, and improvement to the classroom culture was a process. Sometimes, frustration reared its ugly head among several students as they fell back into the I-can't attitude. Even more prevalent was the anxiety many students experienced. They felt overwhelmed with meeting deadlines for all their classes and struggled with knowing how to organize and manage their time to complete their work. It was in this context that I first introduced the daily planning matrix described earlier. My role as a teacher goes way beyond knowing and carrying out the English language arts curriculum.

An important part in creating a positive classroom culture was my use of praise. It was important for students to set attainable learning goals, and we celebrated the completion of each learning target. One student in particular was a slow reader who needed more time to complete his learning goals. Once his learning goals were met, he danced around in a circle as his classmates roared with applause. Over time, students had learned to build each other up rather than tear one another down. They had become a family. A tone of respect had emerged.

MY GIFTED UNDERACHIEVERS

Fully one-third of my class could be called gifted underachievers. Five of my boys tested in the gifted range in reading on the NWEA (Northwest Evaluation Association; www.nwea.org), a computer-adaptive assessment we use to measure students' skill development in reading and math. Yet, at the beginning of the year, they never completed work on time, they often threw in the towel in the middle of a project, or they never even attempted to start a new project. I realized that these learners were completely unaware of their capabilities, and furthermore, they did not know how to take ownership of their learning. They were products of their earlier experience with "sit and get" education, and as a result, they had been turned off from school long ago.

How could I change their mind-set? Above all, I recognized how strong they were verbally. I was amazed at the depth in which they would delve into topics connected with their interests and passions. So, I created opportunities for them to talk, converse with each other, and present and share their knowledge with the class. They needed to be heard. It was phenomenal to see how their ideas led to rich class discussions, which of course benefited everyone. Their knowledge on certain topics inspired other students to pose their own questions and to search for the answers for themselves. An incredible transformation was taking place in my classroom. These five students were engaged in their own learning and were encouraging others to do the same. The motivation came from them. I was no longer the "sage on the stage" but was now a "guide on the side." Learning is transformational. My greatest joy is in watching learners grow, change, and have an impact on others.

YOU MATTER

One example of how my students became a family is the way a student who had formerly been a loner came to be integrated into the family. Of the three girls in my class, two worked together as a learning team nearly all the time. The third always sat by herself and worked alone. Much of her writing focused on crafting fantasy tales of princesses and unicorns. It was a considerable challenge for me to engage her on the required standards like *understanding the author's purpose* and *opinion and argument writing.* I talked with her former teachers, but no one had any ideas on how to motivate her into a deeper engagement in the curriculum. I conferred with the guidance counselor, and together we examined the cumulative-record folder. We discovered that this student had no disabilities and had an above-average intelligence, but we also discovered that she was a strong visual learner with poor auditory skills. Aha! That was my clue to planning instruction that would work for her.

I sat down with her privately and shared what I had discovered about her as a learner. I joked with her that when I spoke in class giving multistep directions, she may have heard "blah, blah, blah." After "hearing" the directions, she probably asked herself, "What did Ms. Raymond just say?" This girl smiled and nodded in affirmation. I went on to tell her that she was a capable learner, and I expected her to be successful in my class with some help. For instance, I would present every assignment visually to her and follow up by checking her understanding and asking her to repeat the directions to me. She was agreeable to this, and it worked. It did not take a rocket scientist to determine what this student needed. It took a teacher to care, to expect the student's best effort, and not to allow her to withdraw during class.

From that point on, she was cooperative and eager to complete any task given. The key to her engagement was in my staying connected with her by helping her identify her strengths as a learner while offering suggestions on how to improve in the weaker areas. Daily check-ins and conversations with this student proved invaluable on her road to success. She needed to know that she mattered. One of the most heartwarming moments in this class was the day the two girls in the back of the room invited the third girl to be a member of their table. Their laughter drew my attention as I witnessed that she was finally part of a group and no longer a loner. The sight gave me goose bumps!

INSTRUCTIONAL DECISIONS

Once we laid the foundation for the classroom culture and continued to practice its components of respect, responsibility, and commitment, we could begin to learn in earnest. I have learned that in my student-centered classroom, *voice and choice* are vital to engage learners. I encourage my students to follow their passions and delve deeply into what interests them. In addition, the students have a choice in how they show what they know. They use a variety of media to present their knowledge, for example, through essays, skits, videos, blogs, demonstrations, debates, posters, and podcasts.

My mantra is *transparency, efficiency, and acceleration.* I work to perfect a classroom environment in which students know exactly what they need to do and have the resources available to move on in their learning when they are ready. This work includes teaching standards that are aligned with the Common Core State Standards.[1] All seventh-graders in my English language arts classes work toward a minimum of proficiency, but they usually go beyond proficiency to an advanced set of skills, knowledge, and reasoning processes for their learning targets.

My responsibility as the learning facilitator is to ensure that all students in the classroom have what they need to work efficiently toward the completion of the learning targets. For example, I use a capacity matrix, which is like a road map that guides students through the levels of performance, ranging from foundational knowledge to more complex reasoning skills. Each day, my students set goals and manage their time to complete their learning targets. Figure 6.4 shows a capacity matrix for plot development.

The students and I also developed a flow chart that we put up on one wall of the classroom that reminds us every day how to use our learning time efficiently (figure 6.5).

Because learning is the constant and can happen anytime and anywhere, I created a class Web site that includes the capacity matrices, instructional videos,

FIGURE 6.4   Capacity matrix for plot development

Content area: Language arts Standard: Literature Measurement topic: Plot development		Learner: Learning facilitator: Ms. Raymond Step: 3	
Learning targets EL.07.P01. RP5.01.03*	**Assessment items**	**My evidence**	**Teacher check**
Level 4 learning targets (knowledge utilization): I can predict what would happen if different conflicts altered the plot.	I can create a new conflict that significantly changes the story and can describe how the events would change the outcome of the story.	5. Write a short story where different conflicts dictate the plot and alter the outcome (e.g., person versus machine, fate/destiny, the unknown), OR create a new conflict that significantly changes an existing story, and describe how the events would change the outcome of the story.	
Level 3 learning targets (analysis): I understand the types of conflict.	I can trace the development of the conflict in the plot using the four types of conflict (person versus person, self, nature, or society).	4. Read a novel. Create a story board to trace the development of the conflict in the plot.	

(continued)

FIGURE 6.4   Capacity matrix for plot development *(continued)*

Learning targets EL.07.P01. RP5.01.03*	Assessment items	My evidence	Teacher check
Level 2 learning targets (retrieval): I know the types of conflicts such as person versus person, self, nature, society, the unknown, technology/ machine, or fate/ destiny. I know subplot.	I can define conflict in relationship to person versus person, self, nature, or society.	3. Complete quiz 2, "To Build a Fire" story, and video 1. Watch conflict video or slide show, or participate in teacher lesson.	
Level 1 learning targets: With help, I have the level 2 content.	N/A	N/A	

*The code *EL.07.P01.RP5.01.03* identifies a learning target from the school district's English Language Arts Scope and Sequence. *EL* identifies the content area (English Language Arts); *07* identifies the grade level (seventh grade); *P01* identifies when the learning target is taught (Pod 1, first trimester); *RP5* identifies the topic (Reading Plot Step 5); *01* identifies the learning target from the RP5 list (first learning target); *03* identifies the version of the learning target (third version).

rubrics, and other resources needed for each learning target. The students can access our class Web site from anywhere so that they can continue with their learning outside of the classroom.

The learning targets and the deadlines for completion are posted on the walls in the classroom. This allows my students to move through the learning continuum at or ahead of my teacher pace. Additionally, students track their progress on the learning targets chart, also posted in the classroom (see figure 6.6 for an example).

FIGURE 6.5   Daily work flow chart

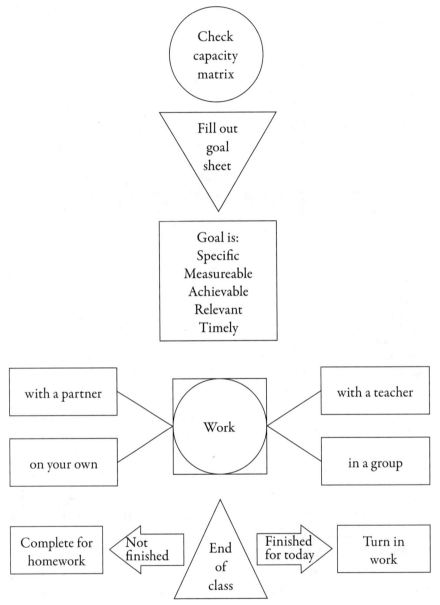

FIGURE 6.6   Sample learning targets and their deadlines

CHARACTER DEVELOPMENT
• I understand that events influence goals and motivations and contribute to character development.
• I understand how and why characters change over the course of the story.
Due November 20.
COMMAS
• I am skilled at using commas in a sentence.
Due December 4.

My classroom looks very different than it did before my transformation from teacher-centered instruction to the kind of student-centered teaching that I do now. I seldom lecture, and I rarely teach the entire class at the same time. Typically, I give direct instruction to small groups of students who are learning at the same pace on the same learning target. Generally, students are working independently, in pairs, or in small groups. Students who have earned proficiency on a learning target can offer to help a peer in the classroom, or they can move onto the next learning target. Also, I offer one-on-one interventions with students who are struggling with a learning target or are falling behind teacher pace for the learning target. Since I implemented a student-centered model, my students are much more engaged in their learning, are more invested in their own learning, and are performing at higher levels of thinking in accordance to Marzano's taxonomy.[2]

TODAY'S DIGITAL NATIVES

I know I have to meet today's students, all digital natives, in their own world if I am to help them learn most efficiently. These students speak their own digital language, are experts at multitasking, and can receive information at lightning speed (as long as it's delivered digitally). I try to provide rich learning experiences that tap into these digital learners' passions. For example, I encourage them to use blogging, online simulations, wikis, and strategy games and to create and edit videos. Giving students choices of what medium they can use to show what they know is highly motivating for my students. Many of these tools are ones that my students taught me how to use. For example, when students have to demonstrate their understanding of character development and plot in a work of literature, several choose to demonstrate their knowledge by using online tools such as storyboards, blogs, and virtual posters. One student uses Glogster (www.glogster.com), an online tool that creates interactive posters showing the creative expression of ideas and knowledge.

Another engaging tool that my students use to demonstrate their understanding of, for example, conflict in literature is Storyboard That (www.storyboardthat.com). The storyboards the students create look like multipanel cartoons depicting the characters in the story. The students label the panels and provide dialogue balloons depicting what the characters are saying about the particular conflict they are experiencing.

Another online tool that is very popular with several of my students is Fakebook (see www.classtools.net). This tool allows students to create Facebook-like profiles of the characters in a book, and through these profiles, the students chart the story's intertwining plotlines.

Some of my students use blogs to communicate with each other in their reading groups. I can see from reading their blog posts that when they communicate this way about the events and characters in the novel, they are better able to make sense of the text they are reading and are developing their metacognitive capacity.

LEARNING IS TRANSFORMATIONAL

I firmly believe that developing strong relationships with my students is the single most important quality in my student-centered classroom. As I work to develop these relationships, several important outcomes emerge. First, the students can see and, more importantly, can *feel* that I care about them and that I am committed to helping them become successful learners. Second, I learn what motivates them, what topics they are passionate about, and what their current aspirations are for their future. All of this informs my decisions about the topics I can suggest to them later for research projects, for example. And third, learning about their aspirations inspires me to work even harder to make a genuine difference in their learning and in their personal growth. I'm committed to empowering my students to use their knowledge to enrich their own lives and the lives of others as well.

For example, one of my students selected the topic of animal testing for various consumer and pharmaceutical products as the focus for demonstrating her proficiency for the standard about opinion and argument writing. She delved into the topic deeply, not only reading arguments on both sides of the issue, but also interviewing experts on both sides of this controversial issue to form her own opinion and to write about how she formed that opinion. She resolved personally never to hurt animals in any manner, and in addition, she convinced her family to join her in becoming a vegan.

Another one of my students this year saw himself as a poor reader and a poor writer. As I got to know him, I discovered what a young entrepreneur he was with raising and selling chickens. He had earned for himself every popular electronic gadget (a smartphone, an iPod, and a MacBook, to name a few) from the profits of his business. When I encouraged him to connect his passions and interests with his learning, he created a "How to Make a Chicken Coop" video for his informative and explanatory writing project (aligned with the Common Core State Standards).[3]

This same student conducted research on the congenital condition that afflicted his younger sibling because he wanted to learn all he could about the syndrome and to better understand how it was affecting his family. He created a set of essential questions, which led to other questions as he researched the syndrome and learned more about all of the possible manifestations it might have and how those might affect his sibling's heart and longevity, for example. This student chose to do an oral presentation and slide show to demonstrate his proficiency with the research process, and he wowed the class with his knowledge about the syndrome and with his personal reflection on how it had affected his own and his family's life. This was a pivotal moment for this student, who had begun the year believing he was a poor reader and poor writer. He now could see himself as a capable learner with strong reading, writing, and communication skills.

My digital natives do not always choose to demonstrate their proficiencies in a strictly online format. One of my students had a history of honest-to-goodness meltdowns in class when he had been asked to write. He had an extreme contempt for writing, and his fear of writing only intensified his underlying anxiety. He was a kinesthetic learner, preferring to move, perform, and do hand-on activities instead of picking up a pencil and paper. We're fortunate in Maine to have laptops for all of our seventh- and eighth-grade students, as we have had for years. Using his laptop, this student created a video of himself to demonstrate what he had learned in his research project on medieval weaponry. He created Styrofoam swords to explain, by demonstrating, the various fighting techniques and strategies that medieval warriors used in battle. This video showed his proficiency with the informational reading and writing standards of the Common Core.[4] He no longer struggled with completing research projects and composing informational pieces. His laptop also helped him complete a report on another of his research projects, the Battle of Thermopylae.

MOVING AHEAD

Communicating with parents is an important part of how I maintain a student-centered classroom. The mother of one of my above-mentioned "gifted under-achievers" asked me late in the year whether this was the "low class" because her child "did next to nothing in the sixth grade." My response: "Absolutely not. The majority of the students in the class are proficient in reading, and five are proficient with distinction, according to NWEA data" (see www.nwea.org).

Throughout the year, I communicated weekly with parents regarding their child's progress in achieving proficiency on the learning targets, and I believe this was a key factor to each student's overall success. My personal phone calls to let parents know how well their child was doing allowed the parents to reinforce what the students were hearing from me at school about their progress.

One mother who knew quite well her child's ability asked me why the school had not previously been able to see his exceptionality. As with most parents, she wanted answers. Her questions were legitimate. I knew exactly what this mother was feeling and thinking. Parents want what is best for their children and count on teachers to provide the education that the children deserve. My own son has a diagnosis on the autism spectrum and is consequently a nontraditional learner. I asked similar questions all through my son's schooling. He's now in college, having completed high school through the adult education program, which implements a fully student-centered learning philosophy, and he's doing quite well in the college environment.

I'm committed to meeting my learners where they are and to inspiring, motivating, and supporting them to achieve more than what they have previously accomplished. I have confidence in my skills and experience as a teacher; I know I can help my students learn, grow, and increase their own confidence in themselves as learners. In my school, we have no room for the blame game among our colleagues. We're all in this together. The students belong to all of us, and we're all responsible for all of them. In the past, we've seen that the chemistry of a class can be challenging for a teacher who may have felt that he or she had to handle it all alone, but this insular approach was detrimental to everyone involved—the teacher, the students, and the rest of the school. Now we reach out to each other for strategies and suggestions that could improve our practice. This practice is helping all of us to become even better teachers.

As the end of this school year approached, my students asked if they could stay with me for their eighth-grade year. This was the greatest compliment ever paid to me as an educator. I told them how proud I was of their achievements in completing all of the sixth-grade and seventh-grade learning targets this year. What an incredible feat. They are at the point where they have taken ownership of their learning. These students are ready to take off their training wheels and meet the challenge of soaring down the hill on their own! I am confident that they will successfully meet the challenges ahead. The eighth-grade English language arts teacher offers a really creative program and has much to offer and teach them. I am excited for their futures, and I am grateful for our time together this year. It was a year of deep learning for all of us.

CHAPTER SEVEN

Grade Eight Special Education

Charting the Course to Proficiency-Based Learning

SHANNON SHANNING

As I started to run up the hill, I glanced at the road before me. I had run this route before, but today the hill felt much larger and the course much longer. Looking at the road ahead, I realized the enormity of this endeavor. For a few fleeting seconds, I began to panic and allowed the running demons to whisper their negative thoughts. *This hill is too big. You are not a runner. It will hurt. You can stop.* Just as I contemplated stopping, I looked down at my feet. While my mental demons tried to deter me, my feet continued to move, one in front of the other, as if on autopilot. In that moment, I realized that despite feeling completely overwhelmed, I knew intrinsically what I had to do. Rather than looking at the hill, I began envision the finish, the end of my run. For me the finish isn't necessarily the physical location of where my course ends, but rather an ending point, a goal of where I want to be. The hill, while daunting, is really only one part of the course. By focusing on where I wanted to be, I was more motivated to continue. Just as quickly as those demons entered my mind, they left, leaving behind optimism and hope.

People often ask me, "What is it like to be a teacher?" When I try to explain the complexity of what I do, the only way I know how to describe it is to compare it to my experience as a runner. *Runner,* such a funny word, continues to elude me, as I can never seem to identify myself as one. Being a teacher is no different. Despite having been in the classroom for more than fourteen years,

I grapple with feelings of uncertainty every single day. As a teacher, I find that the course is constantly changing and the hills seem more frequent. While I try to focus on the finish—that end point of getting every student to where he or she needs to be—I find myself frequently chasing out those demons and pushing on. Just as my feet carried me up that hill, as a teacher I rely on my instincts, my core.

Making the transition to a student-centered, proficiency-based model was a really big hill for me. As a special education teacher, I had been providing a student-centered curriculum to my students for quite some time, but I always struggled with finding that careful balance of implementing grade-level standards on the one hand and meeting the individual needs of my students on the other. Given all of the chatter that was happening in education at the time I piloted this model, proficiency-based learning didn't just feel daunting; it felt insurmountable. As a runner, I tend just to lace up my sneakers and hit the ground running. My approach to implementing this model was no different. While I had researched and even toyed with the idea of piloting a hybrid proficiency-based model in my special education classroom, I expected that other colleagues I knew would do it first and I would follow their lead. Instead I found myself taking on this challenge, the only runner on an uncharted course. It is my core that propels me up those hills, those values and beliefs I know to be true about teaching.

THE STARTING PISTOL WENT OFF, BUT I WAS STILL STANDING AT THE START LINE

When I first decided to become a runner, I knew it meant that I would eventually have to run a race. While I often talked about it, the reality of signing up and training for one meant not only that was it going to happen, but also that I had to put my words and beliefs into action. Similarly, when schools make the commitment to be responsive in their approach to student needs, teachers must be prepared to respond. It is fair to say that although I believed in this approach to education, I was not entirely ready to respond.

It was a Saturday, not just any Saturday, but rather *that* Saturday. The Saturday before school starts. *That* Saturday, which usually follows a sleepless Friday night, is perhaps is the most anxiety-driven Saturday of the entire year. Teachers—I dare say, more so than students—are often plagued with back-to-school anxiety, which usually rears its ugly head in the form of the infamous back-to-school nightmare. While students' dreams often pertain to clothing, or lack thereof, teachers' dreams revolve around not being prepared or in control. My dreams began in July that summer and increased in frequency, making sleepless Friday live up to its name.

That Saturday, I was doing what I typically do every year on that day, bargaining. I was trying to bargain for those last few seconds of summer. Families of teachers know that even during the summer, school is still very present. However, in those final hours of vacation, it consumes every waking moment. So there I was, bargaining. My classroom was set up, the first few weeks planned, and my first-day outfit was pressed and hanging on the back of my closet door. With nerves in high gear, I decided to do some more planning. I chose to work while sitting on my deck. It technically is outside, and if any member of my family caught me, I could easily say that I was enjoying the beautiful weather. I had convinced myself that if I dedicated just a few more hours to schoolwork, I would take the next day off. Thus, the bargain. Little did I know that in a few moments, I would not be able to fulfill my end of that bargain.

The sun flickered through the leaves, causing shadows to dance across my face. I was too distracted by the IEPs fanned out on the blanket in front of me to appreciate the warmth on my skin. I shuffled through the books stacked up around me, looking for my notebook of ideas and resources. It no longer resembled a notebook at all, but rather had grown into a three-inch binder. I have heard of how writers keep pads of paper near their beds in case they wake up in the night with that perfect idea. Teachers, perhaps cut from a similar cloth, also have in their possession writing tablets, which frequently are carried with them on the off chance they will be inspired to create the perfect lesson. My notebook, or three-inch binder, is full of these papers, which are ever so carefully stacked in between curriculum maps, guides, and lesson-planning templates. I opened my notebook and began flipping through the pages, looking for one page in particular. To an untrained eye, it would appear to be a jumbled mess, but for me, it was perfectly organized. Aha, I found it! The page where I had been brainstorming how to incorporate the Common Core Standards for English language arts with IEP goals in a way that supported our year-long theme of survival.[1] My coveted notes, which might be mistaken as nothing more than chicken scratch, provided me with the final key for my reading unit.

Just as the sun and those leaves created a harmonious dance across my face, my fingers gracefully tapped their way across the keyboard creating a masterpiece, a curriculum map. Before me I now had my theme, essential question, targeted core standards (the need to know versus the nice to know), and a list of books, articles, short stories, and videos (all of which I had been collecting for more than three months). I placed my laptop down beside my glass of iced tea, which was now a watered-down version of its former self, and began to examine those IEPs again. I needed to review the students' academic levels, evaluation data, goals, strengths, and weaknesses, so that I could carefully select the appropriate timeframe to introduce and implement strategies. As if struck by lightning, I realized I would need a chart. I pick up my laptop again and feverishly begin creating an instructional chart that would merge all this information. I was on a roll, and for the first time, I started to think that this year I would uphold my end of the bargain. I would be ahead of the game, and just once, I would take that day before school off. As I began to entertain the notion that *this* Saturday was different than in years past, I heard that familiar *ding* indicating that I have mail. Given that it was three days before the start of the school year, this ding sound was happening a bit more frequently than a month ago. Glancing down at my email, I saw that it was from my principal. The subject header read, "A Proposal." Intrigued, I opened it.

As my eyes darted across the screen, I suddenly realized that in a matter of seconds, what I had envisioned for my school year was now going to be rather different. Dramatically different. Given the recent increase in enrollment, and with the growing number of special education students who required direct instructional services for math (fifteen), my principal was proposing that another special education teacher and I coteach these students for one math block a day. He suggested that not only would we perhaps pilot a cotaught model, but doing so would enable us to implement a student-centered curriculum, which the other teacher and I had supported in the past. Clearly, the time frame to plan wasn't ideal (!), and considering that I wasn't slated to teach any math blocks that year, I must admit that I was momentarily paralyzed by the idea. It felt as if the starting pistol had just gone off, but I was still standing at the start line. Suddenly all of the runners were miles ahead of me and I was starting the race so very far behind everyone else. It would be easy in that moment never to start. However, once I make a commitment, I find it difficult not to follow through.

I had made a commitment to be responsive in my approach to education. It had been my long-standing philosophy to do whatever it took to give students what they need to be successful. Not only was I a proponent of individualizing instruction (even if it required using outside-the-box methodologies), but I had actually also served on committees that explored an alternative approach to education. Now it was time to put those words into action. The starting pistol did indeed go off. The race had started, and it was now my turn to run.

THE FIRST MILE

The first mile of any race is usually spent not only getting a feel for the course, but also getting your body and mind into a rhythm. Those initial steps, while awkward at first, quickly fall into a cadence. It also is a time of sheer optimism. Pace is good, legs are strong, and the finish line, which is still miles away, seems within reach. Such was the case those first few weeks of piloting our cotaught, student-centered math program. The idea of a proficiency-based special education program in and of itself was brilliant. As the coteachers of the class, my colleague and I not only are skilled, but also strongly believe in this philosophy, and given that both of us are visionaries, we could see the finish line, or ultimately the potential. And we were optimistic. Very optimistic. Disgustingly so.

After I got over the initial paralysis of what I was about to embark upon, optimism fluttered in with incredible force as I began to realize the possibilities. As a teacher, I am the guru of making lists. Immediately after hitting the "send" button confirming my desire to teach this course, my mind kicked into high gear. And I began generating a list, the first of many that year. The list contained all the reasons why this proposal, and my participation in it, was a good idea, in fact, a *great* idea.

Student-Centered Cotaught Math Program: The Pros

1. This type of instructional approach is the right thing to do for students.
2. Every year, although some students make gains, I always wonder whether they could progress even further. This type of model might serve them better than past approaches have served them.

3. I would be teaching with my colleague, who is perhaps one of the best math teachers I have ever observed. Most importantly, she knows kids. Not only does she have an incredible knowledge of the middle level Common Core Math Standards, but she also knows how to modify and implement the essential standards so that even students years behind grade level have access to this content.

4. I have worked with this teacher before on both our special education team and on an ad hoc committee that explored implementing an alternative programming model. I know both that we have a similar mindset and that she would be open to piloting ideas around best practices.

5. We could integrate STEM (science, technology, engineering, and math) projects that would both allow us to focus on an integration of science and math and provide opportunities for our students to learn to work collaboratively.

6. Our administrator believes in us.

And just like that, my head was swirling with possibilities and optimism.

Those first few weeks were spent getting into our own groove, finding our rhythm, and stumbling through the initial awkwardness of uncertainty. While we clearly had our work cut out for us early on, we were propelled by the initial optimism, not to be deterred from our course. The students that we would be working with had an incredible range of challenges, including not only academic, but also behavioral and emotional needs. We also knew that as is often the case with special education, the number of students in our class would more than likely increase rather than decrease. This made it imperative that we create a strong foundation.

After hours of brainstorming, which included an idea trail that covered three dry-erase boards and multiple pages of chart paper, my colleague and I had our foundation. We knew what we wanted our program to be, even if we didn't know how we were going to do it. Our classroom ultimately needed to meet the needs of *our* students. Both of us had observed student-centered, proficiency-based classrooms in other schools, and we knew which pieces of this model would be most effective for our students. We decided not to use scripted language or educational jargon that our students couldn't understand; instead, this program would be real. We wanted to acknowledge our past successful practices and infuse them with the main goals of a proficiency-based model.

Our program would target individualized goals, group work, and team building. We would provide remediation skill building, introduce and teach essential Common Core Standards, and provide participation in STEM opportunities.[2] The program would also need to be engaging. Many of our students have struggled for so long that they were reluctant to engage in any type of learning, never mind something that may require them to be more self-directed.

Above all, we needed to build a relationship with our students and engage them as collaborative partners in the process before we could even get to the math. We knew that the light of curiosity and desire to learn was not entirely extinguished, but perhaps was buried beneath the rubble of past failures. We needed to remove the dust and debris and expose our students to the light once again.

The first few days of school were spent doing just that. We provided our students with carefully supported ice-breaker and team-building activities. We introduced nothing that was too challenging, but rather offered activities that allowed them to get to know one another and share their strengths in areas that might not necessarily include math. While the students participated in these activities, we took careful notes. We were able to identify student interests and strengths, as well as areas that were a challenge for each student. Ultimately, however, we were creating a culture of trust and investment. When students invest in the teacher and the class, the children are more likely to invest in themselves. We knew what the course ahead looked like, and we wanted to capitalize on this optimism before exposing the students to the more difficult tasks that lay ahead. Truth be told, just like a runner during the first mile, we were incredibly optimistic too. Overlooking the miles in between, we had our eyes on the finish line.

BE THE TORTOISE, NOT THE HARE

Despite the natural desire to start off fast when running, a fast pace is difficult to maintain and can often lead to fatigue, burnout, and even injury. Veteran runners are notorious for saying that "the body doesn't know pace; it knows effort." In other words, your body responds to the amount of effort that is exerted. The same is true for teaching. It is tempting, when in the beginning stages of implementing a program change, to be energized and motivated by student engagement and progress. However it is important to accept that maintaining that pace doesn't always reap rewards.

So there we were, with a successful start to the school year. We had mastered our initial team-building activities, managed to engage our students, and even had attempted some math lessons that went fairly smoothly. To be completely honest, we were stoked, or unrealistically optimistic. At any rate, both of us had shifted our focus to developing a program that would not only meet the individual needs of our students, but would also allow them to make progress at an exponential rate. With both of us having taught special education at this level for some time, we knew what the expectations were at the high school level, where the students would be next year, and we wanted nothing more than to close those gaps that had somehow metastasized into deep canyons for our students. We had seen all too often how students begin at the elementary level only a year behind grade level, but as the academic and social demands increase, the traditional approach of "making a year's growth in a year's time" leaves them permanently behind.

Every planning block, every hour after school, and, if I were completely honest, every free moment was focused on developing this student-centered curriculum. You see, I was also teaching a reading and writing block at the time, and the curriculum design that we were planning for our math class was too good not to apply to my other classes as well. This process was creative, messy, and grueling to say the least, but after careful research and heated discussions, and with years of experience under our belt, we planned a program. We knew that despite strategic planning, we also had to be responsive and willing to change if things didn't work.

By mid-September, we had gathered initial data (benchmarking) through such formal and informal measures as Aimsweb, NWEA, NECAP (New England Common Assessment Program), and teacher-created materials.[3] After all, we needed this initial data to determine goals for each student and to measure growth. We decided to break our class into two larger groups based not only on their shared IEP goals (which included standards such as solving single-digit multiplication and division problems with 90 percent accuracy, subtracting multidigit numbers that require borrowing or regrouping with 90 percent accuracy, or writing and interpreting numerical equations at a fifth-grade level with 85 percent accuracy), but also on their compatibility in working together. We broke each of these two larger groups (groups 1 and 2) into two smaller groups that participated in two rotations per class. My coteacher focused on the essential Common Core Standards, also known as the *power standards*, as determined by the staff at our school and facilitated a rotation for word problems and practical applications. I provided direct instruction addressing IEP goal remediation and computation, which also included one-on-one goal planning, and another rotation for math fluency and computation. Once a week, I also monitored progress using Aimsweb (www.aimsweb.com) to collect data. Figure 7.1 illustrates our weekly teaching rotations.

FIGURE 7.1   Math group rotations

ESSENTIAL STANDARDS (TEACHER 1) TEACHER-DIRECTED ROTATION *Monday and Wednesday, groups 1 and 2* *Tuesday and Thursday, groups 3 and 4*	IEP GOAL REMEDIATION (TEACHER 2) TEACHER-DIRECTED ROTATION *Monday and Wednesday, groups 3 and 4* *Tuesday and Thursday, groups 1 and 2*
• Introduction to, and teaching of, the "power standards" • Combination of individual and group work lessons and activities • Use of Khan Academy*	• IEP goal direct instruction • Remediation of "gap" skills • Computation instruction • Weekly Aimsweb progress monitoring and feedback[†] • One-on-one goal setting and workshop
PRACTICAL APPLICATIONS (TEACHER 1) STUDENT-DIRECTED ROTATION *Monday and Wednesday, groups 1 and 2* *Tuesday and Thursday, groups 3 and 4*	SKILLS / DRILLS (TEACHER 2) STUDENT-DIRECTED ROTATION *Monday and Wednesday, groups 3 and 4* *Tuesday and Thursday, groups 1 and 2*
• Word problem of the week, with focus on writing in content areas • Hands-on activities or problems related to Common Core Standards • Practical applications	• Five-minute frenzy (fluency drill) • Curriculum-based measure probe (computation drill) • Moby Math: individualized computer program based on student need[‡]

(continued)

FIGURE 7.1   Math group rotations *(continued)*

STEM TEAM-BUILDING CHALLENGE OF THE WEEK
Friday, all groups
Each week, students participate in STEM team building activities such as: • Marshmallow challenge • Egg drop challenge • Catapult challenge • Gingerbread house challenge • Raft challenge

Note: IEP, individualized education plan; STEM, science, technology, engineering, and math.
*Khan Academy (www.khanacademy.org) is a student-directed web-based learning tool that measures individual progress toward the Common Core State Standards.
†For online assessment instruments, see www.aimsweb.com.
‡For Moby Math application, see Moby Max, "Math That Works," www.mobymax.com/Curriculum/Math.

For each teacher, one of the rotations was more teacher-directed, while the other was more student-directed. This balanced approach helped the students learn both to work together and to be efficiently independent. These student skills did not occur naturally, but rather required a gradual release of responsibility so that the students were very clear about what it meant to be a self-directed learner. Traditional proficiency-based models have a strong focus on independence and require a level of self-direction that not all students have mastered by eighth grade. Programs and curriculums have to be carefully structured to honor individual needs as well as the needs of the whole class.

Once a week, we held a STEM team-building challenge, which would include a writing reflection. My coteacher and I understood the benefits of student participation in STEM challenges and the importance of learning to work collaboratively.

Essentially, this mixture of rotations meant that we each were planning two mini-lessons per day, totaling eight per week, not including the STEM challenge. Every day, we had to review the progress that students had made and then make updates and plan accordingly, because this instruction was so individualized. We also added another one-on-one workshop within each teacher-directed rotation so that we could give students feedback and review their progress to support their moving toward mastering standards and continued growth.

We also had to teach students not only to be independent, but also to accept new academic challenges. When new learning is introduced, these students often are reluctant to be independent because of failed attempts in the past. We had to carefully craft our program because what works for other students doesn't always work for these kids. I initially thought proficiency-based learning was primarily student initiated, but our program required a significant amount of direct instruction, classroom management, overall structure and setup, opportunities to honor teamwork and individualized needs, and technology integration. This work was hard and constant, and the pace was lightning speed.

And there we were, running like the proverbial hare in a race. We started to realize that this pace during the first few months was exhausting and barely manageable; it would be difficult to maintain much longer (for us as well as the students). We were so responsive in our approach that we had little time to enjoy what was happening in the classroom. Like a runner's body, our students were responding to the effort that they were exerting, moving through the course quicker than they had during any other race in the past. We were expecting more from our students than they had ever experienced before, but if we didn't slow down, we would never get them all across that finish line.

BREAK UP THE DISTANCE

A common strategy for runners is to break up the distance when they run a race. While there are some benefits for the body, the major benefits are mental. If a runner is focused only on running the total distance, it is easy to become fatigued and perhaps stop. Whereas if a runner breaks the race up into sections (e.g., mile 1, mile 2, the home stretch), the race is much more manageable and allows for celebrating each smaller milestone, which motivates the racer to continue on the course, perhaps even achieving his or her personal best. How runners break up the course is really individual, but ultimately has the same effect. Teachers can learn a thing or two from runners in this regard. Students can be overwhelmed when focused on all that they have to accomplish. But when the requirements are broken into (individualized) smaller steps or chunks, the children are engaged and more likely to stick with the course.

By the time December rolled around, it felt as if we had been running for miles with no mile marker or water station in sight. We realized that despite all our efforts, we were missing a key factor. We were not breaking up the distance or taking time to set these smaller goals, which would allow us to celebrate every accomplishment. One of the greatest motivators for anyone is accomplishment. Our students were accomplishing things every day, some little and some major, but we were moving so fast that we were unable to recognize and celebrate these efforts. We also knew that we were embarking on the toughest part of the course, winter, and if we did not acknowledge these achievements, we would not have the stamina to persevere.

At this point in the year, we had also added two more students and were starting to feel like sardines packed into a very tight space. While the kids had become well rehearsed at grouping and regrouping tables and lugging bins full of materials to each rotation, they were really just going through the motions. Our initial fears of developing a program in which everything was scripted was quickly becoming a reality because we had failed to incorporate personalizing this experience for our students. We had somehow forgotten that for every student, the race was his or her own and we needed to honor individual progress.

We often introduced things in the larger group, but to personalize and individualize the course, we needed to meet with each student individually. This meant looking at the one-on-on workshop time, which was naturally embedded into the teacher-directed rotations. It made the most sense to use the progress monitoring time during my rotation (IEP goal remediation) to meet with students, set goals, and essentially break up the course or set benchmarks. As a lover of lists and charts, I created a template to use to help the students narrow down their goals and to identify both the essential tools and strategies and the barriers to their learning. Figure 7.2 shows the student goal-setting template.

Yes, having the students complete this goal-setting template was incredibly time-consuming and, for the initial round, teacher-directed. It also invited students to be accountable and to develop a sense of ownership of their goals. I reviewed with each student the Common Core Standards that they were working on during the essential-standards rotation, in addition to the work that

FIGURE 7.2   Student goal-setting template

COMMON FORE STANDARD

What is this really asking me to do?

(Unpack the standard, circle nouns
and underline verbs)

*What am I able to do as it
relates to this standard?*

(Use Aimsweb, Moby
Max, Kahn, etc.)

What is my goal?

(SMART goal
format)

*Tool Box of
Strategies*

What will help
me to achieve this
goal?

*What
are my
barriers?*

What prevents me
from achieving
this goal?

Note: Aimsweb (www.aimsweb.com) is a student assessment/progress monitoring tool that
works in conjunction with instructio; Moby Max (www.mobymax.com) is a Web-based
learning tool for self-directed learning; Khan Academy (www.khanacademy.org) is a student-
directed, web-based learning tool that measures individual progress toward the Common
Core State Standards.

they were doing in the IEP goal work/remediation rotation. We examined the
progress that they had made on their Aimsweb monitoring, and we set a weekly
goal for the number of problems that they wanted to get correct. We also set
their projected long-term goal. I kept these sheets in a binder and would check
in with each student during our weekly workshop to see where he or she was
in terms of meeting these goals, and we would discuss any strategies that were

helpful or would identify things that prevented the student's progress. I also would have the student mark his or her projected goal for the week (often a dot) as well as the long-term goal (a star) on the progress monitoring assessments.

Before starting the weekly assessments, we would talk about strategy and pacing, a funny thing that we all do during a race or a test, but we often fail to teach to our students to do. Together we developed the *strike-three* method: Upon receiving their assessment, students would go through all the problems and do the easiest ones first—the ones that they were most secure with and were confident that they could complete easily. Next, the students would complete the problems that they perhaps had a strategy for, but that were challenging and maybe time-consuming. Finally, they would attempt the problems that they were not familiar with, but might attempt to solve using deductive reasoning or another applicable strategy. Given that these assessments were timed and only counted the total number of correct problems, the students felt that the three-strike method was the best strategy.

The students were more motivated to achieve these smaller milestones once they knew their goals, were active in developing them, and could see how the progress-monitoring measures and rotations related to Common Core Standards. Every day, we would give both a verbal shout-out and an online one (via the social learning platform Edmodo; www.edmodo.com) to students who met their goals; we would even go as far as to indicate how much they improved and what more they needed to reach their trimester goals. And just like that, the distance didn't seem so far, the pace was more manageable, and the finish line, while looming in the distance, was again attainable. We were back on track!

DON'T FORGET THE WATER STATION

Water stations are strategically placed along a course. On a 5K race, they are usually found at mile 2, while for longer races, they are spaced out every two miles. Whether you drink the water or not (every runner has a different preference), never underestimate the importance of the water station. As a nondrinker, I use the water station to mentally recharge and refocus. After all, even a well-oiled machine needs regular maintenance. It is safe to say that after a grueling few months in which we did see some incredible progress and goal achievement, we needed a water station. Desperately so.

Our students needed a chance to recharge and refocus; we teachers needed one just as much. Both of us needed to see the progress that each student had made and to determine a plan for the rest of the course. I also knew that plain and simple, numbers matter. I am notorious for disputing the effectiveness of standardized tests as a means to measure growth and achievement for *all* students, particularly those in special education. Nevertheless, I do believe in numbers. Having been a longtime supporter of the "Weight Watchers" effect as it relates to education, I knew that whether it is on a scale, a fluency sheet, a scoreboard, or a timer, numbers hold us accountable. Weight Watchers has an incredible philosophy of creating individualized programs for its members according to their goals and, ultimately, the numbers on the scale. Having been a member multiple times over the years, I have observed firsthand how the program works. Each week, members weigh in, attend meetings, review their progress, and develop a plan of action, which includes goal setting.

This same model holds true for what we were trying to do with our students. Each week, they met with us one on one, recorded their progress, applied strategies, and were measured using a scale. Upon completion of this measure, they then would set a new goal or plan of action. In light of our recent progress, it became increasingly clear that when used effectively, numbers can be a motivating factor for students and teachers. We, however, needed to look at each student individually as well as the group as a whole. While runners often pause at the water station for several seconds, our water station lasted a little more than two days.

For several days in February, we reviewed, during our math block, all of the progress-monitoring measures that we had been implementing and compared this data to the Common Core Standards and IEP goals. While I was tallying the results and meeting with students one on one, my partner was introducing a student-led conference template that would later be used in conferences as a means for students to reflect on their progress and determine new goals. Table 7.1 shows the chart that I designed to help with this process.

What we discovered was that eight out of sixteen students had already met their ending goal, while the remaining students had gone up an entire grade level or more, according to their initial Aimsweb benchmarking measures. For example, one student was able to solve five problems correctly at a fourth-grade level at the beginning of the year, with the grade-level expectation being fifteen

TABLE 7.1 Student benchmarking chart

Student	Benchmark score (student's projected grade level) 10/2013	Original score (based on goal) 10/2013	Ending score (based on goal)	Goal met, or difference	Ending benchmark score	New goal for 2/2014 until 6/2014	Notes
John Smith	Grade 4, 10 correct (expectation for this level: 15 correct)	Grade 5, 4 correct (expectation for this level: 10 correct)	Grade 5, 12 correct (expectation for this level: 10 correct)	+2 Goal met (and exceeded by 2 points)	Grade 5, 12 correct (expectation for this level: 10 correct)	Grade 6, 15 correct	

at this level. At the point of completing our benchmarking measures, this same student was able to solve eight problems correctly at the fifth-grade level (with the expectation to solve ten correctly at that level), passing the fourth-grade-level expectations and increasing one whole grade level over the initial evaluations. While the results weren't as dramatic as we had initially hoped, there was considerable growth. The results also allowed us to discuss both realistic goals as they related to the individual students and external factors, such as snow days, vacations, and special events.

Students focused on making connections between what they were learning and their individual progress. They explored and determined an individualized plan, which focused on the factors shown in Figure 7.3.

FIGURE 7.3   Student progress report and goal-setting plan

STUDENT NAME:	
ROUNDTABLE ADVISOR:	
WHAT I HAVE BEEN DOING IN CLASS:	
☐ I can apply computation strategies. ☐ I am fluent with my math facts. ☐ I can apply problem-solving skills. ☐ I know the "power standards." ☐ I can work collaboratively to solve a problem. ☐ I can apply writing skills to math to reflect on how I solved a problem. ☐ I know my levels as they relate to the standards and my individualized education plan goals and can set goals accordingly.	
ASSESSMENTS	CHECK IF DONE, AND RECORD SCORE
☐ RunMoby (current level) ☐ Team-building challenge of the week (reflection sheets) ☐ Five-minute frenzy (fluency drill) ☐ Khan Academy standards ☐ Practical applications	

(continued)

FIGURE 7.3   Student progress report and goal-setting plan *(continued)*

GOALS	HOW HAVE I DONE . . .? CITE EVIDENCE, AND ATTACH IT IF POSSIBLE.
I can apply problem-solving strategies when working on problems independently.	
I can work together with my group and apply math skills when solving our weekly STEM team-building challenge.	
I can apply writing strategies to describe and reflect on how I solved a challenge or a problem.	
I have mastered the following standards as indicated by my work on Khan Academy: _____ _____	
I know how to apply computation strategies.	
From this data, I set the following goals, using the SMART template: S (specific) M (measurable) A (attainable) R (realistic) T (timely)	

Note: RunMoby (www.mobymax.com) is a Web-based learning tool for self-directed learning; Khan Academy (www.khanacademy.org) is a student-directed, Web-based learning tool that measures individual progress toward the Common Core State Standards.

Our time spent at the water station was incredibly valuable and allowed all of us to refocus on what we wanted to accomplish during the remaining part of the course. Although a runner can never fully anticipate all the obstacles in his or her path, with the end in mind, it is easier to focus on how to complete the race successfully.

THE MIDDLE MILES

For any runner, the middle miles are the most challenging, as at this part of the race, you can no longer see the start line, and the finish is still so far out of reach. This is the only part of the race that truly depends solely on the runner's inner strength or, as some say, blind faith, since the runner cannot see the finish line. Propelling a runner forward during this section really lies in the runner's belief in his or her ability to achieve the goal that was set at the beginning of the race. If a runner doubts himself or herself or can no longer envision the goal, then these miles become impossible. This is the point where, if a runner decides to stop, it most likely will happen. Students are no different in this regard. If a student lacks confidence, he or she will be unlikely to achieve the goals that are set.

It was the end of February. We had our "water station," or time to reflect, refocus, and ultimately determine a plan for the rest of the course. Although we were energized, we also were slightly overwhelmed by the notion that we still had so far to go. As teachers, we knew that we were embarking on one of the most challenging parts of the school year, and while some contest this theory, in New England, late February can be a very difficult time. While the calendar indicates that spring is close, the weather often tells a different tale. For students, this time of year presents its own sets of challenges, as they often cannot get outside and have been confined not only to the indoors, but also to long periods of cold and darkness. In our middle school, we have limited space, particularly in our classroom. Our students had been working incredibly hard, perhaps harder than they had experienced in the past. They too had been cooped up in our small classroom doing this challenging work together. Some of our students experience seasonal depression, which typically peaks at this time of year, while others were fatigued by the demands and expectations and were feeling agitated and confined by the limited space. Given that we worked so closely together reviewing progress and setting goals, they were aware of the work ahead and were perhaps daunted. Thus, our class was about to begin our journey into those treacherous and dreaded middle miles.

While we were determined to keep our program and pace the same, we had to be more strategic about posting our goals so that they were always visible and present in the work that we were doing. Students needed constantly to have their goals in their sight so that they would be reminded of why they were doing the work that we asked. They also needed frequent acknowledgment and praise for their accomplishments, more so now than at any other point in the year. For runners during this section of a race, reinforcements come in the form of the signs of encouragement that often scatter the course, as well as the spectators lined up cheering them on. As a runner myself, I find that these things help me the most during these middle miles. For our students, they too needed these signs of encouragement.

We began to write daily goals on the tops of the students' assessments and activity sheets, giving more shout-outs on Edmodo, and even began each group, rotation, and class with praise and acknowledgment to increase their engagement and belief in their abilities. We also had to provide more structure within our groups, particularly in regard to seating arrangements. We strategically placed students into groups and locations in the room where they could do their best. The cubicles in our classroom were used more during this time than at the beginning, as some students required these quieter spots to stay focused on their goals. We were shifting to a more teacher-directed format to accommodate the needs of the students. While this format was exhausting and required a significant amount of planning, we needed to implement the structures and support so that our students could continue to envision the finish line. Some proponents of a proficiency-based model might argue that we were compromising the integrity of such a program; however, we knew our students and had to honor their needs. Giving ourselves permission to do what we knew was best was hard but necessary for our students to be successful. Had we not put these structures into place, our students, like some runners, would have stopped during these middle miles. Unable to go any further, they never would reach that finish line, compromising everything they had worked so hard for.

SEPARATE FROM YOUR DEVICE, AND ENJOY THE RUN

There are two mind-sets when it comes to running: to use electronics or not. Some runners like me are constantly plugged in. Using an iPod, a Garmin, a phone, or a watch to listen to music and track mileage and progress has become the norm for most runners. Others, however, rely on the good ol' standby, their bodies and minds. During any race, you will see the electronic runners, earbud cords cascading down their arms, attached to their device, which is carefully nestled in their armbands, running to the beat of a strategically selected song on their running mix. The electronic runners frequently glance at their watch or device, using it as a gauge to determine when to run faster and when to pull back, all in an attempt to achieve their personal goal. The traditional runners are free from cords, have nothing attached to their arms, hands, or wrists, yet seem to run in sync with their internal rhythm or cadence, which guides them through the course. Heads held high, these runners are often the most envied during a race, because they know their bodies and achieve their goals by listening to themselves.

While teachers rely heavily on data, devices, and technology, they also know their students. At times it can be difficult for teachers to rely on their knowledge and visceral beliefs and feelings associated with doing what is best for children, but doing so is essential. Just as all runners need to separate from their devices sometime, as it truly does improve performance, so do teachers. Despite relying heavily on data and technology, we too needed to get back to the basics and listen to our internal cadence.

Having barely survived the middle miles, we were able to pull back some of the support and gradually release our students so that they could again be more self-directed learners. Our class was moving into that final stretch, where we all were so focused on the finish that we were forgetting to enjoy the race. Truth be told, my coteacher and I actually hadn't implemented our weekly STEM team-building challenges in over a month, as we were so focused on our students' meeting their benchmarks and goals—goals that wouldn't matter if our students couldn't see and enjoy the purpose of what they were doing.

It was early May when we realized that we were again beginning to lose ourselves in the process of being responsive to student progress as it related to standards. One day, we happened to be planning together and came across a picture of our students participating in a team-building challenge that we had done earlier in the year. We didn't need to look at our lesson plans from this day to know how beneficial this activity was for our students. The picture alone showed curiosity, leadership, critical thinking, collaboration, and perseverance, whereas our benchmarks and test scores showed only numbers. We needed to get back to our core, our foundation for this program. We had carefully created this student-centered proficiency-based curriculum on the belief that team-building and collaboration were essential to our students' success; however, we somehow had gotten so wrapped up in the numbers that we were losing sight of the importance of our core. The foundation of our program really was an intricate matrix that was constructed so that each piece complemented the others; thus when one element or piece was missing, the whole would lose its strength and integrity.

We scrapped our previous plans for the next two days and decided to implement a STEM team-building challenge instead. Integrating some of the standards related to geometry and measurement that we recently had focused on, we had the students complete the catapult challenge in which they had to build a catapult using specific materials so that their catapult would launch a table-tennis ball the farthest. Not only would the challenge be good for the kids, but it would also allow us to see if the students, at this point in the year, could work collaboratively and apply their math skills to other activities or content areas. During these two days, there was laughter, discovery, collaboration, and, ultimately, fun. The kids were talking about math without realizing it and were reengaged in the process. This respite and startling reminder came at just the right time and proved that all these intricate pieces are important.

Being a runner is a careful balance of science and intuition, and for teachers, this balance is no different. While research-based materials and methods are important, so are beliefs and instincts. Sometimes, as teachers, we need to disconnect from our "devices" and rely on those gut feelings that are often more accurate than a GPS tracking device or a progress-monitoring measure.

THE FINISH LINE

The finish line is the most coveted part of the race for any runner. For most runners, it is the only reason that they run a race. The finish line not only provides a sense of accomplishment, but also physically serves as a beacon of hope and a symbol of human strength and perseverance. Runners are cheered on as they approach the finish line and are encouraged to give it their all. For runners, this is the final push, the point where they exert all of their strength and energy, ultimately achieving mentally and physically more than what they thought possible. For students, the end of the school year is often an exciting time as it signifies the end of a journey and a reminder of growth and achievement. In education, this is the busiest time of the year as teachers work feverishly to finish up assessments; create class lists to send to the next teachers; introduce their students to, and prepare them for, high-level standards; and celebrate accomplishments. We needed to take the final few weeks to celebrate our students' accomplishments, to show them the growth that they had made, and hopefully to instill in them the belief that they now had the skills to embark on new challenges, challenges that they never believed they were capable of overcoming.

The final weeks in our classroom were filled with schedule changes, field trips, IEP meetings (which meant that one or both of us had to be out of the classroom), community service days, and promotion activities. Thus, while the calendar indicated that there were three weeks of school left, we knew that we had maybe ten teachable days—days in which our students would be less engaged and perhaps more focused on summer rather than accomplishing the goals set earlier in the year. In addition, we needed to give our students a finish line and therefore a chance to celebrate their growth and to experience a sense of accomplishment. We decided to keep our rotations the same, as many of our students require a predictable routine, particularly when everything else is unpredictable. However, we spent more time in our one-on-one workshops with students, reviewing their progress, benchmarking, and even introducing higher-level standards. Within the smaller groups, we gave the students accolades, encouragement, reinforcement, and other support.

To our delight, the students became the spectators cheering each other on rather expecting this reinforcement to come only from the teachers. Students were able to communicate their goals, discuss their levels, and even talk about future aspirations in math. For the first time ever, we observed our students taking ownership over their learning. Even more than that, their ability to discuss their skills and goals was authentic, not teacher-directed or scripted. Besides just discussing their progress, many students were active participants at their IEP meetings, helping the team to determine year-long goals. Their participation was powerful to watch and unlike anything I had ever seen. Our students were motivated by their progress and were able to cross the finish line.

THE DOMINO EFFECT

When runners cross the finish line, they often experience what is called a domino effect. Endorphins are released, and the athletes are excited by a sense of accomplishment and are eager to tackle the next challenge: the next race. Soon they begin training for the next event, hoping to achieve their personal best, maybe even set a course record. Eventually they start eating better, exercising more, and taking care of their minds and bodies, and this training and rigor starts to spread to other areas of their lives. Such was the case not only for our students, but for us as well. I began to transfer some of the student-centered, proficiency-based methods and structures I was implementing in our cotaught math class to my reading and writing classes as well. The students also began to think differently about their learning. They felt empowered, and rather than looking at learning as something that happened to them, they became an integral part of the process.

Like a runner, I was experiencing success in the classroom differently than I had in years past. For the first time, I saw students actively involved in the learning process. While our program wasn't perfect, I knew that the work we were doing was important and that we were on the right course. Relying on my instincts and what I had observed happening in this setting, I decided to implement a similar type of program in my reading and writing classes.

Taking into consideration that each student, class, and content area is different, I knew that my reading and writing classes would not look the same as our math class; however, I was inspired to embark on this challenge. I began small, using progress-monitoring measures similar to those I had used in our math class. I worked one on one with students and used similar templates and goal-setting measures to chart growth and achievement. I called this our *workshop*. While I didn't have my coteacher in this class, I had an education technician with whom I had worked for a very long time. We both worked as teachers in the room and had similar educational philosophies. She was able to facilitate both large-group instruction and small-group workshops, making it easier to implement this type of program. Often she would do a larger-group workshop on making connections, while I did one-on-one progress monitoring for fluency or a small-group workshop on sentence variation. We constantly grouped and regrouped students according to their goals and progress, allowing them to focus on areas of strength and weakness. Students were able to understand their own levels and abilities and set realistic goals to improve their skills, but they also had a better understanding of how multifaceted the content is and how it applies to the world around them.

Knowing our students, we believed that we should maintain our traditional approach of literature circle, in which we took turns reading aloud, discussing the text, and applying comprehension strategies to improve understanding.

This approach had been highly successful in previous years. It not only engages our students, but enables every student to be heard and encourages and supports higher-level understanding and discussion of texts. We also kept the author-share component of our writing class because this had a similar effect and contributed to the overall tone and culture of our classroom. I found that just like our math class, our past reading and writing classes had features that we needed to preserve, as they had a positive impact on our students. But we also needed to infuse these classes with more student-centered, proficiency-based strategies. Our program was able to shift and change, while honoring our students and the culture we wanted to create in the classroom. And as happened in our math class, we provided a careful balance of teacher-directed and student-directed learning activities. Many of our students did not have experience in being independent learners, and we had to teach them these skills. Although they learned some of these skills in math, we had to model and teach this in every class, rather than assume that they were secure in this area.

Similar to what we saw in our math class, I saw incredible growth and achievement. Reluctant readers and writers demonstrated multiple years' worth growth in both areas, reading fluently, writing multiparagraph pieces, and, for the first time, understanding their abilities and developing realistic goals based on these skills. Students in IEP meetings were able to articulate not just their math skills, but also their skills in all content areas. I also observed eighth-grade students advocating for the type of programming they needed for high school.

The most telling piece of evidence came in the form of a letter I received from a student at the end of the school year. I had worked closely with this student during her two years at the middle school. She had entered my program as a shy girl who was resistant to try most academic tasks because she lacked confidence and exposure to the higher-level skills that we were implementing in our classroom. On the last day of school, she walked down the hall ready to catch the bus. In keeping with tradition at our middle school, we were "clapping out" the eighth-graders. This student walked up to me and put her hand out as if she wanted me to give her five. As I brought my hand down to clap hers, she slipped a strategically folded piece of paper in my hands. Throwing her arms around me, she gave me a hug and whispered, "Thank you, Mrs. Shanning. I will miss you so much." Tearing up, I gave her a hug and clapped her out to the bus. I held the tiny piece of folded paper in my hands, waiting until I got back to the classroom to read it. Half expecting it to be like other end-of-year notes

I had received from students in the past (the notes often contained drawings or bubbly letters and hearts with words like "I'll miss you"), I was surprised to see that this note was quite long and well written. Easing myself into the chair, I began to read her words, noting her complete sentences, beautiful handwriting, and clearly articulated thoughts. And then I read the words. Really read them.

Dear Mrs. Shanning,

I will really miss you next year. You are my favorite teacher not because you were the coolest or the funniest, but because you challenged me. I now know that school for me before I got to Whittier was easy. You pushed me even when I didn't think that I could. By pushing me, you helped me to go up three grade levels in reading. When I said that I couldn't and cried or got mad at you, you were positive. Thank you for not babying me or treating me like I couldn't do it, because in the real world there will be no babying and I will have to do things on my own. Thank you for always pushing me to do the best that I could do. Because I learned to believe in myself I was able to go to the NHD State Competition [National History Day, a competition with a parallel event for special education students] and represent Whittier. I hope that at least one person in your class wins NHD every year to show others that whatever the students in your class set their minds to, they can do it. Because of the work that we did I now have the confidence to go to high school because I am a different person than I was two years ago. I am no longer shy and as you say, "I am not going to let the world pass me by." I promise that I will continue to grow and be a leader. I am very proud of the work that I did in your class and am proud that you were my teacher for two years!

Tears now streaming down my cheeks, I realized that the girl's incredible growth had little to do with me, but rather had to do with the culture that we had created in our classroom. From the beginning, we projected the message that our students were capable of doing great things, and through the process, they too learned that they were. I have this letter in the drawer of my desk and have pulled it out frequently when I struggle with determining what is best for my students. I want every one of my students to feel proud.

Whittier Middle School is a progressive school in part due to its teachers, but primarily because of its administration. In our cotaught math class, we could pilot and implement this type of programming because we had the support of our administrator. As described above, because I was inspired by what I observed in our cotaught math class, I began to implement a similar type of program in the other classes that I taught. Many of the students in our math class were also in my other classes, making this transition easier. However, this domino effect wouldn't have happened if I hadn't had the support, trust, and encouragement from an administrator who believes in his teachers and staff.

EMBRACING THE MIND-SET

Runners often struggle identifying themselves as a runner. I often tell people that I run, but I am not a runner. However, by definition I am a runner. I am a better runner when I embrace the mind-set and accept this title. The same holds true for teachers. For learning and success to happen, teachers need to be empowered. They need to believe that they are not just a teacher, but that they are an effective teacher who, no matter what, will do what is necessary so that students can be successful. While most teachers say and feel that they will do whatever it takes, very few fully commit to this statement. It is time for all of us to embrace this mind-set, not only through our beliefs and words, but also through our actions.

Every year, what I teach is different because my students are different. Our school is responsive in its approach to education, which means that our work is constant, hard, and changing. Our lesson plans, curriculum guides, and other educational documents are living; they can be changed and adjusted according to student need, rather than remaining stagnant. The work is fulfilling, and if I am honest, it is also grueling. However, when I am doing this work, I am at my best. This work requires sacrifice on many levels. I have occasionally had to let go of lessons that I used to teach—lessons that were familiar and comfortable, but not effective. I have mourned the loss of time. I have lost time with my family and for myself as I plan programs and prepare lessons. However, I find comfort in the notion that I am approaching education as if I were teaching my own daughter. What would I want if these were my own children? The answer: I want this level of dedication and commitment because *every child*, not just my own, deserves this. I have given up reading pleasure books for reading professional publications that explore best practices as I work to improve my own practice. And I have changed. I no longer rely on just gut instincts but have added research, practice, and input from my colleagues.

As a teacher, I have had to ask myself on multiple occasions if student-centered, proficiency-based education is sustainable. And when I start to fear that it is not, I ask myself if I would be happy being mediocre, because I know that when I teach this way, I am at my best. Could I be comfortable knowing how to do the right thing, but settling for something less? The answer is no. I made a commitment not just to education, but to kids, and in doing so, I must always act in a way that allows them to succeed. At Whittier Middle School, our advisory groups have taken on a curriculum that explores and develops student leadership. As part of this curriculum, we have developed a theme called *choose to lead*. I find myself asking students, "How will you choose to lead?" and "What will be your legacy at Whittier Middle School?" In thinking of student-centered, proficiency-based learning in education, I would dare to ask teachers, "How will you choose to lead?" I also ask, "What will be your legacy in education, for your classroom, and for your students?" I already know mine.

CHAPTER EIGHT

High School English and Speech

People First, Things Second

ALANA M. MARGESON

In my classroom, I sometimes see the metaphor of train tracks in my mind. At a moment's notice, I need to be responsive to my students' needs. I must be able to momentarily switch the path of learning if it means arriving at the destination in a more authentic and effective way. I need to be aware of the forces swirling within my classroom and those finding their way into our classroom culture—current events, community issues, student concerns, even tragedies. I want my students to feel that I care about helping them find their place—in school, in life, and as citizens of the world.

"You make me believe I can do better. It is clear you love what you do and you make me want to learn. I actually look forward to coming to class because I know I belong here . . . You have inspired me to be a teacher someday, too."

Reading over the note she had left on my desk just before the final bell rang, I realized that this was it. For a teacher, there is no feeling more compelling or gratifying than when a student communicates what your presence and instruction has meant for her.

Each day brings unique challenges and opportunities. Schools are tiny worlds of goals, fears, doubts, and dreams—all mixed together but searching for a common good. It is easy to get caught up in what makes me upset. My students bring physical and emotional ghosts with them to school each day. I want them to work, to think, to achieve. I remember the advice from a mentor and team teacher early in my career: "Treat your students kindly as though you are all they have. Some days, you will be." One of the most touching and profound ideas Cara shared with me in that note is that she felt welcomed in my class—she wanted to learn because she belonged as a human and was challenged to better herself.

When I was a student in the high school where I now teach, our principal, Mr. Ugone, had a sign in his office: "People First, Things Second."

I believe that this mantra was his personal philosophy of administration. I have never forgotten the red laminated poster with black block letters. Eighteen years later, when I was named 2012 Maine Teacher of the Year, a card arrived in the mail from Mr. Ugone, congratulating me on this honor and recalling his belief in me almost two decades earlier. He signed it "Forever a Viking" (our school mascot). Student-centered teaching is creating a welcoming place for students to learn, to face adversity, and to grow from experience. It is creating a home that students may look back on years later as a place that shaped their views of themselves, their relationships, and the world.

Each year, I make it a point to tell my students that we are a partnership. We cannot be successful without communicating with each other and respecting one another. I also stress that each day is a new beginning. When my students enter the doorway to the classroom, I want them to know that if yesterday wasn't great—especially if there were issues I had to address with that student—we start fresh each new day. Negative feelings shouldn't carry over and cloud a learning experience. I want to wipe away any distracters or doubts for students. Learning must be the centerpiece, but learning must be built on a foundation of care, trust, and mutual respect.

In my career, no choice has made a more profound impact on student learning than my decision to make my classroom a place where students want to learn. I know that I cannot control the rate or complexity of changes happening in education any more than I can control the life circumstances of my students. But I can create an inviting space for students to grow academically and intellectually. I can foster habits of mind such as empathy, humor, and resilience that we so desperately need in a world that seems simultaneously promising and terrifying. And I can ask for students' feedback; nothing will provide a richer reflection of my strengths and need for further growth. When I ask students to describe the learning atmosphere in room 201, I hope for feedback similar to the following response from Eddie, a dependable and steadfast sophomore in my period 6 English class. Eddie graciously helps refocus the attention of his more distractible classmates with a smile and a nod.

> The atmosphere in our classroom was without a doubt very welcoming and calm. You may come in with struggles from previous classes, but you leave with a calm feeling and an understanding of the class. I always felt welcomed every day I came, no matter what. Everyone in the class was clearly valued; everyone was always encouraged to grow and their learning pace was honored as being unique. If we had problems, or misunderstandings, we would take extra time to go in depth to clarify, *then* move on. If I still didn't get it, you would go out of your way to meet with me to help. In class I was treated like anyone else, as equal. Nobody was better than anyone else. We all had our time to speak if we wished to, and our questions were always answered fully. I felt honored because if I had an idea that was really good, we would have a class discussion about it.

My plan book is full of learning targets, assessment ideas, instructional resources, and meetings. Yet, the more I teach, the more I understand that students need to know that I care about them as individuals and that I want to be in the classroom to help them succeed. How can I expect my students to want to be in my classroom if I don't make them feel welcome? How can I expect them to show enthusiasm for learning if I fail to show enthusiasm for teaching?

Four years ago, I met Sydney. She was a student in my grade 10 Honors English class, and she was one tough cookie. Her demeanor was defensive, and sarcasm was her main deflective weapon. For the first month of school, I took every barb personally. She was tremendously bright and intuitive, but it seemed much easier to be rude than to talk about what was truly troubling her. But I understood that Sydney didn't trust me—yet. It was imperative for me to be patient and not show judgment. She was testing the waters.

One day, she and another student lingered after class. Sydney shared a bit about a writing piece and the dynamics of her life that were reflected in it. Both students were so open about their frustrations with high school life and goals after high school. I learned that Sydney was a sensitive, caring young woman who had trouble trusting people. And she had good reasons. Sydney and Kyra stayed after class regularly after that. We talked about their part-time jobs, peer relationships, families, and other challenges. It was a time for the girls to just have someone listen and be real. I maintained this rapport with Sydney and Kyra. Nicknaming me "Mama Marge," these girls left me a beautiful gift when they left for college—they created three painted collages filled with inspirational quotes I had given them, images that reminded them of me, and even my husband's and children's handprints. One of the least recognized but yet widely understood ideas about student-centered teaching is that years after the books have closed, a relationship will remain open. It may come in the form of a note, a visit, or an invitation to a wedding.

Just recently, Sydney and Kyra returned from college (Sydney is studying aeronautical engineering, and Kyra is premed), and we had lunch together with one of my colleagues. We talked about college, their social life (or lack thereof), and lessons learned. There was no judgment, just mutual admiration and support. I asked Sydney and Kyra what they remember having learned and felt in my class. Kyra answered:

> In your class, I learned to annotate for greater reading comprehension, to synthesize information in an organized fashion, and to be a critical thinker who can pull the bigger picture or the "so what" meaning from any medium of information sharing. But that's not all I learned in your class. I learned that a teacher can have a sense of humor and be a mentor and a friend, that the material will have relevance to real life, and that it doesn't have to be boring! In your class, I felt reassured that I would have help when I needed it and that I could feel comfortable asking questions. I felt that it was okay to not always know the answer. I felt stressed at times (writing papers isn't exactly my favorite thing in the world), but I felt supported, respected, inspired, and encouraged to do my best in the class and in life itself. I didn't feel like just another student in the class; I felt cared about as a human being.

Finally, one of the most helpful ways I have found to make sure my classroom is a place of academic and human integrity is to ask students to share with me in writing what they believe my philosophy of teaching is. I have learned that my intentions are not always congruent with my messages. At the end of each year, this exercise continues to give me rich feedback.

SOCRATIC SEMINARS

"What do you mean, you'll be in the *outer* circle?" a group of students asks me. "You aren't going to be asking us questions?" The student arrangement I have just set up, wherein one group of students forms an inner circle and a second group forms the outer circle, has put all the students completely outside their comfort zone. The inner-circle students are asked to speak, while the outer-circle students are required to observe the discussion and take notes.

"Who do you think Faber would be in today's society?" I ask. The question settles on the inner-circle participants as the outer-circle members look at one another. You could read it on all the students' faces: *Wow. Great question.* Each member of the inner circle is partnered with a student in the outer circle. While the inner-circle students are using annotations, their own thoughts, and evidence from the text to propel a conversation, students in the outer circle observe. After about fifteen minutes of discussion, members of the inner circle turn and confer with their outer-circle partners, who identify areas of strength and ways to improve their partner's contributions to the discussion. The feedback may target the student's use of textual evidence, questioning, assertiveness, or degree of interactivity or the reflective nature of responses, for example. After this break, the discussion resumes in the inner circle, with members using the feedback to make adjustments, hopefully improving their support for the evolving academic discussion.

"Maybe it's not a person," says one student. "Maybe Faber would be a place . . . or maybe he just represents human desire for knowledge."

"But what if he didn't exist? What if people weren't willing to make sacrifices for knowledge?"

"Well, on page ninety-eight, it says . . ."

As the students build upon each other's ideas and pose follow-up questions, I realize that if I got up and left the room, nothing would change. Students were engaged in academic, intellectual conversation. My presence was secondary to their academically driven conversation. Success! This notion may be the single most powerful testament of student-centered teaching—it means empowering students with skills and strategies that they will use regardless of my presence.

Admittedly, Socratic Seminar was rough going at first. Students were used to looking to me to lecture and lead the conversation. The norm of what a classroom structure was supposed to look like was changed—and change can be uncomfortable. At first, the students struggled—with conversation content and with timing. It's one thing to *write* in response to literature, but to *converse with peers* about personal reactions and points of view is powerful. Socratic Seminar is not about who is right, but rather about how ideas are born and built on through collaboration. Students not only own the learning, but also own the *process* of building understanding that leads to learning. The strategy of Socratic Seminar supports this process. Student-centered learning isn't always using strategies in the classroom that are smooth or easy; rather, it is about making time for practice and the evolution of learning.

Gina, a student in my AP English class, shared her thoughts:

> The first time we did Socratic Seminars, I have to admit it was a little awkward. Everyone was a bit unsure of themselves and what to say, so it didn't go as smoothly as it could have. However, by the end of the year, at our last SS, it went wonderful! I think it was a valuable learning experience because I had to learn how to navigate a conversation with about seven other people while still staying on-topic. I had to be patient and listen while others were speaking, but I also had to be quick and take advantage of openings in the conversation because if I didn't then someone else would.

To build in a mechanism for feedback, I used the Teaching Channel's pinwheel activity model to engage the outer circle of students as well.[1] After approximately seven minutes of inner-circle discussion based on an initial open-ended question, a one-minute half-time is called. Partners in the outer circle huddle with their inner-circle partner, giving feedback on the quality of what the student said and his or her speaking skills and offering specific pointers for improvement. Utilizing the feedback from the outer circle of observers, the members of the inner circle then delve back into the conversation for five to seven additional minutes before switching topics. When we switch topics, the students also swap places, with the formerly outer-circle students becoming inner-circle students for the next topic.

Socratic Seminar, specifically the pinwheel activity, allows students to use text evidence to build support and notes to tether themselves to key ideas. Students generate ideas and conversation; they are not focused on what the teacher deems to be the "right answer." They dig deeply into ideas of *what* and *why*.

They learn to disagree intellectually. Could it be that the epitome of student-centered teaching is the realization that students will learn after I have completely removed myself from the situation?

STUDENTS AS TEACHERS

Near the end of the year, another student-centered activity again empowered students to create individual pathways and to show what they know and can do. This activity was feasible after the students had learned a host of reading strategies. Students developed lesson plans to use in teaching second-grade students one specific age-appropriate reading strategy that could help younger students be better readers. At first, the idea that I would be an observer in the room and that they had to plan and execute an engaging lesson was frightening for them. "What if I mess up?" (You will have a lesson plan as your touchstone.) "How am I supposed to know if they get it?" (Remember you were their age once—what are your ideas about assessment?)

Using the idea that students master learning when they teach someone else, each student chose a children's book to use to model a reading strategy with second-graders. Lesson plans incorporated objectives, a lesson sequence, levels of questioning, practice for the second-grader to use the reading strategy, and some form of assessment (verbal, artistic, a game, etc.). The grade 11 English "teachers" were all deeply engaged with their students. Looking around the classroom, I saw one student, who rarely showed emotion in the high school setting, down on the area rug making a real connection with the second-grade student. My student had lost his father about six months before, and his grades and engagement in school reflected that this young man was struggling to make sense of his great loss. I saw him smiling for the first time in months. He had chosen a book that was personally meaningful to him, and I believe there was a connection with his father. I may never know that for sure, but I do know that Samuel was very mindful about the importance of reading strategies at any age.

WHEN THE GOING GETS TOUGH . . .

I can see it on their faces, I think to myself. They are not sure they can do what I am asking of them.

"Rhetorical analysis?" Ian says. "I've never even heard of that!"

"Okay," I answer, "let me try framing this another way." I decide that to back out of this work at the most challenging phase sends a message that the work wasn't that important in the first place. "Yes, this can be difficult. But my job is to break down the steps for you and give you the tools to be successful. Remember, your job is to be open to learning. Mine is to give you strategies and skills to make that learning accessible for each and every one of you. Let's go."

I notice relieved looks on students' faces. I wasn't going to throw them in the deep end—but they knew they were all getting ready to swim.

One of the best pieces of feedback I have received from students is that I have high expectations for all. Student-centered teaching does not necessarily mean that every student will have the same level of achievement. Nor does it mean that I expect all students to learn in the same ways. Usually, when students tell me they can't do something, it means "I don't know how to do that *yet*." Sometimes, however, it means "I don't want to do that." Student-centered teaching means diagnosing which of these it may be. If students don't know how, I need to give them the tools—not necessarily the answers—to be successful. Sometimes, students (like adults) need to be asked the honest question "Is this really your best effort? I've seen what you're capable of, and this work doesn't represent what I know you can do."

Toby was a cheery and gregarious sophomore in my period 4 English class last year. One of the qualities I most admired in him was his resilience and commitment to producing quality work—even when it was tough. Toby was a member of the basketball team, and during basketball season, he turned in a piece of writing that did not reflect his best effort. I called him in after school and talked to him about it. There was no accusation, just an honest observation. "This isn't your best effort." He agreed and redid the work.

We never spoke of this again, but I was surprised that it came up when I asked Toby what he remembered most about the school year. "It's not really a lesson, Mrs. Margeson," he began sheepishly. "It's that time you called me in when I turned in that horrible assignment. You cared enough to call me on it when I wasn't working to capacity. You had an expectation of me, and that made me care more. You helped me realize that being accountable isn't always a bad thing."

Stephanie, a classmate, shared a similar point of view: "When we began a new skill or learning target, I knew that you wouldn't give up on us or stop helping us until we truly understood. It's good to know that your teacher has high expectations for you, but is also going to give you the tools to feel good about the learning." As simple as it sounds, reassuring students that they can achieve—and that you will help them reach their potential—is one of the greatest strategies I can use in the classroom. Who can't remember the sinking feeling of "Am I the only one who doesn't get this? I would ask a question, but I would be so embarrassed."

Having high expectations for students—and showing them I will help them—is secondary to the importance of having students set high expectations for themselves. One of the self-assessment tools I use often in the classroom is a simple one. At the beginning of a unit, I identify learning targets, and these remain posted in the classroom for students to see every day. I ask students to identify where they are with regard to the learning targets. Using a 1-to-4 proficiency scale, where 4 = *exceeds the standards* ("I know this so well I could teach someone else"), 3 = *meets the standards* ("I know how to do that"), 2 = *partially meets the standards*, and 1 = *does not yet meet the standards*, students identify where they believe they currently are. With multiple learning targets per unit, there is always room for growth. Students identify expectations of learning for themselves. As critical as it may be for me to set expectations for my students—and visibly believe in them even when it's tough—it is much more effective and personally satisfying for students to set expectations of and for themselves.

STUDENT-CENTERED TEACHING IS RESPONSIVE

When I was child, my mother and grandmother would take me to visit family along the Massachusetts coast just south of Boston. This summertime ritual was filled with sandy feet, walking the jetty, lobster boats, and laughter. When we ventured into the city, learning was embedded in the fun—Paul Revere's house, the New England Aquarium, or *Old Ironsides* in the Harbor. Being from rural northern Maine, my vistas of picturesque fields of potato blossoms and green countryside were replaced with the sights of the ocean and the city. One of my favorite things to see was the subway system. Mass transit was a foreign concept to me. I loved peering down into the subway yards to see the vast matrix of tracks. As a young child, I was fascinated with the concept that a train could find its correct path out of a maze of dozens of overlapping rail lines. Each train had a unique destination, but they all had one thing in common—to safely get the passengers to their destination.

In my classroom, I sometimes see the metaphor of the train tracks in my mind. At a moment's notice, I need to be responsive to my students' needs. I must be able to switch the path of learning momentarily if it means arriving at the destination in a more authentic and effective way. I need to be aware of the forces swirling within my classroom and those finding their way into our classroom culture—current events, community issues, student concerns, even tragedies. I want my students to feel that I care about helping them find their place—in school, in life, and as citizens of the world.

Student-centered learning in my classroom is built upon the notion of being dynamic. As much as my teaching is built on clear goals and objectives, I understand that how and when we reach them will vary from day to day and from student to student. When I sense that the students need to get up and move, I quickly change the lesson on, say, independent quick writes to a Smart Board survey or a gallery walk. Admittedly, when I started teaching, I was married to my lesson plans. If it said so in "the book," it must be so. Now, using backward planning and research-based instructional practices that incorporate opportunities for formative feedback, I feel that I listen to my students better and that I am more in tune with their needs.

I continue to find structure and rationale both in building lessons and units with clear learning targets designed with the end in mind and in utilizing multiple opportunities for formative feedback. But compared with my first years in teaching, I now understand that rates of student learning are never constant; I am working with approximately eighty-five individual learners with unique needs each day. Student-centered teaching is not relying on a script; rather, it is incorporating the underpinnings of good teaching in a multitude of lessons that may be swapped out, modified, built upon, and even scrapped at the last moment. It is making changes in response to feedback, assessment, and instinct.

This past year, I experienced firsthand the need for commitment to change and to adjust my teaching. My two grade 10 English classes—just before and just after lunch—reflected very different dynamics. When it came to forming small groups for power strategies for reading nonfiction text, my period 4 class was immediately on-task. When students began to distract their group or other groups, there were inevitably students who brought the distracted students back to the objectives of the day. However, after a few class periods, it became clear that the period 4 students were operating largely as independent learners. They were not stopping at critical points to engage in dialogue and reflect with one another. This development led to a lesson on the crucial nature of collaboration and learning with and from peers. My students, entrenched in a world in which face-to-face communication is often the least desirable format, needed to know how to talk to each other and assert academic voice.

Conversely, in period 6, I was pulling out my hair each day of small-group work. Students were constantly making faces across the room, and some were dominating what little academic conversation was taking place. In this class, I knew it was time to stop and establish student-generated group norms. Once students had a chance to share as a class what good group work should look like—and not look like—we created a simple classroom poster as a visual reminder. Telling them constantly to be quiet was *not* the answer. But allowing students to create the picture of what respectful and fruitful dialogue should be like was a game-changer.

When I began teaching, I felt married to my lesson plans, as I noted above. They were more than comfort—they were scripts. While I look back and hope that I was at least somewhat responsive then, I know that student-centered learning hinges on the acceptance that some lessons flop. Some students do not learn well when I teach a certain way. Some of what I considered the most innovative lessons have fallen short in enabling the students to articulate learning or to transfer skills.

ACTIONABLE FEEDBACK AND HOW-TO INSTRUCTION

Recently, my oldest son, an incoming high school freshman, received first place in 4-H showmanship with his steer at our local fair. Friends of mine, also in education, were standing with me as the judge took the microphone.

"Really close competition here this evening folks," the judge said. "Let's talk about what this young man who took first did well . . . and then I'd like to share how I'd like to see him make some changes to improve for next year."

My friends looked at each other. "That's exactly what we need to be doing in classrooms!" one of them said. "Learners need to be able to reflect on where they are . . . and understand what they need to do to grow!"

So maybe the classroom isn't exactly a show ring, but the idea of specific, actionable feedback for student improvement is certainly applicable. One of the classes I took for my master's degree was in formative assessment. To demonstrate, one of the instructors asked a student to come to the front of the room. "Let's pretend you are a golfer. There is the first tee. Go for it." The student gave it his best shot. "Sorry, but that wasn't very good. Have a seat."

Calling up another student, the exercise was repeated. However, after the student pretended to swing the club, the instructor changed the feedback: "Nice follow-through and posture. Next time, try keeping your feet shoulder-width apart." Next, the instructor turned to the class. "What was different between these two pieces of feedback?" We all agreed that the second example provided ways to get better. This was my introduction to formative assessment. In the classroom, I need to give students frequent opportunities to reflect on where they are in their learning and how they will reach the next steps.

It is easy for me to make assumptions about why students do not improve their work—they aren't trying hard enough, they haven't made school a priority, and so on. But I cannot count the number of times I have witnessed breakthrough moments for students when I help them discover how to get better. "Great job" or "needs more effort" is not clear feedback.

I also need to teach students strategies—the how-to of academic skills. Janet Allen, literacy expert and mentor, hails from Presque Isle, Maine. In working with her and writing for her Plugged-In to Reading series, I came to understand and appreciate her emphasis on explicit strategy instruction.[2] "Students need to know *how to* in order *to*," she would say. This is so true. I assume that students have processes and steps ready for use, but this is often not the case. Consider how many times it may have taken you to drive a standard shift smoothly or to navigate in a new city. Learning takes time and requires knowledge of how to do something, whether the *something* is a physical or mental process.

Evan, a sophomore in an afternoon English class, was described by his mother as "capable" but "stubborn as a bull if he doesn't get it." The last comment struck me.

"What exactly does he do when he doesn't get it?" I inquired.

"He stops trying," his mother said. "It's as though he won't allow himself to admit when he doesn't get it. And he's bright. We've seen this with Evan for years."

Evan isn't alone. I have seen many students over the years shut down emotionally when threatened with what they see as failure or when they are frustrated. When it came to writing, several students, including Evan, really struggled with conclusions. The "sum it up and make it interesting" advice was largely what students seemed to remember about conclusions. But this was still an abstract idea to them. They still didn't understand how to write the conclusion. Using the visual of a triangle wider at the base than the top, I asked students to re-create the figure in their notes and label the parts:

> We remember that an effective introduction looks like an upside-down triangle. You hook the reader and ease him or her into your subject matter, ending with your thesis. The conclusion is just the opposite. Begin by reminding the reader of the main points you want to emphasize, but end with big ideas. This is easiest when asking yourself a series of questions. So what? Why should people care about this topic? What are the risks or dangers of not thinking about what I am saying? What are the implications of my writing? What do I want my audience to remember?

Once I gave students questions to consider and answer, the mystique of conclusions was replaced with confidence. When I looked at Evan's revision, I noticed a marked difference in the quality of the conclusion. "A thought-provoking ending to your piece," I wrote on the paper. "Can you trace your thinking here? I would love to hear about how you did this so I can share with others." Evan enthusiastically shared with me after class that he simply used the questions and triangle diagram to guide his writing.

"I had to stop and think about what I was really trying to say," he said. "But I knew that I needed to end with that 'so what?' factor you talk about all the time. I still don't like writing conclusions all that much, but at least I know how to do them. That's better than before."

Okay, so maybe not all students will love all things English. But it should be a choice or preference, not because I left students frustrated and in the lurch!

TAKING RISKS AND ALLOWING STUDENTS TO CREATE UNDERSTANDING

"I need to be honest with you all," I told my students one day. "I am not sure if this lesson is perfect. I changed it when an idea popped into my head last night. I'd like to introduce the concept of synthesis to you, but I would like to do that in a rather unconventional way. I think you are up for the challenge."

With desks in groups, I passed out rather random objects to each group— a geode, a stopwatch, an ostrich egg, and a tiny painting, to name just a few.

Students' reactions were a cross between amusement and disbelief. Then, I issued the challenge: "Find a common idea or concept among all of the items on your desk. You have five minutes, and it starts now."

The buzz of student chatter filled the room, but everyone was focused. When time was called, the responses were amazing.

"Artistic items have the ability to inspire the imagination."

"Some of the world's most powerful objects are also the tiniest."

"Nature produces beautiful things."

Students blew me away with their ability to find cohesive ideas in a variety of objects pulled from my curio cabinet, home office, and my children's bookshelves.

"Congratulations," I said. "You have just illustrated the idea of synthesis beautifully. So what do you think the definition of synthesis is?"

"Creating something from parts, or pulling ideas together?" one student asked. Suddenly, my struggle to clearly explain an academic writing idea that seemed so complex seemed so simple. My students had created understanding and clarified their own definition of a complex concept. Not bad for 9:30 on a Wednesday morning.

"Exactly."

When students use inductive reasoning to create understanding, a process of mental construction creates a framework for understanding. Instead of frontloading students with definitions and requiring them to remember this material, I have found that allowing opportunities for students to collaborate, brainstorm, and construct definitions themselves solidifies the learning much more than feeding students with information that may be forgotten soon after.

When I started teaching fifteen years ago, I believed that it was a teacher's job to create understanding. Today, I believe it is much more effective for students to take the lead. Perhaps this student-led practice isn't as much taking a risk on my part as it is allowing students to rise to a challenge.

LEARNING BEYOND THE CLASSROOM

If asked where learning takes place for students, many people would answer "in the classroom," or "at school." True, engaging instruction is happening in classrooms across America. Especially with the help of technology, students may learn about—and with—others regardless of the confines of geography.

When students can share their perspectives and unique points of view, both students and community benefit. In a time when many municipalities are facing shrinking budgets, it is all too easy for schools and educational funding to become targets of public ire. Sadly, there are often misconceptions about what is actually happening in classrooms and how education continues to evolve and prepare students to become civic-minded, engaged, and productive members of society. For me, student-centered learning means that I give students opportunities to expand their education beyond classroom walls. Students and communities mutually benefit when youth are engaged in learning about local history, culture, and issues of concern. Here are some examples of how my students have experienced learning beyond the classroom and have amplified their voices in the community.

Student-Created PSAs

After the students have read a novel in which the main characters faced issues such as sexual abuse, drug addiction, and alcoholism, I asked my students to compare how different characters handled adversity and how they, the students, would have done so. During a class conversation in which students shared their ideas, they expressed a desire to share the lessons of the novel—to target those in need of help and provide information about where to get it. They contacted a local radio station, which agreed to record and run public service announcements that my students had created. After studying the attributes of a PSA, the students wrote their own announcements and recorded them at the station. The students reported a great sense of satisfaction with empowering others to take action in ways that characters in the novel did not. They also loved hearing their own voices randomly on the radio! This particular radio station was so impressed with the quality of the PSAs and the enthusiasm shown by students, it invited my class this year to create PSAs for the station. After learning from the chief of police about a local drug abuse problem that has become prevalent in our area, the students will create PSAs focusing on awareness and describing resources for help.

Public Speaking

Another opportunity for learning outside classroom walls arose in the form of a school seminar on what community means. Speech students who spoke on this topic and shared suggestions for improving their community benefited from feedback and insight from invited audience members, who included the city manager, a state senator's local office manager, and the director of the Parks and Recreation Department. Building on feedback offered by the students' classmates on speaking skills, the community members offered their own feedback about public speaking and shared their own experiences and lessons as public speakers. Having outsiders listen to their ideas and give specific, honest feedback was validating and valuable for my students. In the words of Marcus, a senior, "it made us understand that public speaking and voicing our opinion intelligently isn't a school thing—it's a community value."

Loring Air Force Base

To learn more about local history, all juniors at my school tour the former Loring Air Force Base, located nearby. During the height of tensions between the United States and Soviet Union during the Cold War, Loring AFB held the largest stock of nuclear weapons in the United States, because of northern Maine's proximity to the U.S.S.R. Upon the closing of this base in 1994, our local communities faced many difficult changes in population and culture. Students and community came together to preserve rich local history and to keep future generations informed of the critical role of the base. Students in my AP English class interviewed several area veterans—from firefighters to B-52 pilots and others who served on the base in many capacities. Students videotaped these interviews, which were archived in DVD form and distributed in the community. Local citizens who remembered duck-and-cover drills and the impact of the base shared their stories. A colleague's father was declassified at the same time the archiving of this local history began; he was a guard at the top-secret nuclear storage facility that was not revealed to the public until recent years. Together, Mr. Atcheson and I created a Loring AFB tour, using his expertise as a primary source to give students a firsthand account of what it was like to work at such a facility and have the same security clearance as the president of the United States. A B-52 bombardier and civil engineer, both whom worked on the base, also continue to take part in the tour for all juniors each May. Students continue to learn about local history, share their learning, and keep the history alive. It is one thing to learn about the Cold War in social studies class or to analyze a political cartoon on McCarthyism in English class. But taking students to a place where local history dovetailed with national security is powerful and memorable. Student-centered learning allows for unique opportunities such as these to come alive and to serve as a bridge between school, community, and even the world.

Puccini's La Bohème

One recent outside learning experience offered my students some multidisciplinary opportunities for learning. I recently secured a grant from Target to take twenty-five students to see Puccini's *La Bohème*, broadcast live in high definition from the Met, at the Collins Center for the Arts, on the campus of the University of Maine at Orono. Several colleagues and I collaborated to create a learning experience that incorporated all our content areas. The music teacher, Mrs. King, discussed the idea of opera and how music uses not only lyrics, but also tone and volume to express the emotions of the story. The history teacher, Mr. Atcheson II, discussed with students the historical and cultural context of mid-nineteenth-century Paris. Mrs. Theriault prepared students in her French classes. As an English teacher, I asked students to analyze the opera as a whole as if they were analyzing a text. What was the message or central idea of the opera? What techniques were used to effectively deliver the message?

Feedback from the students was overwhelmingly positive. In addition to the pleasure of sitting at a restaurant discussing the opera with students afterward, my colleagues and I learned from students that spending time with teachers outside of the classroom—while not always feasible—is a definite way for us to express passion for education and lifelong learning and to deepen our relationships with students. They loved that their teachers shared a meal with them and cared enough to give up a Saturday to go to the opera with them. When given such amazing opportunities to expand knowledge, work collaboratively with colleagues, and get to know students better, I consider the time spent applying for the Target grant time well spent.

THE POWER OF COTEACHING TO BENEFIT STUDENT LEARNING

For two years, I have cotaught one class of junior English with my colleague Ms. Quinlan, whose classroom is next door to mine. While coteaching required thoughtful scheduling on the part of my principal, he was accommodating and enthusiastic about providing more opportunities for students to experience individualized attention and the dynamics of two facilitators of learning. At first, the notion seemed a bit overwhelming—how would we account for our unique teaching styles? How would we share responsibilities? Now, I only wish more teachers could experience the synergy and professional reflection that happens as a result of coteaching.

Maine passed L.D. 1422 in April 2012—legislation designed to implement proficiency-based education for college and career preparation in Maine schools. As we continue the work of recognizing that students learn as individuals at different paces, and reject the notion of just moving on, even if students are missing critical strategies or pieces of information, it becomes clear that this work cannot be done alone. Focusing on clear learning targets in our unit on figurative language and how history is reflected in text, Ms. Quinlan and I used the anchor text *The Great Gatsby* in our first coteaching unit.[3] (An anchor text is the book all the students read at the same time. It serves as the central focus for all the learning activities in the class for a certain time.) Immediately, we recognized the strength—not the challenge—of having two teachers work with a group of students. Such a dynamic allows for more in-depth discussion and examples based on our unique training and teaching experiences.

Coteaching allowed us to be more responsive to student questions and needs. For example, if a group of students was still rating their proficiency level at a 2 (partially meets the standards) for how an author's diction affects tone, one of us could drill deeper and work in a more concentrated way with that group of students, catching them up with more individualized attention. Because we both love teaching but have different areas of passion within the discipline, we would discuss in our planning who might take the lead with certain topics, skills, or learning targets. We shared a rich cache of resources that we had each compiled and were pleasantly surprised to find out we used many of the same online resources. Why hadn't we done this before? we often asked ourselves—it just made such sense.

With new standards, proficiency-based education, and a shift in state assessments, many changes coming from outside were afoot. Combining our knowledge and skills created a learning environment where I believe I learned as much about being an effective educator from my colleague as students did from the two of us offering instruction, support, and modeling strategies and positive rapport. As Ghent, a junior, told us at the end of the school year, "I liked how if one of you was busy with another student, I still had someone else to get help from. You obviously liked working together and had fun—that made our learning fun. When it was time to hunker down and get to work, there was one more person there to make sure you kept moving forward in your learning."

In the words of my esteemed colleague, Ms. Quinlan:

> As an educator, I found coteaching to be an invaluable experience. As with any collaborative effort, the ideas that were generated—from lessons, to goals, to delivery systems, to assessments—were far more creative, thoughtful, and, overall, more effective than when I was working alone. When two motivated educators are given the opportunity to share ideas and collectively work on common goals and objectives, the best from the two individuals is combined and yields noteworthy results for the students.

The obvious benefits of coteaching are the extra set of hands, eyes, and ears in a single classroom. What is less obvious, but what I found to be most rewarding (for both the students and the educators), is the extra brain and heart that coteaching provides. Effective teachers are able to quickly assess students' understanding of a concept when it is introduced. The coteaching classroom allowed students to hear explanations and examples from two sources. I often noted that my coteacher and I approached a topic (everything from definitions to ways to think about a complex concept) quite differently; our different approaches mirrored the diverse ways that students in that class seemed to process information. While a single educator can certainly address the various learning styles of his or her students in the classroom—an ability essential in a student-centered environment—coteaching allowed the differentiated instruction to occur more seamlessly and naturally.

In our coteaching classroom, Ms. Quinlan and I modeled learning strategies for students in a more responsive way. For example, if a model I used for writing a thesis statement during whole-group instruction did not make sense to some students, Ms. Quinlan was able to explain the same idea in a different way. Consequently, we were better able to meet the individual needs of our students, thus moving each of them forward as they worked toward proficiency with the learning standards.

An essential component of a student-centered classroom is the ability to group and regroup students according to their needs at any given time. Coteaching allowed us to break the class into smaller groups more often. Grouping in a coteaching classroom meant that students had to wait less time to meet with a teacher for clarification or instruction. The shortened wait time thus removed some of the challenges that a teacher often faces when trying to work with groups with only one teacher in the classroom. Having more accessibility to an instructor meant that the groups were vastly more productive and effective in reaching their goals.

Another result of coteaching is more difficult to measure, but was nonetheless apparent in my coteaching experience. The presence of two adults in a classroom seems to improve student engagement. The banter and mutual respect shown by the two educators toward each other was palpable in the classroom, and I found that students laughed more and learned more in this environment. After all, most students learn more when they're having fun, and witnessing the teachers having fun at the same time only adds to this possibility.

FORMATIVE FEEDBACK FROM STUDENTS

I've described a number of examples of how I try to live my philosophy of caring for students as people, of working to engage them in learning, and of teaching the skills they'll need so they can learn in any context. I'm not always sure that I'm succeeding in these commitments, so from time to time, I ask for feedback from the students to keep me on track. I recently conducted an anonymous poll with my students using Survey Monkey (www.surveymonkey.com). A sample of their responses suggests that the students do experience my commitment to these ideals.

> "I feel like Mrs. Margeson values me as a student and a person. I have never felt more welcomed, safe, or valued than I do when I'm in her class."
>
> "Mrs. Margeson influenced me to analyze more both in and outside of the classroom, which in turn helped me in my other courses."

"Being in Mrs. Margeson's class makes me work a lot harder and understand that I'll get out what I put into my assignments."

CREATING A CLASSROOM COMMUNITY IN SPEECH CLASS

Offering a speech class for the first time in over fifteen years at our high school,
I looked out at the interesting mix of students representing grades nine through
twelve. After asking students to complete a quick write about why they chose
to take the class, I learned something that surprised me—most students were
scared to death of public speaking! What all students had in common, however,
were two things: a recognition of the importance of public speaking in career
and community, and a desire to overcome their fear and self-doubt.

Working with a common body of learning targets, but focusing on a specific one each week, this semester-based elective course turned into one of the
most transformative teaching and learning experiences in my sixteen years in
education. Acknowledging the fear from the beginning, the students and I
created a classroom community that devoted itself to taking academic risks in
spite of the fear.

For one senior, Darcy, being class salutatorian did not mean that all academic skills came easily. Public speaking was something she struggled with,
yet knowing she wanted to take over the local family business after college, she
signed up for the challenge. She was a naturally garrulous young woman, but
anyone could tell, from the hives creeping up her neck when she gave a speech,
that talking in front of an audience was downright terrifying. I sat with students in the audience as we followed each speech with specific feedback about
what the student did well in terms of the learning targets and made specific suggestions for improvement. As the weeks went on, the body of academic vocabulary, specific examples, and learning targets grew with encouraging feedback.
Because the students had empathy as learners and public speakers, the classroom
became a place where students gained more and more comfort not only with
speaking in public, but also with giving and receiving feedback. The students
were kind, but also honest. Even students giving the speech critiqued themselves on their own satisfaction with their speaking; honesty about amount of
preparation and practice also became part of our conversations. Because the

classroom was a community of learners, there was safety in admitting room for improvement and a synergy of celebration concerning growth. Sitting with students as part of their learning community, validating their feedback, and encouraging honesty, reflection, and academic risk created a place of learning where competition was replaced with support. This is the type of classroom I want for my students. This is the type of environment I wish to work in as an adult.

As the semester went on, we upped the ante, inviting members of the community as well as other classes to be audience members and give feedback. Instead of dreading the thought of what others had to say about their speaking skills, my students genuinely welcomed it. "I knew how, and if, I was getting better when I listened to others," said Theo, a senior who chose to take the class because he believed effective communication with the public would be key as a future game warden.

During the very last capstone speech of the course, students used the TED Talk model to create a ten-minute speech with visuals, speaking from the stage of the community's Performing Arts Center. After choosing an "idea worth sharing" from their life lessons and experiences, one student decided to speak about the importance of self-acceptance. During this speech, looking out at the audience of peers who had supported her academically and socially throughout our eighteen weeks as a little family, she used her last speech to also share with students that she was gay. When the speech concluded, students did exactly what they had done all semester long—they gave her feedback on her speech. They shared with her what made her speech effective and powerful. Here is a sampling of the comments:

> "You balanced your pathos well."
>
> "You had us laughing and on the verge of tears."
>
> "You clearly practiced this speech."
>
> "Your pacing was effective, especially when you wanted to emphasize key points."
>
> "Great job."

After about five minutes of supportive student feedback (and hugs), one of the students spotted me a few rows back and became immediately apologetic.

"Mrs. Margeson! We totally took that over, didn't we? You probably had something to say, too."

Actually, I didn't. They had touched upon every single piece of academic feedback I had as well. It was one of those moments in a teacher's life, when the clouds part and the sun shines through—when students take ownership of the processes of growth, giving and receiving feedback and supporting one another.

At graduation, Darcy's salutatory speech was superb and was described by one of my veteran colleagues as "one of the top graduation speeches I have heard." Watching Darcy stand confidently at the podium, I couldn't help but marvel at the transformation from hand-wringing and hives to poised and poignant. While her speaking skills were impressive, it was in what she shared with the audience that day that resonated most: "Practice kindness. We all remember being left out on the playground or not getting invited to the slumber party. In the words of Maya Angelou, people will forget what you said, they will forget what you did, but they will never forget how you made them feel."

Perhaps this was the ultimate lesson of the semester. A student-centered classroom is one in which students feel safe and supported—by the teacher and each other—to take the greatest academic risks for the greatest academic growth.

CHAPTER NINE

Sophomore English

Creating Meaning

CHRISTIANE CULLENS

BACKDROP PHILOSOPHIES

An incredibly quick and fabulously curious sophomore once asked me an interesting question as he settled into the old, beat-up red armchair by my desk. "Ms. Cullens," he said, "because I respect what you think, I want to know and I really want the truth." He looked me directly in the eyes and inquired, "What exactly is the whole point of it all?"

Caught, I began to babble, processing and reaching out loud for some sharp, witty existential rationale to satisfy both his soul-baring innocence and razor-sharp scrutiny. Suddenly, I realized how ridiculous I sounded, and it occurred to me that I did have an answer, although I'd never once articulated it to anyone—myself, least of all. I laughed out loud, exhaled, and said, "To create meaning, Jarrod. For yourself and for others. It's about the inherent responsibility we all have to create meaning, and boy, that's some really hard work."

Jarrod nodded thoughtfully and replied, "I can live with that kind of work."

I agreed, and we laughed at the simplicity and magnitude of it all. I sighed and offered, "Well, it's a really good thing *you* are awesome."

He smiled, and we both knew it.

The Role of Humor

In the sixteen years that I've taught sophomore English, I've channeled my kaleidoscopic life experience into an effective practice that directly demonstrates to students how literacy and meaning-making support critical thinking and personal development. To this end, I must consistently create authentic tasks and offer supportive, deadly honest feedback through the all-important lens of a forgivingly wicked sense of humor.

Why is humor so important? Humor performs several crucial functions in my practice and needs to be carefully qualified. It's not at all enough to be funny—I'm not interested in entertaining students as a classroom management tactic, but I do actively use humor to engage and challenge them in a provocative and safe way.

Turns out that humor is a crucial part of how adolescents genuinely think and interact with the world. I once had an aspiring sophomore comic who now writes for Second City (go, Murphy!) research the role of humor in adolescents and society. He found that on average, a fourteen-year-old will laugh between 90 and 110 times a day. The average adult will laugh maybe 20 or 30 times a day. For real. Why is this so? And honestly, with whom would you rather work?

What makes us laugh is equal parts surprise and revelation. In short, something strikes us as funny when it comes to us as an unexpected truth. In this way, humor provides a kind and benign means to explore and discover. It simultaneously disarms and comforts.

Laughter enlivens a classroom and creates an environment where kids are more willing to express themselves and engage. When kids can laugh and contextualize their own process within the parameters of humor and forgiveness, they are literally *more alive.*

Modeling is crucial. For example, the word *punitive* came up on a class-generated vocabulary list. From the quizzes, it was clear that students were using the word incorrectly, as a noun. Clearly, I hadn't made the usage explicit enough. I didn't take points off the quiz, but I made sure to address the issue directly the next day. I asked the kids, "Okay, what sounds totally bizarre about this sentence?" On the board, I wrote: "My friend Yolanda is totally bummed; she's got the punitive."

Barely stifled giggles rippled around the room. Finally, brave extrovert Jacob piped up: "That makes it sound like she's got an . . . *STD*!" Waves of laughter followed, then Marni added over the din, "That must explain why my hand burned when I wrote it!" Paroxysms of hilarity. After a minute, I found the natural ebb and explained how if one doesn't use the right variant, at best, one could land oneself with a nasty case of misunderstanding and at worst, start really terrible rumors. The correct use of variants was very carefully observed from that point forward.

Laughter and the use of humor are contagious and create a repartee effect that, when channeled and contained effectively, can generate a great amount of energy in an inclusive learning environment. Ultimately, humor is about discovering unexpected truths: about books, culture, language, and, in the end, ourselves. Modeling humor as a strategic skill set inherently encourages and demonstrates a practice of self-directed learning. It also turns out that laughter may be the only truly universal emotive sound. And that's just funny.

No Shame

There is a mantra I have in my class from day one: "NO SHAME!" I make students repeat it with me until they are dizzy with giggles. We talk about our collectively bizarre, hypocritically perfectionist culture where folks feel responsible for what they do not and cannot know, yet. I make the kids say it over and over throughout the semester, in all sorts of contexts.

To illustrate, I explain to students how we will "do" vocabulary. Vocabulary acquisition should come from students' lives and should reflect specific criteria of what makes a good vocabulary word *for each individual student*. I ask kids to interview a trusted elder about why we *all* should learn new words and to reflect on this short interview in a paragraph. From those paragraphs, we create a shared chalk talk and identify key thematic reasons why learning vocabulary might be valuable, and we generate ideas on how we each could do it well. Inevitably, students come up with rationale for what good vocabulary words should do for them:

Make me (sound) smart

Allow me to be more precise when I describe something

Help me communicate more clearly

Then, we talk about where the words should come from. Usually, they agree that new words should come from their own lives: music, movies, friends, and elders. The inevitable collective complaint arises: "This is so much work! It's too hard to ask people about the words they use. I'll sound *dumb*! Just give us words! *Puleeze?*" Here's the crux, the trust, and the challenge. There is *no shame* in asking anyone about a word she or he has used. There is no shame in looking up a word you have sung one hundred thousand times in a song, unsure of what it really meant. And there is certainly no shame in asking Ms. C about that crazy weird word she just wrote up on the board during a lecture.

The very act of asking reveals both ignorance and the *drive to move beyond that ignorance*. It can initially seem like an insignificant thing, but to a sophomore, this is huge. It is a stepping-stone to self-awareness, self-advocacy, and self-directed learning. Each student researches and teaches a new word to the class weekly; the lesson includes the word's etymology and derivatives, how to use it correctly with usage notes, and an explanation of its real-life source. This student-led practice creates an arena for students to showcase their discoveries in a seemingly small, but very real way. Collectively, they are all accountable for not knowing and taking the steps to knowing and then sharing that knowledge—an approach tantamount to creating the sort of culture and environment that supports student-directed learning.

Modeling Effective Reflection

Every classroom is a laboratory on many levels. Strategies that have worked beautifully with one group utterly fail with others. My best critics are my students, and I share this observation with them, explicitly and often. They begin this course learning that most of the tools we use have been actively informed by years of sophomores who have come before them. I liken it to a natural biological phenomenon: each year, the plants of our world take seed, grow, bloom, fruit, and go back to seed, and on the outside, they appear not very changed. But this is untrue. Each wave of sophomores has something a little different to offer, some shift in perspective, some cultural marker that makes the current generation better able to negotiate an ever-evolving world. I need to notice these changes, listen well, and take active heed if I am to teach my students anything at all. I consistently ask for reflections and feedback, both informally and formally, but all the responses influence my instruction, timing, and choices. Tools to cull feedback from kids can range from eyes-closed votes all the way to incredibly thoughtful and evidence-based midterm or final reflections and student-led conferences. I never have a set semester syllabus; it would be blown to pieces within a week because I'm usually reacting to class dynamics and the students' needs and thus restructuring my plans. This does not mean I don't have a plan, goals, and scope—but I recognize that when I am working with a group of human beings, their individual and collective education is more important than a deadline.

Power of Limited Choice

Throughout the tools and texts presented in class, I embed a great deal of choice—from offering up to ninety minutes of in-class free reading time per week in an independent reading program to allowing students to choose how to approach an assignment, to offering various basic motifs within a text for students to focus on, to modeling several prewriting and revision strategies. Student-centered approaches like these are incredibly important in recognizing students' individuality and in giving students even greater responsibility for their own learning needs.

Revise, Retake, Resubmit

I embrace a living policy that all students can revise and resubmit any piece of work until they have come to a place of learning they can recognize using rubrics and scoring guides tied to the Common Core Standards. I make it clear to students and parents that the first three to four weeks of class are spent acclimating students to the culture and tools of the course. We use the first set of double-entry journals (DEJs), roundtable discussions (RTDs), on-demand writing, and vocabulary drops and quizzes as diagnostic to determine an individual's strengths, challenges, experience, and interests. Once students have received their first wave of documented feedback using scoring guides, they can then reach for official grades based on clear evidence, while they still understand, as noted above, that they can revise and resubmit work if necessary. But it doesn't stop there. Students need space and practice to gain perspective on their own process and work. For these reasons, they are regularly encouraged to revise and resubmit their work and retake quizzes, and once they feel they can trust the process, they do trust it. They feel free to hand in work that they fear may not meet the standard the first time, knowing they will receive feedback and have the chance to revise it with support. Because this is a living policy and

I depend on a computer program that accounts for grades, I never average the grades a student earns; I replace them.

Standards, Tides, and Students

My practice has weathered through three state mandates and two national directives concerning what "the educational powers that be" think kids should know and be able to do if and when they graduate from public school. I am fortunate enough to work in a district that prioritizes student needs over legislative vicissitudes. As a trusted professional, I am expected to consistently corroborate, reflect, and revise curriculum with my colleagues to prepare students for just about anything modern life can throw at them. With great freedom comes great responsibility and a great deal of work. Standards are only useful when they are clearly articulated and purposeful, are accessible to students, and can be clearly assessed with evidence. Regardless of what initiatives come down, my sophomores will always need to express themselves, learn how to listen well, think and read critically, and self-reflect. With the Common Core State Standards, my colleagues and I are currently working with identified essential standards and creating a proficiency-based model and practice that works for our district, school, and community. Reference to the Common Core in this chapter reflects that work and our shared priority.[1]

THE FRAME

Identifying Needs: A Letter to the Teacher

For their first assignment, I explain to students that despite how school may seem to them, I as a teacher work for them, and as my clients, the students both have individualized needs and collectively inform a class dynamic and experience. With this premise, I'll ask the kids to write an informal letter to me about what they feel they need from me as a teacher, from each other as peers, and from themselves to be successful in the class.

Many students are so grateful at getting a chance to identify and articulate their needs that they are totally forthcoming. Others, not so much. Students who have been hammered with labels of lazy or procrastinator will often minimize their responses and parrot what other adults in their academic lives have told them with heartbreaking defeatism. To address a range of student attributes and to encourage lateral trust, when I share class feedback anonymously, I explain that I don't buy into the cultural phenomenon that uses laziness as both an excuse and an accusation. I suggest that procrastination is merely a form of perfectionism. I also share that boredom brings on a very real and constant source of pain for many of us and might just be the most destructive force in the universe—a force that fuels our most desperately poor choices. Often, students will visibly relax upon hearing these comments. To prime students for their letters, I share former students' responses, which range from the most concrete and universal to the most bizarre and specific. The idea is to demonstrate that it's totally acceptable to have individual needs, no matter how outlandish they might seem:

> "You need to know that I eat constantly. If I get hungry, I get really angry, so it's not you. If I look mad, just ask me if I've eaten, I can forget to."
>
> "I really need you to not look over my left shoulder when I'm working, it freaks me out because of some stuff that happened when I was a kid."
>
> "I'm really good at being invisible. I might need you to check in on me when I don't hand work in. I won't like it, but I might need it."

This stark honesty demonstrates to me the power of simply asking. I also ask students to handwrite these responses, as you can also tell quite a bit about them by their script. When I read these letters, I conjure up what they wore in class and how they chose to sit and with whom. I begin the process of "Sherlocking" to get a sense of their comfort zones, interests, and potential challenges.

Once the responses come in and I share them anonymously, we talk about and actively synthesize them to agree on classroom norms and post them in the classroom for easy reference and as visual confirmation. It's important to keep these norms universal, yet in language that is organic from the letter exercise for a sense of shared ownership. At the inception, students appreciate having a voice in expectations and how things get done. This past semester's norms were the following:

Respect each other's ideas.

Keep it about the work.

No drama!

Ask the Right Essential Question

Over the years, my colleagues and I have grappled mightily with how to best utilize essential questions. The right ones should cohere the curriculum in a meaningful way. Like most noble intentions, the process has suffered growing pains. At first, we called the essential question "the quest"—noble, but not really a question. The texts that all sophomore teachers used at the time had a quest theme, which was not so student-centered as it was convenient to the books we'd already ordered. The essential question then evolved into "investigating the other," but this proved to be a developmentally inappropriate nightmare for a population of fourteen- to sixteen-year-olds who wanted nothing less than to seem "other." Again, the central idea did not resonate or originate with the kids. It was well intended, but totally missing the mark. The question that has spoken the most clearly and consistently to and for the kids and has given me enough tooth, structure, and flexibility to include and challenge all of my students has evolved into "How does storytelling inform our lives?"

Having the right essential question serves a number of purposes. It lays down a baseline of inquiry, meaning, and focus for students to grapple with over the whole semester. It answers the challenge "How am I going to use this in *real life?*" It supports the structure and space for kids to learn, refer to, and revise their answers to the essential question over time. With proper documentation, the question can also provide them with a map showing how and why they got to their ideas. Documentation, intermittent referral, and reflection are key to the students' understanding of themselves as learners of English. In my experience, effective essential questions need to do the following:

> *Be developmentally appropriate.* Sophomores cannot directly focus on themselves. Biologically, they are so much a bundle of hormones and mushrooming brain growth that they often lack the language and metacognitive tools to recognize their own growth without focusing primarily on something else. Between the ages of fourteen and sixteen, most adolescents' prefrontal cortexes are blooming at a rate these regions of the brain never will again. This explains why most sophomores are so focused on a sense of identity, social justice, and others' opinions of them.
>
> *Be relevant to the sophomore experience.* A teenager's social experience is very different from the biological aspect described above, but is directly

related. A relevant question has much more to do with how that mushrooming brain manifests in pop culture, school culture, and class dynamic. For example, I have no personal interest in rap music, but it's important that I understand how my students both listen to it and use it to self-identify and express themselves. Doing so helps me make choices and build bridges to their experience.

Be universal enough so that most students feel as though they can begin to answer the question. If every student can weigh in on the essential question, it helps create a classroom dynamic to which everyone can be held accountable. The question "How does storytelling inform our lives?" does this for my sophomores.

Picking the Texts

Although all students are accountable to wrestling with the same essential question in their own individual way, flexibility and accountability to a group community are also important components of a class dynamic. Even within the same semester, I have used different texts in response to the individual readiness and interests of different class sections of the same course.

The class that this chapter primarily refers to was composed of eighteen boys and five girls. When I initially ran this class of students through the diagnostic tools to get to know these kids, I quickly realized that there would be no Shakespearean romances or art projects running amok for this group. These students would instead benefit from as much role-playing and out-of-seat time as possible, with a slow, steady, and supported movement from concrete, sequential, evidential thinking to more philosophical, abstract thinking. They would also need lots of practice in how to articulate their ideas to each other in a meaningful, respectful way.

I chose to go with *Oedipus Rex* first in combination with a simplified version of Aristotle's *Poetics* to give students both a concrete set of classically tragic criteria and the room to affirm or refute the idea that within the confines of those criteria, the play was still effective to a modern audience.[2] Next, we moved on to *Macbeth*, where students could choose from several motifs in the play, from very concretely symbolic to the abstractly paradoxical, to extrapolate Shakespeare's possible intent in employing their chosen motifs.[3] Last, we tackled Hesse's *Siddhartha*, and I knew this one would be a risk.[4] Eighteen boys and a novel about the Buddha? Really? Yes, and we did it with a focus on how our preconceived ideas about how learning, teachers, experience, desire, and suffering are all interconnected. *Siddhartha* ended up being the text and the vehicle that allowed students to reflect on their own self-directed learning in a thoughtful and circumspect way.

THE TOOLS

Students often confront me with, "How is what we're learning relevant to my life and getting a *real* job?" They are right to be concerned and doubly right to ask. What my students are really begging me for here is a sense of authenticity and validation that their energies, explorations, and, ultimately, the risks we're asking them to take will pay off for them in the end. For this reason, I employ several tools to help students with their self-directed learning.

Elder Interviews

Developmentally, sophomores are particularly prone to grappling with the huge philosophical questions and will often seek out trusted elders with whom to safely test their ideas and feelings. These elders are not often teachers. I'd always suspected that the sometimes-problematic triangulated communication between school, students, parents, and community harbors hidden potential; it only needs the right frame and clarified purpose. In response, I have created and incorporated a core practice of having students interview elders within my sophomore curriculum.

Sophomores are first asked to consider an adult (over the age of twenty-seven, please!) with whom they can reliably communicate regularly, who knows them well, and who cares about their overall growth. Sometimes elders are parents, but very often, they are not. A fair number of students do not choose direct family members, for valid reasons. Talking directly with a parent about big ideas that could affect school can be a very scary prospect for some students. Some of my students are effectively homeless because of drugs or poverty and need to seek an elder elsewhere. Some students differ so widely from their families' basic philosophies that these conversations can serve as incendiary devices in an already tense home life. Therefore, elders can be family members, friends of the family, people who live nearby, or someone from across the world. They can be former teachers, coaches, bosses, or clergy. Some students opt to Skype or exchange emails with extended family members from across the country or across the planet.

Occasionally, a student has become so withdrawn that he or she may be at a total loss about whom to ask. It may take some work, but because I work in a district that supports students first, we have always been able to connect students with a nonthreatening elder who is within the system and who can work under the auspices of "school." Quite often, these relationships bloom into mentorships of sorts, despite what the student or elder may have initially anticipated. Most important, the adults need to be consistently available to engage the process and the student must trust them. Without these criteria, the process will fail.

Once the elder is identified, students invite him or her to a semester's worth of interviews and discussions that introduce and connect the texts' larger themes with the real world in a philosophical, but tangible way (see the sidebar "A Sampling from the Semester's Interview Questions and the Texts They Informed"). Throughout the nineteen weeks, there are usually six to seven interviews, usually two to three weeks apart. The very first interview centers around the essential question for the course. The class's responses provide me with a sense of how individual students grapple with large ideas and how the kids might interact in a class dynamic. Through their choice of elder and responses, I get to know a great deal about which basic philosophies feel the safest to the students, which ideas might be the most provocative, and how they handle differences of opinion, even with someone whose opinion they trust. These interviews happen simultaneously as I am initiating the first sets of diagnostic on-demand writing tasks, roundtable discussions, and double-entry journals (more about these tools to follow). The diagnostic information I gather sets parameters, goals, and priorities for each student.

A SAMPLING FROM THE SEMESTER'S INTERVIEW QUESTIONS AND THE TEXTS THAT INFORMED THEM

Oedipus Rex: Many stories grapple with the tension between how much free will and fate have an impact on our lives. Which has more sway, and why?

Macbeth: If you were told that you would achieve or receive your heart's desire, how would this information affect the way you lived your life?

Siddhartha: In what ways do people seek out enlightenment, learning, or personal advancement? What motivates folks to do so?

Over time, students take on large questions that relate to the texts we read. Ultimately, these questions help the students connect their own lives with the texts. As students gain experience with the tools that I describe here, they become better versed in their own metacognition, strategies, and self-advocacy.

A large part of the success with this process is recognizing how students negotiate the content of their interviews. The frame offers them many outs but, at the same time, reveals a great deal about who they currently are as learners. Having information come from trusted elders serves students in a number of ways. Students uncomfortable with wrestling with these kinds of questions alone can rely almost explicitly on the elder feedback and report back the content in a "book report" sort of way that keeps with the expectation of the process. For kids who thrive on this sort of philosophical extrapolation, the interviews offer them even more food for growth.

Having gone through several semesters of this process, I have come to appreciate a few key outcomes of the elder interviews. Teenagers spend the vast majority of their time with their own peers. The assignment (or opportunity) to make meaningful contact with folks from another generation offers students the chance to empathize, connect, and understand not just where others are coming from, but where they might eventually want to go in their own futures. When I create space for individual voices from other eras and other perspectives in our classrooms, I honor all aspects of the communities that give shape to personal development. The exercise provides a protocol for tolerance, questioning, exploration, and learning not only on a shared-classroom level, but on a level that honors each student's personal process, who they are, where they come from, and who they can be.

On-Demand Writing

Even though they've been warned for days, this snowy steel-gray morning in early February finds my twenty-three sophomores shuffling into the dark cave of Room 101 blinking in utter disbelief at today's agenda on the board: "First On-Demand Essay, Yay!" Some stop slack-jawed in their tracks, roll their eyes, and offer groans to the ceiling as they flop themselves into their desks. Once I've waited for most of their eyes, I reassure the kids that they all can use their laptops, but that they don't have to. I let them vent and shift around for a moment, and then I hearken back to an earlier class discussion titled "Why In-Class Writing Assignments Often Suck" to remind them that the prompt on the blackboard behind the pull-down screen has been developed and informed by many sophomores before them. The lowing complaints die down as ears prick up. I remind them that like all our initial assignments, this is a diagnostic and that the point in writing an expository essay or narrative story in response to a prompt is to deliver on what one promises to do. With these assignments, students have eighty minutes to show me something about how they approach writing. They do so by focusing on something they all are experts on: their own opinions. The kids now begin to lean in, and I can tell they are all actively wondering what could possibly be behind that screen. I pull the screen down a little and up it flies, revealing the age-old philosophical dilemma of . . .

Who's cooler?

- Pirates
- Ninjas
- Aliens
- Knights

The students lean back to take it in and then break out into barely stifled smiles and guffaws. The whole mood of the room gels, and the kids bodily lighten up. They look at me and to each other in disbelief and for reassurance that this is really what I'm asking them to write about. "Really? That's the prompt?" "Dude, pirates!" "No way, aliens!" "You're full of it!" "This is going to be so wicked easy." It usually takes about three to five minutes for them to recover from the shock. The topic doesn't seem to have anything to do with school, and of course, that's precisely the point. Every sophomore knows deep down what he or she personally means by "cool," and nearly every student has some predilection and experience with one of the four archetypes that inform that opinion. Whether the kids have ever been asked or taken the time to really identify their own criteria of cool and use those criteria to explicitly support the superiority of ninjas, pirates, aliens, or knights in a story or an exposition—well, that's another thing altogether.

Before they settle into the task, I remind them of a few things: It's totally expected that these pieces of writing will be messy; that's not only okay, but encouraged: *no shame!* I need evidence of some sort of prewriting or revision strategy, or both, that shows me how each student got to his or her best ideas within the time allotted. If kids need to finish up in a study hall, they can, but the work must be in my inbox by the end of the day. Students who need to work in an alternative space give me the nod and leave. I put on the classroom kettle for tea as they begin to contemplate cool, make assertions, and dream up plot points to show what they really think.

Later, I will read their work and, from it, develop thematic feedback to share with the class as whole. I use a scoring guide designed to give each student specific feedback on what's happening with the process and suggestions on what might work for future writing. Even though there is often a wide variety of responses and strategies, a prompt like this reveals clear pitfalls in argumentation and levels of complexity in both the narrative and the expository styles. This awareness of the pitfalls can help kids see how argumentation and narrative reflection can really work to answer such a prompt or won't—*yet.* Depending on the class dynamic and response, the feedback can be administered immediately or more often, after at least one full week has gone by. Given too soon, the feedback won't help kids to effectively objectify their own writing to clearly see what happened. If it's given too late, the humor and competitive spirit of the challenge can dissipate.

When they have duly forgotten about the prompt, I hand their responses back to them with scoring guides and individualized feedback. I first ask them to read through their own work with a pen to indicate parts that they really like and the parts they find unclear or less powerful than they had imagined when they first wrote. Once it's time, we vote on who thought which was cooler to regain a sense of levity and fun with the assignment. The voting also gives students a chance to see with whom they share similar opinions, especially if these other students are not friends. It also provides them with scaffolding to make a promise to themselves about what they will do the next time to make a more successful response.

Students revisit their responses and feedback from me with an eye to specific strategies they used (or didn't), and we brainstorm ways not to succumb to those pitfalls again or to tweak them to strengthen thinking and writing. I offer them two graphic organizers: one for a narrative and another for expository. I model how to use lists, "verbal mcvomit," outlines, and drawing notes/illustrated thought-webs as further options. Considering these strategies and where students are in their process, they write out two to three promises to themselves about new strategies they'd like to try the next time we do on-demand writing. When the next such assignment comes around, I will hand these scoring guides and self-promises back to students to help guide their writing process. Every two to three weeks through the first two-thirds of the semester, students engage in an on-demand writing prompt that in structure looks like the "Who's cooler?" assignment. That is, the students are asked to make choices, create criteria or stories or both around those choices, and defend their choices, but the content is often directly related to the texts and larger concepts we are grappling with as a class, such as these:

What best defines a hero? Achievement, service, sacrifice, or the ability to be a role model?

What best defines success? Financial wealth, adventure and travel, relationships, or achievement?

What contributes most to your sense of identity? Media, peers, family, or school?

At this point in the class, my work with on-demand writing evolves from identifying individual and class needs to suggesting individualized writing strategies and introducing the purpose of revision. Students have made clear promises to themselves to play with a few prewriting strategies, to get comfortable with making supportable assertions, and to identify narrative constructs that illustrate thematic purposes, like symbolism or characterization. The process is about creating awareness of audience, voice, and purpose. It's also about students being confident that they can deliver on what they promise in their writing. All of this practice also serves as a foundation and practice for the formal literary thesis writing that will come in the final quarter of the semester.

When students receive feedback on their third on-demand assignment, I ask them to retrieve previous samples of the task from their writing folders. Because we have practiced some pattern recognition in double-entry journal writing, I can ask them to reread their pieces with an eye to patterns that work and those that don't work so well with their strategy, organization, and content. I ask them to identify one emergent pattern that they like, one they don't, and one that might just baffle them. Students then revisit their own pattern recognition, decide where on the continuum their writing piece falls, and identify steps they need to improve. In addition, I coach students on how to consult me effectively about revision. Too often, students will come up to my desk, hand back a paper with plenty of marks with a scoring guide or rubric stapled to it and say, "Um . . . what do I need to fix?" Nothing makes me nuttier. When students are looking for pattern recognition, I also ask them to go through my marks with a highlighter and, if they do not understand what I meant, to highlight them and write down the question to bring with them to conference. This way, in conference, we both stay on task and students practice the self-advocacy they need.

Students share with me the patterns they recognize and choose one piece to revise with three specific things they'd like to do to improve the piece. When their revisions are completed, students hand in their first drafts, the original expository or narrative on-demand scoring guides with original feedback, and individualized revision scoring guide. This way, I can document how well they've met their identified revision goals and how well this helped them address the standards outlined in the original scoring guide. Over the latter half of the semester, we will use at least two of these revisions that were based on the on-demand assignment. Doing so provides a context and practice for the students' formal literary thesis papers, a key common assessment for which sophomores need to meet standards to graduate.

Double-Entry Journals

One of the most challenging things to ask sophomores to do is to look at their own engagement with the texts they read. Reading for information, for understanding, or for meaning can all look very different and yet suspiciously similar to a sophomore brain. Even among the most voracious readers and articulate extrapolators, clarity of purpose can get muddled with how and why we read for pleasure, respond to assigned texts, and even negotiate the nuances within social media. It's nearly impossible to ask students to use the writing process to think critically if they cannot critically engage with a text or reflect on a growing ability to read well.

The myriad of ways in which a student engages with a text tells me what he or she understands, if and how the student questions or predicts, and how well, if at all, he or she can personally connect with what the student reads. The double-entry journal tells me if and how a student can reflect some truth from the world beyond the classroom. It tells me a great deal about who the student is, where his or her biases live, and where the student's challenges and strengths as a reader reside. The double-entry journal is a tool I've blatantly stolen and tweaked from a host of thousands of other English teachers worldwide. Its strategy is to document student engagement with, and comprehension of, a given text. Using a guiding question or motif, students identify and isolate relevant quotes from their reading to support their inferences and the meaning they find in the direct relationship between the quote, the guiding question or motif, and their own developing understanding. Students copy the quote in the right-hand column on their paper, and in the adjacent left-hand column, they write their understanding of the quote's meaning in relation to the guiding question or motif. When used consistently with clear feedback and models, the journals serve as a foundation and an ongoing process that individuates and motivates students and provides them with evidence of increased engagement with a text and their own critical process.

I warn the kids. I tell them up front that double-entry journals will feel messy, unwieldy, laborious, and probably even tedious at the beginning—but that this tool also provides the foundation for the whole course and the emerging writing process and that the journals are wicked, wicked important. Because they are. They comprise a regular part of the students' weekly homework timeliness checks and their preparation for roundtable discussions, and they inform formal papers and support complete projects. The good and fabulous truth is, the students will be practicing how to do these journals all semester long with every text we read. To shamelessly parrot the unfortunate villager from Monty Python's famous drowning-a-witch scene, "It got better!"[5] And it does get better, because unbeknownst to each student at the onset, double-entry journals will also provide each with a sense of routinized, shared class culture. Students can commiserate over the journaling tasks and receive tons of feedback. The journals also provide evidence that students can use to reflect and determine who they are as readers. Finally, the students use double-entry journals to eventually create strategies for getting more from what they read.

Maintaining the journal is a process, and like most of the tools described here, the end product at the end of the semester can look a lot like fabulous student-directed learning. To sophomores, however, the beginning can seem like a lock-step cage with infuriatingly dictator-like language. Students initially need something concrete to look for as they determine key clues, criteria, and questions while they read. For *Oedipus Rex*, for example, we focused on Oedipus's character development and connecting this to Aristotle's criteria for effective tragedy. In the beginning, the guiding questions and criteria are very clear, concrete, and recognizable. These initial clear guidelines are important, because they give me a baseline on where students are in their comprehension and ability to follow how character complexity drives plot and a how a theme develops over the course of a text.

At this point, students receive feedback on a small number of double-entry journals partway through the first reading to determine what support they might need and what questions to ask to push their thinking ever more critically. Students also keep their original scoring guides so that I can see changes that they have made to their journals as they engage with the rest of the text.

Once the first text has been tackled and students feel that they understand the expectation, it's time to move on to *Macbeth* and more opportunities for choice and voice. *Macbeth* is a great midcourse text primarily because it offers (as all complex and classic literature should) comprehensive opportunities on several levels. Also, Shakespeare is *hard*. The language intimidates, and the canonical reputation looms large. Yet, if sophomores can get this, their confidence skyrockets, and confidence is key.

In an effort to combat the ease of SparkNotes and the like, I offer them openly to students with the caveat that these shortcuts really won't help all that much for what *we* are doing with the text. With this particular class, we began each text (*Oedipus Rex* and *Macbeth*) in the school's theater, where I assigned roles and the students acted out the parts before we ever began our close reading. We do this by having students read their roles onstage as I direct and stage-manage their movements. If students can identify with at least one character and understand the major plot points, reading Shakespeare becomes a learning experience instead of torture. I also offer them several movie versions to bolster understanding and wonderful audio support to use while they are reading.

I've been taken to task for these approaches. Some people would condemn such support as enabling or even cheating. To these reproaches, I contend that when students feel cornered, they will resort to anything possible and (im)plausible to avoid looking bad or, worse, stupid. The sheer availability of various types of Internet support will surely trump any sophomore's good intentions and erstwhile academic integrity. To put it simply, I cannot afford to teach in a rarified atmosphere. Real students struggle with Shakespeare and deserve help. Besides, what I ask students to do with Shakespeare can hardly be touched by any Internet support, and I will immediately know when they try to use less-than-honorable means to comprehend the Bard's intentions behind his literary choices. When these attempts inevitably cross my desk, they deserve a larger conversation, not punishment and judgment. After all, this is really about creating the foundation and support so that students become better readers, not grifters.

Macbeth offers a number of thematic motifs that students can choose from to follow throughout the text. The motifs range from the already familiar and relatively concrete elements of tragedy to character development, to a new, more complex level of blood or clothing symbolism, to the more esoteric motifs of the role of masculinity or paradox. Because students already know what happens in the story, they are primed to find, follow, examine, and form ideas about what Shakespeare had in mind as he wove these motifs through Macbeth's tragic tale. Students are asked not only to make a choice, but also to defend it and infer what Shakespeare may have had in mind.

At this point with *Macbeth*, we are also introducing and practicing the skill of pattern recognition toward an intended goal with the motifs. Once students have completed eight to ten double-entry journals, it is time to go back, reread, reflect, and test out ideas about how and why Shakespeare employed the motifs as he did. Of course, what we have here are the bare bones of a literary thesis paper with quotes and inferences to support those ideas.

Roundtable Discussions

Perhaps nothing terrifies most sophomores more than speaking out loud in class, especially when they know they will be graded on it. I ask kids to reflect on the purpose of classroom discussions and what has gone well for them in prior classes and perhaps not so well. The students often respond that while they really value the opportunity to express their opinions and love to listen to others to deepen understanding and widen perspective, they also complain—a lot—about getting graded on what should be the free expression of their opinions. To many sophomores, being graded on what *should be* a spontaneous assertion of their views stands as a profound conflict of interest. They grouse about the vocal minority who often dominate the conversation and an environment where students will often simply reiterate a point only to earn points toward their personal grade. Others voice frustration at those who would simply piggyback off the discussion to cover themselves because they have not read in preparation. It became clear to me that I needed to talk explicitly about how preparation; identifying personal style, goals, and strategies; and reflection could help inform not only a personal investment and performance in a discussion, but also the success within a classroom dynamic.

It's also important to clarify the actual purpose of classroom discussion in a way that incorporates each student's experience and voice in helping to shape that purpose. Often, academically biased observers (teachers) are shocked by the diversity of opinion on this seemingly elusive purpose. To begin, I ask my students to write a 250-word piece, using their own experience and a very short interview of an elder, on what they think the purpose behind classroom discussions is. I ask kids to pull out two to three key findings and to share them in a chalk talk. We use those responses to determine, refine, and develop criteria of what a good classroom discussion should look like. Getting their honest reflections out in the open is crucial.

Often, the developing criteria involve deepening understanding, sharing ideas, and benefiting from others' perspectives and interpretations—all valid. Inescapably, however, students' frustration also bubbles up. When we talk about past challenges in class discussions, the floodgates really open up—students begin to feel relieved and validated by each other's vexations with being graded on what they feel should be a free experience. Their body language softens, and they begin to address their comments to and with each other rather than just me. They complain about silly and ultimately useless grading systems, where they earn points by saying anything at all. They bitterly recount being trounced by those who would transform the discussion into a personal battlefield to argue and win. They begin to get mad, which is utterly fabulous.

This hurricane of raw frustration provides me with the opportunity and emotional investment to really give roundtables an individualized and shared purpose. As a class, we can define what the discussions should look like to meet the agreed-upon goals and criteria. I can also assemble these criteria into understandable and accessible standards for my students (table 9.1).

The roundtable discussion on the purpose of discussion itself creates a common language and concrete, accessible goals that students have generated and for which the students can find meaningful connections within identified standards. Offering students the gift of voice and purpose behind their work and then validating that investment with external standards tends to create much more student buy-in toward self-advocacy and self-directed learning. It's messy, but can also become deeply meaningful.

TABLE 9.1   Roundtable discussion goals that correspond well to Common Core Standards

Student-generated goals: elements supported by good discussions	Applicable Common Core Standard
• Thoughtful questions • Fully explained ideas • Logical persuasion • Timely and appropriate comments • Appropriate responses • Provocative comments and questions from others • Clear reference to text for support of ideas • Connections between texts, comments, and ideas • Use of text to persuade • Use of text to clarify • Listening well to others • Following up on comments with questions • Contributing to flow of discussion • Appropriate gestures • Eye contact	SL 9-10: 1. Initiate and participate effectively in a range of collaborative discussions with diverse partners on grades 9–10 topics, texts, and issues, building on others' ideas and expressing their own clearly and persuasively. c. Propel conversations by posing and responding to questions that relate the current discussion to broader themes or larger ideas; actively incorporate others into the discussion; and clarify, verify, or challenge ideas and conclusions. d. Respond thoughtfully to diverse perspectives, summarize points of agreement and disagreement, and, when warranted, qualify or justify their own views and understanding and make new connections in light of the evidence and reasoning presented.

We then talk a little about the spectrum of speaking and listening styles, from introverts to extroverts, and how some folks use talk to process, how body language can inform an exchange within a class dynamic, and how, with the right support and preparation, we can encourage the more reticent kids to share. This sort of discussion opens up the fact that students (and teachers!) all have different styles, needs, strengths, and challenges when it comes to collaborative learning like a roundtable discussion. We then talk about different styles of collaborators and the advantages and disadvantages of those styles.

Right after this short lecture, I have students reflect on what kind of a speaker and listener they identify themselves as and on possible reasons why they may have evolved in this particular way. Students tend to be very open about their own interpersonal tendencies and histories. They often come to identify really valid reasons for their development:

> "I hate talking in front of the class. I'm more of a covert learner, but if I'm not right in what I do say and I still said something, does that mean I get a bad grade?"

> "I hate it when it gets too quiet; it makes me nervous and that's why I always end up talking too much. I know kids get mad at me for talking, but if they said more, I wouldn't have to."

> "I *love* debates! We have them at dinner all the time, and it's great when I can beat my dad at them. I don't know why other kids don't like them."

> "I like listening, but I feel like I need time to write about it later to figure out what I really think about it. By the time I know what to say, the conversation has moved on."

At this point, it's important to talk about the role of preparation, how to take notes, and how to use reflection critically. Many students are bewildered at the suggestion and confess to not having a clue as to how to prepare for a discussion. Often, they assume that reading the assigned material should be enough.

From many years of being faced with challenges of all stripes, I have designed, tweaked, and redesigned the preparation template for roundtables, and I will continue to work it as a tool that gives kids the room to process and fine-tune what they might bring to a discussion and to reflect or take notes to account for listening and critical thinking skills. Each discussion has a guiding question and room for a personal goal. All students are responsible for preparing questions, quotes, and thoughts to address (see the appendix at the end of this chapter for the template).

During the actual roundtable, I use a wondrously archaic tool that I have tweaked endless times and will surely continue to tweak. Using a very fancy yellow legal pad and ballpoint pen, I complete a live scoring sheet that gives both me and my students relatively quantified hard data and clear evidence of what actually happened during the discussion itself. I have found that recording by hand gives me a more accurate record of the discussion, as a computer screen just distracts me mercilessly. I list all the participants' names in order, creating enough room to record the following keys:

?	question
Q	quote referenced
CP	counterpoint
R	response
DR	disagreeing response
*	provocative or fabulous

I also record the title of the discussion, the prompt, the date, and the totals of each student's responses. I often add a crude little graph that plots how many students engaged in how many responses and add little observations, like 10 percent of the class engaged in 50 percent of the discussion, or 15 percent of the responses used quotes to back up what they said. I take particular care not to set quantitative goals for the students or the class as whole, because this information is to help shape reflective thinking on their individual and collective goals—not to articulate goals. This approach gives each student collective and personalized evidence and data on their contributions during the roundtable discussion. The day after a discussion, students hand in their preparation templates (see the appendix at the end of this chapter) and their reflections on how the discussion went for them individually and collectively. When I return the material, I attach a scoring guide grounded in Common Core Standards and a copy of the roundtable class record. See tables 9.2, 9.3, and 9.4 for examples of individualized scoring guides.

TABLE 9.2   Roundtable discussion scoring guide and student feedback for
Common Core Standard 9-10 1a

Approaching standard	Meets standard	Exceeds standard
• Partial completion and/or use of template for reflection • Partial engagement of goals in actual roundtable discussion • Responses, questions, or comments are not fully developed • Imbalance of response to preparation For example, "Shane, it was clear that you had a lot to say, and there are many examples in the text to corroborate your ideas. Your template was barely used, and completing it would have benefited your contributions."	• Full preparation for roundtable discussion to address literature, questions, and personal goals • Reference to preparation to formulate questions, to support and clarify ideas, and to persuade	

By the end of the semester, students will have had six to eight official round-tables. They will also have preparation templates, record sheets, and reflections from all of those discussion to track their own individual goals as well as whole-class collaboration. Drawing from these documents, students can get a clear picture of what individually works for them well and what doesn't when it comes to collaborative learning.

For me, this endeavor is constantly evolving. I was always told, "You can't assess classroom discussions. It's too subjective. There are too many moving parts. It's too hard!" I agree with only part of this protest. I can and do assess

TABLE 9.3 Roundtable discussion scoring guide and student feedback for Common Core Standard 9-10 1c

Approaching standard	Meets standard	Exceeds standard
• Repeats ideas or questions without further development • Disjoints fluency of discussion • Muddles others • Faulty logic in challenge • Only dips into discussion without committing to ideas	• Pose and respond to provocative questions • Relate a current discussion to a broader theme • Contribute to the flow of a discussion by listening well and responding appropriately For example, "Ruby, in light of your reflection and contributions in the roundtable discussion, it's clear that you not only posed a number of provocative questions, but also listened well enough to others to have their ideas influence the direction of your own."	

discussions. The assessment is not subjective if I provide kids with the tools, skills, and models they need to improve. There *are* a lot of moving parts, just as any other authentic task should have. Yes, the assessment is hard, but most things worth learning are hard. This is part of the reason why I have spent years trying to design a systematic way to instruct and assess how students use communication to create better understanding. Just this past semester, while I was discussing the process with a mentor and fabulous editor, it occurred to us that were I to make a PDF of the record sheet of that day's roundtable discussion, the students would have immediate access to relatively quantified data regarding their performance to better inform their reflections. It is definitely something new and worth trying in the fall.

TABLE 9.4   Roundtable discussion scoring guide and student feedback for
Common Core Standard 9-10 1d

Approaching standard	Meets standard	Exceeds standard
• Rigidity to challenging perspectives • Faulty summary of points to agree or disagree • Inability to articulate rationale for views • Debate trounces discussion	• Respond thoughtfully to diverse perspectives • Summarize points of agreement and/or disagreement • Qualify own views • Relate new connections in light of new perspective	For example, "Josh, even though you didn't talk about the huge shifts in thinking in the roundtable discussion, your reflection shows how much our discussion changed your ideas about Macbeth's own culpability in his own downfall. Way to be open and use the process!"

Revision Spirals

As the last four weeks of the semester loom large, students have accumulated a great deal of writing and have increased their ability to productively self-assess and to identify strategies that work with their interests and emergent styles as writers. Each student has a clear running commentary to account for the five to six pieces of on-demand writing he or she has completed and at least two revisions based on these. This process allows each student to knowledgeably advocate for his or her own strengths and challenges as a formal writer.

The students will also have three drafts in varying degrees of completion of formal literary thesis papers based on the literature we read over the first part of the course. By the time we get to *Siddhartha*, most students have created one full first draft based a thesis map produced from their double-entry journals. Once all three drafts or prewrites are done, it's time to choose which one the students would like to bring to standards.

The act of reflecting and choosing is important. I meet with the students to discuss which of the three drafts they have chosen and why they have chosen it. Students are coming at this final revision from many entry points. The kids have all done some version of a draft, and each version has been scored using a rubric or scoring guide that is also their final rubric for the task in the end. This feedback is important for consistency and continuity of process. The literary thesis paper rubric or scoring guide has four Common Core Standards that my department and I have set up in a taxonomy spiral that supports the comprehension, prewriting, drafting, and conventional aspects of formal writing. Basically, if a student does not understand what he or she reads, we cannot expect the student to be ready for the next standard. If another student cannot articulate a thesis or find appropriate quotes, this is the moment for a conference rather than asking him or her to write draft without direction. This scaffolding also allows for generally thematic and personalized feedback over the course of the three drafts to identify individual strengths and challenges.

Even though this may seem like a lot of juggling, when students actively use their writing folders, organization follows. It can be relatively easy for kids to retrieve, reflect, and choose and create individualized revision plans in light of all that we've already done with the on-demand writing revisions. Like the gears in any mechanism or the human beings that create a classroom culture, the consistency of practice, feedback, reflection, choice, and tools makes the writing process truly student centered.

The Final Roundtable Discussion: How Does Storytelling Inform Our Lives?

I have found that offering students a shared sense of closure and learning that will go far beyond sophomore English is the key to ending the course effectively. As a class, we started out with a great essential question and have grown together through numerous texts, tools, protocols, and other processes. Now the time has come to reflect deeply on how the students' experiences in the class will help them come up with a shared, yet personalized answer to our essential question. To prepare, I have students do three things. First, they need to review all the texts we have read and all the writing they have done to make concrete connections to how the stories we have studied have informed our own process in class. Then, I will ask them to conduct one final elder interview, where they will recap their initial interview and discussion and review those answers through the lens of what they've learned since. Finally, I have them watch Tim Burton's masterpiece, *Big Fish*, which they usually adore. The film was especially well received a recent class, in which a fair number of the boys had experienced challenges in communicating with their fathers.[6]

In many ways, the story of the character Edward Bloom in *Big Fish* and his use of storytelling, sense of fate, need for experience, ambition, and humorous embellishment strike meaningful connections to all of the texts we've studied. Yet, because Edward and Will are ostensibly just "regular" people in a modern American era, those themes, criteria for tragedy, and the power of storytelling and relationships tend to resonate especially well with sophomore brains and hearts. The viewing gives students one more fresh platform from which to think, but also offers enough connections that it can pull in the other three texts quite nicely. For their final roundtable, students are encouraged to pull from interviews, texts, on-demand tasks, and anything else they deem valid enough to bring into what ends up being the most orbital discussion yet. Consider these student comments:

> "It's so weird how these wicked old stories like Oedipus and Macbeth are still relevant. I guess part of what I've learned is that really good stories do two things—they connect you to a specific place and time in history, but are also about what is universal and what will never change. I really like that."

> "What I liked best was how Sid and Vasudeva both knew that wisdom was incommunicable, yet we know that Govinda really understood that Sid had reached enlightenment at the end with the kiss. It was metaphoric and it had to be. Hesse could never have explained that exchange in an expository way that wouldn't sound totally stupid. It had to come naturally from the story itself. I think that this is why telling stories is so important, by using stories to teach—you can communicate incommunicable wisdom and experience."

> "It's the same with Edward and Will. Edward couldn't stand dying a regular old normal death and he needed Will to 'pick up the torch' and tell his death story to him like it was a huge party by the river even though it never really was. By doing this, Will finally understood that Edward told stories to communicate his perspective and love of life, not to deceive anyone."

Toward the end of the class period, I kept an eye on the time to make sure we have enough time to do a classroom whip, where everyone gets one last say on how each felt that storytelling has informed his or her life. Responses vary, but there was one lasting theme that I know each student will take far beyond this classroom, and no one could have said it better than Thomas: "It seems to me that if we give stories enough time, thought, and telling, they will reveal to us how hard and worthwhile it is to try to become fully human."

THE FINAL EXAM: REFLECTION, EVIDENCE, AND STRATEGIES

I give students two to three weeks' lead time to review, prepare, and choose evidence for their final exam. Their task is to review their own personal trajectory, struggles, and improvement through the tools and protocols of the class and to write four essays on reading, writing, speaking, and listening. The essays need to document, with evidence from their own work, not only improvement, but identified personal strategies they will take with them well beyond this class.

To get started, I offer them a model essay and time in and outside of class to confer with me through the process. We also go over *everything* we did in class—the texts, double-entry journals, elder interviews, on-demand writing, revisions, vocabulary, literary thesis papers, roundtable discussions, independent reading, small-group work, and lectures. This listing is very important. Sophomores tend to live in the moment, and getting them to appreciate the heft of their own investment can prove challenging. I make it a very big deal and talk to them about how proud I am of them and highlight moments that I've collected about each student and share these moments aloud with the class. It's a little sentimental and a little hokey, but they get the clear sense that the class is ending and here is the last chance to really finish fabulously. I also make it a point to tell students that even if what they got out of the class wasn't specifically academic, if they feel as though it was bona fide learning and it has evidence, then by all means, they should write about it! I then hand them back what have by now become very fat writing folders so that the kids can begin to sift through the small mountains of data.

IT NEVER REALLY ENDS

Through my practice, I have come to appreciate the power of how literacy, storytelling, and the writing process inform academic and personal efficacy. Even though my methods are solidly grounded in rigorous expectations and standards, they are only truly successful when tempered with a great dose of humor, forgiveness, and the offering of practical, resilient tools with which students can own their own process, thoughts, and feelings. It is a process of creating meaning that, thankfully, never really ends for my students and certainly not for me. Becoming increasingly human is very hard, very worthwhile work. Work well.

Roundtable Discussion Template

Personal goals for this roundtable discussion: _____

_____

Literature discussed: _____

_____

Roundtable topic, guiding question, or motif: _____

_____

Formulate two provocative how and why questions that you think will inform this discussion. (Note: Just because you do not ask your question, you can still react to similar questions that others pose!)

Question:	Notes on class reaction:
1.	
2.	

Choose and paraphrase three relevant quotes and inferences (can be bulleted!) to share in the discussion. (Note: Again, even if you do not share your specific quote or inference, you can still take notes on similar themes or thoughts.)

Page number and quotation	Inference and notes to self	Notes on class reaction
1.		
2.		
3.		

TONIGHT: REFLECTION!

Self-reflect on how the roundtable went for you in terms of the following criteria. You may write the reflection here or attach another page. Paragraphs should be three to seven sentences each.

First paragraph: Describe how you did individually. Did you meet your goal? What evidence can you cite that you did meet it, or what got in the way?

Second paragraph: How did the class do as a whole? For example, did a few students dominate, or was it a discussion rather than a debate?

Third paragraph: Offer suggestions to make the class dynamic more inclusive and thought-provoking.

Fourth paragraph: Describe how your thinking has been supported, qualified, or refuted by the roundtable.

CONCLUSION

"Yet"

BILL NAVE

How many times do you remember seeing that little word *yet* in the chapters? The teachers are not done perfecting their practice *yet*. The students have not mastered all they need to learn to succeed in school and in life *yet*. You have not decided how to respond to what you've read here *yet*. We hope we have intrigued and inspired you to think deeply about how you will respond beyond merely saying to yourself, "My, those teachers sure are doing some interesting things with their students."

The introduction made a statement that I repeated for emphasis: the nine teachers whose classroom portraits are included in the book began their careers as ordinary teachers, but as you have seen, somewhere along the way, they made a commitment to become more student centered, and in doing so, they became extraordinary. The events that catalyzed their change of direction varied, from subtle to profound. For Suzen Polk-Hoffses, it was the Peace Corps guest speaker. For Mary Graziano-Glynn, it was reading the research on how poverty affects students' ability to learn in the traditional school setting. For Shelly Moody and Cynthia Raymond, it was engaging in the Reinventing Schools Coalition training. For Susan Carpenter O'Brien, it was the course on bringing the sea into the classroom. For Karen MacDonald, it was the Outward Bound camping retreat. For Shannon Shanning, it was the email invitation from the principal. For Alana Margeson, it was the poster that read "People First, Things Second." And for Christiane Cullens, it was a simple question from a student, "What exactly is the point of it all?"

WHAT'S COMMON ACROSS THESE CLASSROOMS

You no doubt have some impressions of the several commonalities across the nine classrooms. You may also be a bit surprised that a laser-like focus on academic learning above all else is not one of the commonalities. Recall Suzen's three R's—she had her own three R's, and as a result of that powerful memory, she became "the teacher who would focus on academics, with an understanding that . . . students' home life does affect their learning."

These teachers build relationships and supportive classroom cultures. They know their students well and attend to social-emotional growth in addition to academic growth. The teachers support student voice and choice, which fosters agency, autonomy, and authentic learning. Students know that their teachers care about them, not in some abstract way, but personally.

Relationships

Remember what Mary said at the end of the story about Brent, the eleven-year-old runner:

> "Brent might be just one student, but I shared his story because he is just one example of what I do with all of my twenty-plus students each year. I build relationships first. Once the relationships are built, the academics fall into place."

Others commented explicitly about the importance of building relationships:

> "As their teacher, I consider it critical to establish a strong relationship with every student and her or his family. Family relationships and communication are important ways to improve student learning." (Susan)

> "My job is to build relationships with students, parents, colleagues, administrators, and community members, all in an effort to support student learning. Above all, students must trust the teacher. If they know I will support and nurture them, they are willing to come along with me on the journey." (Karen)

Classroom Culture

A classroom culture does not just emerge organically for these teachers. They consciously and carefully create the culture at the very beginning of the year.

Answers to the question "What does the ideal classroom look like, sound like, and feel like?" emerge from these nine teachers' chapters:

> "The routines we create together at the beginning of the year lay the foundation for the students to be self-guided and engaged during our work times all through the year." (Shelly)
>
> "If I want to build a community of caring, responsible children and help each of them develop a sense of agency, I need to remember that I'm only one piece of the puzzle. There are still twenty-five-plus other pieces joining me, and *together*, we have to make the community our own." (Mary)
>
> "Ultimately, however, we were creating a culture of trust and investment. When students invest in the teacher and the class, the children are more likely to invest in themselves." (Shannon)
>
> "Along with my colleagues, my job is to create and nurture a classroom culture that encourages all of us to treat each other with respect." (Karen)

Knowing Students Deeply

Christiane explained that many student experiences in her complex suite of activities are designed to support her "Sherlocking" the students, that is, getting to know them deeply so that she can tailor the classroom assignments to move each of her students individually along the ambitious learning continuum that she plans for them. Others describe their Sherlocking metaphorically or more directly:

> "Each child is a story, one that I have to read and study and learn about. No story is the same, yet I am a character in each of them, a character that has many roles. I am a teacher, a coach, a role model, a cheerleader, and an advocate." (Mary)
>
> "I learn what motivates them, what topics they are passionate about, and what their current aspirations are for their future. All of this informs

my decisions about the topics I can suggest to them later for research projects, for example." (Cindy)

"While the students participated in these [ice-breaker] activities, we took careful notes. We were able to identify student interests and strengths, as well as areas that were a challenge for each student." (Shannon)

Whole Child, Social-Emotional Growth

Mary's description of one aspect of her "whole-heart teaching" describes what's explicit or implied in each of the classrooms you've visited through these pages.

"I am always searching for new ways to make learning meaningful and relevant to each of my kids. I view each student as a whole child, and I understand that not only do they have academic needs but they have social and emotional needs as well. I know that if any of them is struggling socially or emotionally, then an academic struggle is inevitable. I can't possibly teach my students every fact there is to know, but I can show them just how much potential they possess and how very valuable that potential is."

Caring

My first teaching job was in a large intermediate school (grades 6 to 8, around fifteen hundred students) in the Ocean Hill–Brownsville section of Brooklyn, New York. At that time, the school department had created three small sub-districts as local-control pilot projects to see if neighborhood-based governance could lead to better learning outcomes for students. About half of the newly constituted faculty consisted of veteran African American teachers who transferred there from other parts of the city, and the other half was a motley collection of young white teachers who were committed to "the Cause," as we called it. I still vividly recall a stern lecture from one of the veteran teachers, addressing us white teachers: "We don't need you to love our children. We can love our children. We need you to teach our children." I knew what had prompted these impassioned comments because I had heard some of my white colleagues saying that their students needed love. But I also knew in my core that unless my students knew I cared, they would not be motivated to learn. This belief is also evident throughout these nine chapters in the words of the teachers:

> "I remember the advice from a mentor and team teacher early in my career: 'Treat your students kindly as though you are all they have. Some days, you will be.'" (Alana)

> "I want my students to feel cared for and valued by all the important people in their world." (Susan)

> "The students can see and, more importantly, can *feel* that I care about them and that I am committed to helping them become successful learners." (Cynthia)

> "Yet, the more I teach, the more I understand that students need to know that I care about them as individuals and that I want to be in the class-room to help them succeed. How can I expect my students to want to be in my classroom if I don't make them feel welcome?" (Alana)

Choice, Voice, Developing Agency

Shelly instituted a special thirty-minute block of time at the end of each day; during this time, students selected a weekly focus. Some did research on a topic that interested them. Some worked on mastering a learning goal that had so far eluded them. But however they used that target time each week, the choice was entirely theirs. To them, it became an almost-sacred time that they were unwilling to give up. Their commitment to target time is an indicator of the degree to which the experience enhanced their sense of academic agency.

Suzen's students chose which signs of spring to record when they went outside with their iPads. Mary's students chose which health and wellness topics they wanted to become experts in for their health and wellness fair for the community. Cindy's students chose how they demonstrated their mastery of learning targets:

> "I have learned that in my student-centered classroom, *voice and choice* are vital to engage learners. I encourage my students to follow their passions and delve deeply into what interests them. In addition, the students have a choice in how they show what they know. They use a variety of media

to present their knowledge, for example, through essays, skits, videos, blogs, demonstrations, debates, posters, and podcasts." (Cindy)

WHAT ARE YOUR NEXT STEPS?

We wonder—what events have catalyzed your interest in improving learning outcomes for students? We know you have that interest because you took the time to read this book. We would like to act as an additional catalyst by posing some questions and making some suggestions for simple things you might do to get started.

For Teachers

Which of the student-centered strategies or practices that you read about do you already do in your classroom? Which ones do you plan to try next? We encourage you to pick out one that feels as if it might work with your students and to try it out. When Shannon was visiting classrooms last year as a member of the Teacher of the Year selection team, she took pages and pages of notes on the strategies she was observing. She tried out many of the strategies she had seen when she returned to her classroom. Some worked, and some didn't work so well. She had been trying one strategy for a couple of weeks, when one day, she finally stopped midsentence in class, looked at her students, and said, "This isn't working, is it?" They all laughed and gave Shannon a resounding "No!" We invite you to have the courage to try some of the strategies with your students and see how the approaches fit. In fact, be fully transparent with your students, and ask them to help you pick out a student-centered strategy to try—this in itself is a student-centered strategy!

Reach out and share the student-centered strategies you're using and that you know work with your students. Invite colleagues to come and observe. Look around your school. Who among your colleagues is also doing student-centered kinds of things? Ask if you could sit in and observe, and then invite this colleague to observe you as you try out something you saw in his or her room.

Pass this book on to a colleague, or better yet, organize a book group and read this book together for the purpose of supporting each other in becoming more student-centered in your classrooms. In short, embrace student-centered teaching, steal strategies, and continue to tweak your own.

For Parents

If your child's teacher has not already done so, work to create an open line of communication. Ask how you can best support your child's learning as a partner with the teacher. Ask to meet with the principal, and bring a copy of this book with you. Ask the principal how she or he supports student-centered teaching in the school. If the response is a bit fuzzy, loan this book and ask to meet again in a week.

For Principals

Reflect on how you create and support a culture that encourages the kind of student-centered teaching you see in these pages. Perhaps you could take the suggestion we made to the teachers and use some of the school's professional development time to read and discuss this book and talk about how you as a staff could move the whole school in the direction of robust student-centered teaching. If you have not already done so this year, spend some time in each teacher's classroom and develop a catalog of the student-centered practices you see. Provide a framework for your teachers to observe those strategies in each other's classrooms. Teachers thrive in a school that is teacher centered in the same way that classrooms are student centered—that is, the whole staff working collegially for the benefit of all the students.[1]

For Superintendents

In some ways, our suggestions are like a set of nested Ukrainian dolls. Identify how you create and support a culture among administrators and teachers that encourages what you have read in these pages. What aspects of your district might be hindering movement in this direction, and how might you and your team begin to move those barriers? For example, do your principals and teachers experience such pressure to improve student scores on standardized tests that the culture is one of single-minded test prep that leaves no room for teachers to implement any of the student-centered strategies you read here? Students in the classrooms featured in this book show improvement in test scores, and it's not due to time spent on test-prep activities.

For School Board Members

Resolve to invite all members of the board to read this book and then talk about its implications on the kinds of policy decisions that consume your meeting time. Discuss with your administrators how the district can work toward providing all students with experiences like those in the classrooms described here. For example, has your district created a schedule that provides time for teachers to observe each other's classrooms or to plan together in designing student-centered strategies for their particular students? Does your community seem to believe that if your teachers are not in the classroom all the time, then they're not working—not doing the job they were hired to do? Have you worked with your administrators to create a teacher evaluation framework that includes a commitment to increase the frequency of student-centered strategies in your classrooms?

For University Professors in Schools of Education

Redouble your efforts with your preservice teachers to give them the desire to implement student-centered teaching when they have their own classrooms. Ensure that these teachers have access to the experiences during their practicum and student teaching time to observe quality student-centered teaching.

For Preservice Teachers

Reflect on the experiences that led you to teaching, and embrace them. Let your wide and varied experience inform your professional personhood. Find a mentor or, better yet, several mentors—official or unofficial—as you begin your first teaching job, and stick with them over time. Answer Shannon's question: "I would dare to ask teachers, 'How will you choose to lead?' I also ask, 'What will be your legacy in education, for your classroom, and for your students?' I already know mine." Keep Shannon's metaphor of the race in mind, and keep that finish-line vision of becoming highly skilled at student-centered teaching, even though you know you are still in the first mile.

For Legislators and Other Policymakers

Spend time in classrooms, not just for a brief visit, but for a day. At the end of the day, ask the teachers about their most pressing challenges as they work to assure that *every* student learns to her or his potential. Then ask them what kinds of policies might help them to meet those challenges.

For Taxpayers and the Rest of the Public

Attend a school board meeting. Ask the board members how they are supporting student-centered teaching in your district. If they don't seem to know what you mean, ask them to read this book or other books on student-centered learning like *Anytime, Anywhere.*[2] Find opportunities to create meaningful bridges with teachers and students in the form of mentorships, internships, or volunteering. Seek out ways to maximize the capacity of schools to be community centers.

THE FINAL WORD, OR PERHAPS THE START OF YOUR RUN

We are born with an innate drive to learn. Schools can support that drive or squelch it, and we've all had experience of both during our time in school. The portraits of classrooms that you have read here provide powerful examples of how student-centered teaching supports our innate drive to learn. Please, please, commit to do your part in helping to make that experience more and more universal for students in every corner of the country. To rephrase Shannon's question: What will be your legacy in this challenge?

Introduction

1. Maine Revised Statutes, Title 20-A, Chapter 207-A, Section 4722-A.
2. Maine Department of Education, *Learning Results: Parameters for Essential Instruction*, Regulation 132, 2007, www.maine.gov/education/lres/pei/ch132-2007.pdf.
3. Ibid.
4. Rebecca E. Wolfe, Adria Steinberg, and Nancy Hoffman, eds., *Anytime, Anywhere: Student-Centered Learning for Schools and Teachers* (Cambridge, MA: Harvard Education Press, 2013).
5. Ibid.
6. Ibid.
7. Shannon's Shanning's special education class was in a very small room, and furthermore, we did not want to upset the delicate cultural balance that she had established and that my presence may have precipitated (chapter 7).
8. Wolfe, Steinberg, and Hoffman, *Anytime, Anywhere*.

Chapter 1

1. Aleksei Tolstoi, *The Great Big Enormous Turnip* (Danbury, CT: Franklin Watts, 1969).

Chapter 2

1. Timothy Rasinski, *The Fluent Reader* (New York: Scholastic, 2003).
2. Johann Goethe, as quoted in Justin Pikunas, *Human Development: A Science of Growth* (New York: McGraw Hill, 1961).
3. Sean Covey, *The 7 Habits of Happy Kids* (New York: Simon and Schuster, 2008).
4. Lisa McCourt, *Chicken Soup for Little Souls: The Goodness Gorillas* (Deerfield Beach, FL: Health Communications, 1997).
5. The students did not know that the letter was from me.

6. They also didn't know that this project addressed the curriculum topic of human body systems or the standard of informational writing.
7. *Bed-to-bed stories* is a term we use. It means the students write about every boring detail that happened to them from the time they wake up until the time they go to bed, with no real meat or focus.
8. Irene C. Fountas and Gay Su Pinnell, *The Fountas & Pinnell Benchmark Assessment System* (Portsmouth, NH: Heinemann, 2010).

Chapter 3

1. Maya Angelou, quoted in Bob Kelly, *Worth Repeating: More than 5,000 Classic and Contemporary Quotes* (Grand Rapids, MI: Kregel Publications, 2003), 263.
2. Richard A. DeLorenzo et al., *Delivering on the Promise: The Education Revolution* (Bloomington, IN: Solution Tree Press, 2009).
3. Dr. Suess, *Oh, the Places You'll Go* (New York: Random House, 1960).
4. Charles Schwahn and Beatrice McGarvey, *Inevitable: Mass Customized Learning; Learning in the Age of Empowerment* (Amazon: CreateSpace Independent Publishing Platform, 2012).
5. Carol S. Dweck, *Mindset: The New Psychology of Success* (New York: Ballantine Books, 2006).
6. Pearson Education, "Developmental Reading Assessment, 2nd Edition PLUS (DRA2+)," Pearson Instructional Resources, accessed December 2014, www.pearsonschool.com/index.cfm?locator=PSZ4Z4&PMDbProgramId=23661&prognav=po.

Chapter 4

1. Roger Bybee, *Achieving Scientific Literacy: From Purposes to Practices* (Portsmouth, NH: Greenwood Publishing Group, 1997); Arthur Eisenkraft, "Expanding the 5E Model," *NSTA WebNews Digest*, August 15, 2003.
2. Jean Fritz and Tomie DePaola, *Can't You Make Them Behave, King George?* (New York: Coward, McCann & Geoghegan, 1977).
3. Scholastic News Staff, "A Case for Equality," *Scholastic News*, February 17, 2014, edition 5/6, 4–5.
4. Scholastic News Staff, "Malala's Dream," *Scholastic News*, November 11, 2013, edition 5/6, 4–5.
5. Myra Sadker and David Sadker, *Failing at Fairness: How Our Schools Cheat Girls* (Toronto: Simon and Schuster, 1994).
6. David Sortino, "When Boys Get More Classroom Attention than Girls," *Santa Rosa (CA) Press Democrat Blog*, December 13, 2012, http://davidsortino.blogs.pressdemocrat.com/10161/when-boys-get-more-classroom-attention-than-girls/.

7. Valerie E. Lee, Helen M. Marks, and Tina Byrd, "Sexism in Single-Sex and Coeducational Independent Secondary School Classrooms," *Sociology of Education* 67 (1994): 92–120.

Chapter 5

1. Melba Beals, *Warriors Don't Cry: Searing Memoir of Battle to Integrate Little Rock* (New York: Simon and Schuster, 1995).
2. Walter Dean Myers, *Malcolm X: By Any Means Necessary* (New York: Scholastic, 1994); Walter Dean Myers, *The Greatest: Muhammad Ali* (New York: Scholastic, 2000).
3. National Governors Association Center for Best Practices, and Council of Chief State School Officers, *Common Core State Standards for English Language Arts and Literacy in History/Social Studies, Science, and Technical Subjects* (Washington, DC: NGA Center and CCSSO, 2010).

Chapter 6

1. National Governors Association Center for Best Practices, and Council of Chief State School Officers, *Common Core State Standards for English Language Arts and Literacy in History/Social Studies, Science, and Technical Subjects* (Washington, DC: NGA Center and CCSSO, 2010).
2. Robert Marzano and John S. Kendall, *The New Taxonomy of Educational Objectives* (Thousand Oaks, CA: Corwin Press, 2007).
3. National Governors Association Center for Best Practices & Council of Chief State School Officers. (2010). *Common Core State Standards.*
4. National Governors Association Center for Best Practices, and Council of Chief State School Officers, *Common Core State Standards.*

Chapter 7

1. National Governors Association Center for Best Practices, and Council of Chief State School Officers, *Common Core State Standards for English Language Arts and Literacy in History/Social Studies, Science, and Technical Subjects* (Washington, DC: NGA Center and CCSSO, 2010).
2. Ibid.
3. For these assessment instruments, see www.aimsweb.com; www.nwea.org; www.measuredprogress.org/necap.

Chapter 8

1. Teaching Channel, "Pinwheel Discussions: Texts in Conversation," accessed December 2014, www.teachingchannel.org/videos/high-school-literature-lesson-plan; Teaching Channel, "AP English Lesson Plan: Pinwheel Discussion," accessed December 2014, www.teachingchannel.org/videos/ap-english-lesson-plan.
2. Janet Allen, "Plugged-In to Reading Series," Stenhouse Publishers, accessed December 2014, www.janetallen.org/Plugged-in_to_Reading.php.
3. F. Scott Fitzgerald, *The Great Gatsby* (New York: Scribner's, 1925).

Chapter 9

1. National Governors Association Center for Best Practices, and Council of Chief State School Officers, *Common Core State Standards for English Language Arts and Literacy in History/Social Studies, Science, and Technical Subjects* (Washington, DC: NGA Center and CCSSO, 2010).
2. Dudley Fitts and Robert Fitzgerald, trans., *Sophocles, the Oedipus Cycle* (New York: Harcourt, 1977); S. H. Butcher, trans., *Aristotle, Poetics* (New York: Hill and Wang, 1960).
3. Barbara A. Mowat and Paul Werstine, eds., *Macbeth*, by William Shakespeare (New York: Simon and Schuster Paperbacks, 2009).
4. Hermann Hesse, *Siddhartha*, trans. Hilda Rosner (New York: Bantam Books, 1971).
5. Michael White et al., *Monty Python and the Holy Grail* (Burbank, CA: Columbia TriStar Home Entertainment, 2001).
6. Richard D. Zanuck et al., *Big Fish* (Culver City, CA: Columbia TriStar Home Entertainment, 2004).

Conclusion

1. Rebecca E. Wolfe, Adria Steinberg, and Nancy Hoffman, eds., *Anytime Anywhere: Student-Centered Learning for Schools and Teachers* (Cambridge, MA: Harvard Education Press, 2013).
2. Ibid.

Bill Nave, EdD, is a program evaluation and research consultant living in Winthrop, Maine. From 1968 to 1993, he taught science to students in New York and Maine in grades 6 through 12 and created programs for at-risk students and high school dropouts. He was selected as Maine's 1990 Teacher of the Year, was a finalist for National Teacher of the Year, and received a Milken Educator Award for his work in the River Valley School for dropouts. Since completing his doctorate at the Harvard Graduate School of Education in 2000, he has conducted program evaluations of teacher professional development programs and curriculum development programs, among others, with a primary focus on science and math programs.

Christiane Cullens, MSEd, NBCT, teaches English to sophomores, juniors, and seniors at Mount Desert Island High School in Bar Harbor, Maine. From 1998 to the present, she has collaborated and mentored with colleagues and the community to create meaningful and effective curricula to meet a wide spectrum of student need. She was selected as a semifinalist for the 2014 Maine Teacher of the Year and is most currently an active advocate for student-centered learning within a standards-based model. Christiane is also working to support the implementation of restorative justice practices throughout her school and district.

Mary Graziano-Glynn, BS, currently teaches fourth grade at the Hartland Consolidated School in Hartland, Maine. She has taught elementary students in kindergarten through grade four since 2001. Mary was a finalist for the 2014 Maine Teacher of the Year. Mary's passion is literacy instruction with a goal for her students to be ahead of grade level by the time they leave her classroom. She also provides afterschool drama experiences and running experiences for students in her school. Her colleagues look to Mary for leadership as the school works to implement a fully proficiency-based system of instruction and a new teacher evaluation framework.

Karen MacDonald, BA, MS, NBCT, teaches English language arts to students in a grade six and seven loop at King Middle School in Portland, Maine. She has a Maine English Language Learner endorsement, which is important because students in her school speak more than twenty languages. Karen has taught in Portland since 1979, and she was one of the first teachers to implement the Expeditionary Learning model of student-centered teaching when King Middle School adopted the model in the early 1990s. She plays an active leadership role in the national Expeditionary Learning Network. Karen was selected as Maine's 2014 Teacher of the Year.

Alana M. Margeson, BS, MSEd, teaches English to sophomores and juniors and AP English to seniors, as well as an assortment of elective courses at Caribou High School in Caribou, Maine. She has taught since 2000, beginning with middle school special education and eighth-grade English language arts, math, and social studies. She moved to the high school in 2005. For a number of years, Alana has written for colleague Janet Allen's *Plugged-in to Reading* and *Plugged-in to Non-Fiction* literacy series. Alana received the University of Maine at Presque Isle Distinguished Alumni Award in 2012 and was named Maine Teacher of the Year for 2012.

Shelly Moody, MEd, is an upper elementary teacher at the Williams Elementary School in Oakland, Maine. During the past fifteen years, she has taught third, fourth and fifth grade, as well as a fourth and fifth multigrade classroom. In 2004, Shelly earned her master's degree in literacy from the University of Maine with a literacy specialist certification. In addition to her work in the classroom, Shelly enjoys leading professional development trainings with pre-service and veteran teachers across the state focused on proficiency-based education and differentiated instruction. She is currently working as an instructional coach supporting new teachers in their implementation of a standards-based, student-centered learning environment. Shelly was Maine's 2011 Teacher of the Year.

Susan Carpenter O'Brien, BS, MEd, currently teaches fifth grade at the George B. Weatherbee School in Hampden, Maine. She has taught fifth grade for the majority of her thirty-four years in teaching. Sue was a semifinalist for the 2014 Maine Teacher of the Year. Her passion is science, and she uses that passion to engage her students in learning all subjects. The fifty-five-gallon saltwater aquarium in her classroom never fails to engage student interest. Sue has established unique outreach partnerships with several science and environmental-based organizations to bring hands-on, real-life educational opportunities to her elementary school students. These experiences help her students learn the kinds of environmental stewardship that is essential to preserve our natural world.

Suzen Polk-Hoffses, MEd, is an elementary education teacher living in Jonesport, Maine. She served from 1991 to 1993 in the Peace Corps in Paraguay as an early childhood educator. Upon her return to the United States, she worked for five years as a Head Start teacher in rural Maine. Since 2000, she has been teaching kindergarten in a rural K–8 elementary school on the Downeast coast. She is actively involved in issues of poverty and its impact on education, in promoting the importance of early childhood education, and in closing the opportunity gap in student learning. Suzen has been instrumental in establishing the Comienza en Casa program to provide school readiness skills in the home via the use of iPads and monthly parent meetings that are held at her school.

Cynthia Raymond, BS, is currently a middle school English language arts teacher who lives in Augusta, Maine. Cindy taught in a sixth-grade self-contained classroom on the coast starting in 1983 before returning to her hometown in 1989 to teach at the Hall-Dale Middle School in Farmingdale, Maine. She has taught here ever since, including math, remedial reading, social studies, and English language arts. In 2014, Cindy was a semifinalist in Maine's Teacher of the Year program. As she embarks on her thirty-first year of teaching, her core values remain the same: education must be tailored to meet every student's needs by honoring the student's strengths, interests, and preferred learning style.

Shannon Shanning, BS, teaches special education at Whittier Middle School in Poland, Maine. She has been teaching special education students since 2001, first in grades 4 through 6 at Poland Community School and then at the newly consolidated Whittier Middle School when it first opened just down the road in 2010. Shannon works to provide her students with opportunities to make connections with the community, while simultaneously encouraging community members to actively engage with their local schools. For example, she established a partnership with the local fire department to create the MidKnight Fire Slayer Program. The students visit the firehouse weekly to learn about firefighting, safety skills, and good citizenship.

INDEX

academic achievement, 103, 129, 130, 162, 165

academic growth, 78

academic language, 119

acceleration, 141

accomplishments, celebrating, 125–127, 162

accountability, 45

achievement gap, 15

actionable feedback, 189–191

active learning, 20–22

affinity diagram, 64

agency, 7, 40, 239–240

Aimsweb, 159, 163

alternative programs, creation of, 4–5

Anytime, Anywhere, 6–8

assessments
of achievement, 103, 129, 130, 164, 231
NWEA, 78, 139
prior knowledge and, 68–69

at-risk students, 4

authentic work, 117–123, 128–129, 204, 212

back-to-school anxiety, 152–153

benchmarks, 162, 165–167

blogging, 146

book clubs, 115–117

boredom, 209

boys, attention given to, 104–106

Burnt Island Lighthouse, 89–92

capacity matrix, 141, 142–143

career paths, 28–29

caring, 238–239

Casco Bay High School, 5

celebrations of learning, 125–127, 162

check-in points, 121

choices, 50–52, 117, 141, 207, 239–240

Civil Rights Movement, 109–110, 115

classroom
as community, 38, 57, 62, 140–141, 199–201
culture, 62–67, 102–103, 130–131, 135–136, 139–141, 157, 180–181, 237
discussions, 139, 221–231, 233–234
happy habits for, 40–46
learning outside of, 24–32, 89–94, 192–195
norms, 209
observations, 9–10
use of technology in, 17–20, 145–148
Web sites, 141, 143

collaboration, 41, 76–77, 115–117, 120–122, 157, 171–172, 195–198

Common Core Standards, 110, 116, 141, 148, 153–154, 158–159, 162–163, 207, 208, 223

communication, 100–101, 116–117, 148
community
    classroom as, 38–40, 57, 62, 140–141,
        199–201
    learning, 112–114
    support from, 29–30
community meetings, 114
community service, 4
compassion, 41, 46, 49
confidence, 128
constructive critiquing, 46
cooperation, 64–65, 135–136, 138
coteaching, 154–178, 195–198
course objectives, mastery of, 3
credit by appointment, 3
credit by objective, 3
crew groups, 112–113
culminating events, 123–127
current events lessons, 96–98
curriculum
    flexibility in, 2
    maps, 154

daily planning matrix, 133–135, 139
daily work flow chart, 141, 144
deficit model, 16
digital natives, 145–146
domino effect, 173–177
double-entry journals, 207, 218–221
dynamic learning, 188

Edmodo, 164
efficiency, 141
elder interviews, 212–214
email communication, 100–101
emotional growth, 46–49, 238
empathy, 41
empowerment, 38, 43, 52, 69–71
encouragement, 169–170

engagement, 8, 18, 38, 73–75, 82–83,
    98–99, 118, 133, 198
English language learners, 16, 109, 111,
    120
essential questions, 210–211
Expeditionary Learning model,
    111–131

Fakebook, 146
families, relationship building with,
    100–101, 113, 128
family dinners, 4
family responsibilities, 3
feedback
    actionable, 189–191
    formative, 188, 198–199
    from interviewees, 122–123
    loops, 66–67
    mechanism for, 184
    respectful, 130
    from students, 119, 180–181, 198–
        199, 206–207
field trips, 24–32, 89–94, 194–195
five-step learning cycle, 88–89
fixed mind-set, 75–76
flexible schedules, 2, 3
formative feedback, 188, 198–199
Fresh Fruits and Vegetables Program,
    22
future, visions for, 3

gardening, 20–22
gender differences, 104–106
gifted underachievers, 139–140
girls, attention given to, 104–106
Glogster, 146
goal setting, 40, 42, 43, 133–135, 141,
    162–165, 167–169
goodness gorillas, 47–49

grade eight special education, 151–178
grade five, 81–106
grade four, 33–56
grade seven, 133–149
graduation requirements, 5
grant proposals, 30–32, 93
group work, 102–104, 115–117, 145,
    158–159, 188–189, 198
growth mind-set, 75
Gulf of Main Research Institute, 93–94

habits of mind, 75–76
hands-on learning, 20–22, 83–94, 99
high school
    English and speech class, 179–201
    sophomore English class, 203–232
high school dropouts, 2, 4
home life, 4, 13–14
home visits, 113
how-to instruction, 189–191
humor, 204–205

I-can statements, 43
individualized instruction, 17–20, 155,
    162
individual learning plans, 67–68
individual needs, 208–211
inductive reasoning, 192
inquiry-based lessons, 84–89
instruction
    authentic work and, 117–122
    collaborative, 76–77
    hands-on, 20–22, 83–94, 99
    how-to, 189–191
    individualized, 17–20, 155, 162
    organization of, 67–75
    transparent, 71–73
instructional decisions, 141–145
interviews, 117–123, 212–214

intrinsic motivation, 99
invention reasoning, 70–71
invisibility, 3
iPads, 17–20
I-wonders, 50–52

journals, 44, 207, 218–221

kindergarten, 13–32
    active learning in, 20–22
    learning environment in, 15, 22–24
    nutrition education in, 22–24
    out-of-school learning experiences in,
        24–32
    teaching strategies for, 16–22
    use of technology in, 17–20
kindness, 46–49, 64
King Middle School, 5, 10, 107–131

laughter, 204–205
leadership opportunities, 70–71
learning
    See also learning opportunities
    celebrations of, 125–127, 162
    dynamic, 188
    goals, 40, 42, 43, 71–72, 133–135, 141,
        162–165, 167–169
    hands-on, 20–22, 83–94, 99
    individual learning plans, 67–68
    passion for, 99–100
    proficiency-based, 5, 152, 160, 161,
        170
    real-world, 16–17
    self-directed, 133–135, 171, 173
    student-centered. *see* student-
        centered learning
    teacher-directed, 137–138, 160
    as transformational, 146–148

learning community, 112–114
learning environment
   See also classroom
   in kindergarten, 15, 22–24
   students' views on ideal, 138
   welcoming, 180–181
learning opportunities
   authentic work and, 117–122
   challenging, 128–129
   engaging, 114–117
   obstacles as, 56
   outside of school, 24–32, 89–94,
      192–195
   for students living in poverty, 15–16
learning principles, 59–60
learning targets, 143, 145
learning targets chart, 187
legislation, 5
legislators, 243
lesson plans, 188
lessons
   dynamic, 188
   individualization of, 17–20, 155, 162
   inquiry-based, 84–89
listening skills, 41
literature circles, 174–175
looping, 113
Loring Air Force Base, 194–195

MacDonald, Karen, 10
Maine Cohort for Customized
   Learning, 75
Maine Learning Results, 5
meaning-making, 204
media, 4, 141, 146
mentors, 112–113
middle school classes, 107–131
mind-set, 177–178
morning meetings, 102
motivation, 2, 8, 43, 99, 168–169
multiage classroom, 57–79

academic growth in, 78
classroom culture in, 62–67
collaboration and, 76–77
developing Habits of Mind in, 75–76
organization of instruction in, 67–75

National Board for Professional
   Teaching Standards, 103–104
Northern Main Children's Water
   Festival, 93
Northwest Evaluation Association
   (NWEA) assessments, 78, 139
nutrition, 22–24

on-demand writing, 214–218
online tools, 146
opportunity to learn model, 16
oral history project, 117–127
oral language, 16, 17
organizations, partnering with, 29–30
out-of-school learning experiences,
   24–32, 89–94, 192–195
Outward Bound Expeditionary
   Learning, 5, 10

parents
   communication with, 148
   meetings with, 101
   next steps for, 241
   relationship building with, 100–101,
      113, 128
parking lot, 66–67
passion, 99–100
perfectionism, 209
perspectives, teaching different, 96–98
picture books, 16
Pierce, Derek, 5
Poland Regional High School, 5
policymakers, 243

poverty, 6, 12
  impact of, 15–16
  students living in, 6, 12, 15–16, 37–38
power standards, 158–159
praise, 139
presentations, 123–127
preservice teachers, 242
principals, 241
priority setting, 40–41, 43
prior knowledge, 68–69
proactive, 40, 42
procrastination, 209
proficiency, 78
proficiency-based learning/teaching, 5,
  152, 160, 161, 170
progress monitoring, 165–168
public service announcements (PSAs),
  193
public speaking, 193–194
Puccini's *La Bohème*, 195
punishment, 45

reading achievement, 55–56
reading instruction, 35, 174–175
real-world learning, 16–17
reflection, 118, 126–127, 129–130,
  206–207, 231
Reinventing Schools Coalition (RISC),
  59
relationship building, 33–40, 46, 83,
  100–101, 113, 114, 128, 146–147,
  157, 181–182, 236
research projects, 50–52, 88–89
respect, 130–131, 138, 139
responsiveness, 187–189
revisions, 207–208, 228–229
risk taking, 191–192
River Valley School, 2–4, 5
roundtable discussions, 207, 221–231,
  233–234
routines, student-led, 65–66

rubrics, 119, 129, 207

school administrators, 176–177,
  241–242
school board members, 242
school engagement. *See* engagement
science experiments, 83–89, 94–96
self-assessment, 187
self-directed learning, 133–135, 171, 173
self-reflection, 43–44, 61, 129–130
Seven E's model, 88–89
The 7 Habits of Happy Kids (Covey), 40
Seven Happy Habits in Our Classroom,
  40–46
shame, 205–206
small groups, 102–103, 104, 115–117,
  145, 188–189, 198
social-emotional growth, 46–49, 238
social experience, 210–211
social studies, 96–98
Socratic Seminars, 183–185
sophomore English class, 203–232
special education, 151–178
standardized tests, 103, 129, 130, 165,
  208
STEM opportunities, 160, 171–172
Storyboard That, 146
strike-three method, 164
student-centered learning
  See also student-centered teaching
  experiences of, 2–6
  in grade eight special education,
    151–178
  in grade five, 81–106
  in grade four, 33–56
  in grade seven, 133–149
  in high school, 179–201, 203–232
  in kindergarten, 13–32
  in middle school, 107–131
  in multiage classroom, 57–79
  practices, 7

student-centered learning *(Cont.)*
  student choice and, 117
student-centered schools, characteristics
  of, 6–7
student-centered teaching
  See also student-centered learning
  commonalities in, 236–240
  in cotaught math program, 155–178
  definition of, 9
  development of, 10
  efficacy of, 6–8
  environment for, 10
  Expeditionary Learning model,
    111–131
  in high school, 179–201
  in kindergarten, 16–22
  philosophy of, 79
  as responsive, 187–189
  tools for, 212–231
student choice, 117, 141, 207, 239–240
student-created PSAs, 193
student-led routines, 65–66
students
  acting out by, 136, 138
  at-risk, 4
  creating understanding in, 191–192
  diversity of, 36–37, 109
  ELL, 16, 109, 111, 120
  empowering, 38, 43, 52, 69–71
  engagement by, 8, 18, 38, 73–75,
    82–83, 98–99, 118, 133, 198
  expectations for, 186–187
  feedback from, 119, 180–181, 198–
    199, 206–207
  gender differences in, 104–106
  grouping and regrouping, 76–77, 198
  home life of, 4, 13–14
  learning about, 237–238
  living in poverty, 6, 12, 15–16, 37–38
  motivations to learn of, 2, 8, 43, 99,
    168–169

  needs of, 208–211
  as partners, 180
  prior knowledge of, 68–69
  relationships between teachers and,
    33–40, 83, 100–101, 114, 128,
    146–147, 157, 181–182, 236
  as teachers, 185
student tracking, 107–109
success, 128, 137
superintendents, 241–242
Survey Monkey, 198

target time, 73–75, 78
taxpayers, 243
teachable moments, 46
teacher-directed learning, 137–138,
  160
teachers
  back-to-school anxiety of, 152–153
  caring by, 238–239
  collaboration by, 76–77, 115, 155–178,
    195–198
  engagement by, 98–99
  expectations of, 186–187
  influence of, 57–58
  mind-set for, 177–178
  next steps for, 240–241
  planning by, 116, 153
  preservice, 242
  reflection by, 118
  relationships between students and,
    33–40, 83, 100–101, 114, 128,
    146–147, 157, 181–182, 236
  student-centered, 57–59, 79
  students as, 185
Teaching Channel pinwheel activity
  model, 184
teaching philosophy, 182
teaching practices
  individual learning plans, 67–68

student-centered. *see* student-
    centered teaching
team building, 157, 158, 171–172
teamwork, 21, 41
technology, 17–20, 145–146, 147–148,
    170–171
texts, 211–212
transformational learning, 146–148
transparency, 71–73, 141

uncertainty, 152
underachievers, 139–140
university professors, 242

validation, 212
vocabulary, 16–17, 21, 87, 205–206
voice, 8, 141, 239–240

water safety, 27–29
Web sites, 141, 143
Whittier Middle School, 151–178
whole-heart teaching, 37, 38–40, 55,
    238
win-win situations, 41
wonder wall, 50
writing strategies, 52–55, 95–96, 120–
    121, 174–175, 214–221, 228–229